HAWAIIAN APARTHEID

HAWAIIAN APARTHEID
Racial Separatism and Ethnic Nationalism
in the Aloha State

By
Kenneth R. Conklin, Ph.D.

Kenneth R. Conklin, Ph.D.
46-255 Kahuhipa St. #1205
Kaneohe, HI, 96744

Ken_Conklin@yahoo.com

http://www.angelfire.com/hi2/hawaiiansovereignty

E-BookTime, LLC
Montgomery, Alabama

Hawaiian Apartheid
Racial Separatism and Ethnic Nationalism in the Aloha State

Copyright © 2007 by Kenneth R. Conklin, Ph.D.

All rights reserved. No part of this book may be reproduced or transmitted in any form or by any means, electronic or mechanical, including photocopying, recording, or by any information storage and retrieval system, without permission in writing from the copyright owner.

Library of Congress Control Number: 2007923618

ISBN: 978-1-59824-461-8

First Edition
Published March 2007
E-BookTime, LLC
6598 Pumpkin Road
Montgomery, AL 36108
www.e-booktime.com

Contents

Preliminaries – *Purpose of Book; Who is Ken Conklin; Diacritical Marks* 13

Chapter 1 *Introduction – The Gathering Storm* 17

    The Big Picture 17

    Environmental and social paradise threatened by apartheid and ethnic cleansing 20

    How did the present trouble come about? 22

    How unity, equality, and aloha are defended 24

    How the Evil Empire fights back: Historical grievances, victimhood statistics, and charges of racism 25

    Attitudes between ethnic Hawaiians and others 27

Chapter 2 *Mixed Metaphors* 29

    Evil Empire 29

    Cancer spreading 30

    Family where one beloved member is spoiled rotten, has handicaps and is a drug abuser 32

    Broken rainbow and the Aloha Spirit 33

    Boiling Frog 34

    Hawaiian Jihad (aggressive religious fascism) 35

Contents

Chapter 3 *Racial Separatism in Hawaii, Past and Present* 42

Summary 42

Caucasians were full partners in the Hawaiian Kingdom (government and culture) 44

Racial separatism in the politics of 1874 to 1902 48

Racial separatism in the alii trusts, and Department of Hawaiian Homelands 51

Kamehameha Schools (Bishop Estate) 56

Office of Hawaiian Affairs 60

Ceded lands 63

Over 160 racially exclusionary federally funded programs 66

Racial separatism in Hawaii's "Public" schools 67

University of Hawaii 70

Sandwich Isles Communications 73

A Tale of Two Islands: Kahoolawe and Niihau 74

Racial separatism gone wild – The Akaka bill to create an apartheid government and fuel a secessionist movement 77

OHA's Plan B 80

Degrees of separatism: Four models for the relationship between "indigenous" people and everyone else 81

Contents

Chapter 4 *Ethnic Nationalism* 86

    Hawaiian ethnic nationalism, secession, and multiplicity of sovereignty theories 86

    Race is the core 87

    Four levels of political and economic rights depending on race and long-ago circumstances 88

    If the Kingdom has maintained its continuity (although ineffectively in limbo), then why would today's Asians and Caucasians born in Hawaii not be Kingdom subjects fully equal to ethnic Hawaiians? 93

    The situation in Fiji is also a cautionary tale. 97

    Decolonization – Is Hawaii legitimately the 50th state? 99

    Tax evasion on grounds that Hawaii is not really part of the United States 105

    The Akaka bill as a pathway to secession 108

Chapter 5 *Historical Grievances (and falsehoods)* 112

    Two kinds of grievances, and how they are exploited for wealth and power 112

    Genocide 113

    U.S. "armed invasion" in 1893, and U.S. apology resolution in 1993 117

    Fake Presidential Proclamation alleged to be by Grover Cleveland 124

Contents

Hawaii puppet regime had no legitimacy to offer a treaty of annexation 135

Illegal annexation 139

Anti-annexation petition signed by 95% of ethnic Hawaiians 140

Hawaiian language was made illegal 143

"Treaties are the supreme law of the land." 145

Hawaiian flag publicly torn into souvenir pieces given to the Caucasians, as a way of humiliating ethnic Hawaiians at the time of overthrow or annexation 149

Mauna Ala (The Royal Mausoleum in Honolulu) today remains sovereign territory of the Kingdom of Hawaii, and U.S. law does not apply there 156

Is Hawaii legitimately the 50th state? 159

Chapter 6 *Current Victimhood Claims (Junk Science Fueling the Hawaiian Grievance Industry)* 161

What claims are being made, and for what purpose? 161

A few examples of some specific victimhood claims and their debunking 164

Kamehameha Schools PASE – the Daddy Warbucks among tycoons of the Hawaiian grievance industry 169

Why ethnic Hawaiian victimhood statistics are unreliable or misleading, and what terrible prescriptions we must write if they are correct 172

Contents

Reductio ad absurdum: left-handed breast cancer 183

The solution: a welfare system based solely on need regardless of race 185

Chapter 7 *Anti-American, Anti-Military Activism* 186

Most ethnic Hawaiians reject both racial separatism and ethnic nationalism, and are patriotic Americans 186

Degrees of anti-Americanism 187

Some supporters of the Akaka bill might be patriotic Americans with distinguished military careers 188

Historical grievances against the United States produce a simmering anti-Americanism even among wealthy Hawaiians and well-established institutions not (yet) seeking independence 190

Racism, threats of violence, and actual violence 195

Hawaiian activists seeking independence by "working within the system" through U.S. domestic activity including the banking system, tax evasion, and "peace" churches 197

Anti-military activism – push the U.S. military out of Hawaii as a first step toward ripping the 50th star off the flag 200

The Hawaiian independence movement at the national and international levels 201

The possibility of Hawaiian espionage or sabotage in collaboration with foreign governments hostile to the U.S. in order to get diplomatic recognition of an independent Hawaii, or to weaken the U.S. thereby causing U.S. abandonment of Hawaii 207

Contents

Tribal status as a pathway to independence and a threat to national security 211

Chapter 8 *Indigenous Rights and Religious Fascism in Support of Hawaiian Racial Supremacy* 213

Introduction 213

Do ethnic Hawaiians qualify as an indigenous people by historical standards? 214

Do ethnic Hawaiians maintain an indigenous lifestyle? 215

Where the bones are 221

A beautiful creation legend now used as a basis for religious fascism 223

The gods, the land, and the ethnic Hawaiians – How Hawaiian religion is (ab)used to assert an inherent right to racial supremacy 224

Deep culture 230

Hawaiian epistemology as justification for claiming indigenous status and for demanding racial separatism in education 232

Polynesian voyaging: religion, epistemology, and racial politics 237

Indigenous intellectual property rights yes; but in Hawaii? 246

He alii ka aina, he kauwa ke kanaka Land is the chief; people are its humble servants 247

The choice between religious fascism or religious freedom 248

Contents

Chapter 9 *Hawaiian Sovereignty Frauds* 251

   New Issue of $1 Billion of Hawaiian Kingdom Bonds in February 2002 (109 years too late) 252

   "Perfect Title" land title search and registration scam 256

   "World Court" allegedly confirms Hawaiian Kingdom still exists ... 262

Chapter 10 *Steps Toward a Positive Future* 271

   Quick review: What is Hawaiian apartheid? Why should it be of concern to people in Hawaii and throughout the United States? 271

   What would a positive future look like for Hawaii? 274

   What steps can we take to rescue ourselves? 275

   Civil War analogy 278

   Conclusion 281

Footnotes 282

Preliminaries

Purpose of Book; Who is Ken Conklin; Diacritical Marks

This book is intended to awaken the sleeping giant of public opinion to the dangers of the Hawaiian sovereignty movement. The gathering storm of racial separatism and ethnic nationalism threatens not only the people of Hawaii but the entire United States. Racial separatists have had legislation in Congress since 2000 seeking authorization to create a racially exclusionary government with land and money taken from the State of Hawaii. The "Akaka bill" threatens to set a precedent for ethnic balkanization throughout America. Hawaii's independence activists want to rip the 50th star off the flag, either by international efforts or through the economic and political power the Akaka bill would give Hawaiians as a racial group. There are more than 160 federally funded programs that are racially exclusionary, plus the $8-15 billion Kamehameha Schools. We must work hard to restore our fundamental principles of unity, equality, and aloha for all. The Table of Contents provides the titles of the chapters and their sections.

I, Ken Conklin, have a Ph.D. in Philosophy. I'm a retired professor, living in Hawaii since 1992. I came to Hawaii for spiritual rejuvenation. I visited Hawaii on summer vacations since 1982 and felt drawn to our beautiful rainbow of races and cultures, especially native Hawaiian. It was easier to feel the presence of the gods in Hawaii than anywhere else. From 1992 to 1998 I spent full time studying Hawaiian history and culture, and learned to speak Hawaiian language with moderate fluency. At first I was inclined to agree with Hawaiian sovereignty activists because their political views seemed grounded in spirituality. I attended hundreds of sovereignty meetings and political rallies, talked with dozens of activists, and asked lots of questions. After a period of growing doubt and gut wrenching inner struggle over the most complex issue I have ever studied, I finally saw the "big picture" and concluded that "There is no historical, legal, or moral justification for race-based political sovereignty for ethnic Hawaiians." I saw the face of evil in the movement, and felt compelled to step forward to oppose it. Following a highly controversial civil rights lawsuit I became the first non-ethnic-Hawaiian to run for trustee of the Office of Hawaiian Affairs in 2000, placing 4th out of 20 candidates for one seat. I have published numerous newspaper letters and commentaries, taught a controversial course on Hawaiian sovereignty at the University, and maintain a huge website at http://www.angelfire.com/hi2/hawaiiansovereignty

There was no written Hawaiian language until 1820. Native Hawaiian adventurers had traveled to Yale University, and were taken in by professors of religion. The Hawaiians converted to Christianity. One of them, Opukahaia (Henry Obookiah), pleaded fervently for missionaries to come to Hawaii. The natives taught the missionaries to speak Hawaiian both at Yale and on the long journey to Hawaii, helping them create an alphabet and figure out some rules of grammar. The written language had no diacritical marks until modern times. The reason why diacritical marks were invented was to help people who did not hear Hawaiian spoken in everyday life (including nearly all ethnic Hawaiians today) learn how to pronounce words correctly. Today professors and students of Hawaiian language insist everyone use the kahako (a bar over a vowel indicating a longer intonation and stress) and okina (apostrophe-like mark indicating a glottal stop). Bills in the legislature requested by Hawaiian sovereignty zealots propose that all government documents, or at least letterheads, be printed with Hawaiian language coming ahead of English translation, and insisting on proper use of the diacritical marks. I speak Hawaiian moderately well, and know from experience where most (but not all) of those marks belong (including the word "okina" which is supposed to be spelled "'okina"). However, I refuse to be bogged down in endless verification of their correct use and endless criticism for their misuse. This book follows the precedent set by esteemed historian Gavan Daws in his book "Shoal of Time." In "A Note on the Use of the Hawaiian Language" at the start of that book, Daws wrote "So that the general reader will not be subjected to undue strain, all Hawaiian words in the text of this book, including those in quotations, have been given standard spellings." The present book differs somewhat, by sometimes showing an apostrophe inside a quotation where the quoted word had an okina. Or sometimes not. Don't stress over it. Can't we all just get along?

Many people of various races have taught me Hawaiian history, culture and language; as well as things about modern law. Some have inspired me. A few helped me in my civil rights activities and in writing this book. They know who they are. None of them will be named here. Many of them will be glad for not being named, so they are spared the vilification that might come from sovereignty zealots angered over a book that dares to "tell it like it is."

Chapter 1

Introduction – The Gathering Storm

The Big Picture

There's trouble in Paradise, and it threatens all of America. Racial separatism and ethnic nationalism are growing stronger in the Aloha State, with the U.S. as current accomplice and future victim.

In a book entitled "The Gathering Storm" Winston Churchill described the rise of Nazi influence in Germany in the 1920s and 1930s. During the early years of the Nazi movement most Germans didn't realize how dangerous it was, and few outsiders knew or cared about it. When Hitler threatened to take over Czechoslovakia by military invasion, British Prime Minister Neville Chamberlain tried to appease Hitler by giving him part of it. Arriving home after a September 30, 1938 meeting with Hitler, Chamberlain stepped off the plane, waved a document in the air, and loudly proclaimed "Peace in our time!"

Hawaii's gathering storm has been building strength for several decades. Most people don't recognize the danger. Some Hawaii politicians and community leaders who do recognize the danger prefer to ignore it, or to appease a growing Evil Empire by giving it money, land, and political power. Sometimes there's talk of a "global settlement" for "peace in our time." Most U.S. Senators were unaware of the issue until June of 2006. That's when the Senate spent several hours discussing the "Akaka bill."[1] Every Democrat and several Republicans voted in favor of bringing to a vote an outrageous bill to authorize an apartheid regime for Hawaii.[2]

Race-based institutions have grown so powerful they now control Hawaii's political establishment. A state government agency, eagerly supported by the Democrat legislature and Republican governor, is pushing Congressional legislation known as the Akaka bill. It would authorize a racially exclusionary government to include 240,000 citizens of Hawaii (20% of the state's population) and 160,000 citizens of other states.[3] Most support for the Akaka bill comes from Hawaii's large race-based institutions seeking to protect the vast wealth and political power they already enjoy. Polls show that 2/3 of all Hawaii's people, including about half of the ethnic Hawaiians, oppose this bill.[4] But the political establishment responds to the money and power of the institutions, and fears to go against a swing-vote of the 20% of citizens who have a drop of native blood and are regarded (wrongly) as a monolithic voting bloc.

Some see the Akaka bill as a path to secession. Most independence activists accuse supporters of the Akaka bill of selling out; yet most supporters of the Akaka bill privately dream of eventual independence for Hawaii. Some independence activists accept the Akaka bill as a short-term pragmatic necessity to acquire ever-larger amounts of money, land, and power to fuel a drive for complete secession of the entire State of Hawaii from the United States. Hawaiian sovereignty activism is similar to "liberation movements" in other parts of the world, such as Quebec (Canada), Northern Ireland, Scotland, Sri Lanka, East Timor (Indonesia), Chiapas (southern Mexico), Kurdistan (southern Turkey and northern Iraq), etc. One wing of these movements appears to seek only self-determination, autonomy, and separatism within the existing system; while a more radical wing loudly demands total independence. The moderates view the radicals as pure-hearted idealists and often give them financial and "moral" support. The radicals often accuse the moderates of being bourgeoisie "sell-outs" but the radicals gladly accept whatever help the moderates give them.

Hawaiian sovereignty activists believe international law supports their demands for independence. They also believe international law provides special rights for indigenous peoples, whereby the 20% of Hawaii's people who have a drop of native blood would be entitled to racial supremacy over the remaining 80%. The general public quietly tolerates and sometimes supports race-based governmental and private agencies. That public acquiescence encourages the activists to believe racial supremacy by law can be obtained peacefully. Over 160 racially exclusionary federal programs, plus massive state government programs, plus private race-based institutions valued at $8-15 billion, already provide a substantial amount of racial supremacy to a group that also shares all the benefits available to everyone else. Racial supremacy by a zealous minority over a much larger but passive majority could continue and expand dramatically if Hawaii were independent from the United States, since there could no longer be interference from the U.S. Constitution or federal courts.

Hawaiian Apartheid

Civil rights activists are struggling to protect the unity of Hawaii and the equality of all our people. One tactic has been to file lawsuits seeking to stop racially exclusionary practices. When race-based programs and institutions are threatened by civil rights lawsuits, politicians eagerly endorse the Akaka bill to shield them by creating an apartheid government.

A "nation within a nation" along the lines of an Indian tribe would require approval by Congress. Tribal governments have sovereign jurisdiction over their people and territories comparable to the powers of a state government, and often have very different laws which state governments cannot override, on important topics like taxation, zoning, divorce, child custody, labor unions, etc. The situation in Hawaii is unlike any other state in regard to the severity of the impact on the population as a whole. No other state has 20% of its people eligible to join a single tribe, whose members would then be active participants on both sides of negotiations between the tribe and state government over money, land, and political power. No other state has an Indian tribe whose reservation lands, under tribal laws, would comprise 40-50% of the entire state in a great number of large and small enclaves scattered everywhere.[5]

The Akaka bill to create a phony Indian tribe for ethnic Hawaiians threatens all America because it is based on a new theory of the U.S. Constitution which would encourage and accelerate the balkanization of our nation into ethnic enclaves. The theory is that the Indian Commerce Clause authorizes Congress to single out any ethnic group (especially if they are "indigenous") and give them group rights similar to an Indian tribe, even if the group has never functioned as a tribe and even if its members are widely scattered and thoroughly assimilated into the general population. If that theory applies to ethnic groups in general, the Amish could seek tribal status, along with Louisiana Cajuns; and perhaps a Nation of New Africa for all of America's Blacks. If the theory is restricted to so-called "indigenous" people whose ancestral lands were engulfed by the United States, then America's people of Mexican ancestry (most of whom have a drop of Aztec or Mayan blood) could demand the right of MEChA to form a Nation of Aztlan controlling those parts of America which formerly belonged to Mexico.[6]

A state within the State of Hawaii (comparable to a state-recognized Indian tribe) would require only the approval of the state legislature. It is being pursued by the State of Hawaii Office of Hawaiian Affairs as a Plan B in case the Akaka bill fails. It's a way to empower a racially exclusionary governing entity which can acquire huge amounts of land, money, and political power. For starters it would gather under one umbrella all the housing, healthcare, schooling, and welfare functions already being performed by various racially exclusionary government and private institutions. With a membership of perhaps 200,000 (OHA's stated goal), this state within a state would have a position of power from which to pursue federal recognition through the Akaka bill, and eventual independence. The Hawaiian state-within-a-state could grow to more than 400,000, as large numbers of ethnic Hawaiians now in "diaspora" return to their "homeland" (where many have never been). At the end of 2006 nearly 60,000 of America's 400,000 ethnic Hawaiians have already signed a racial registry sponsored by OHA that would probably become the nucleus of the phony tribe's membership roll.

Those who think it's acceptable to have a state-within-a-state based on race, ethnicity, or religion should look to the role of Hezbollah in Lebanon. Setting aside the violence, Hezbollah became politically powerful by providing healthcare, housing, and welfare benefits to thousands of people over a period of many years, thereby gaining their zealous loyalty. Hezbollah, like OHA, is an official agency of the government with the legal authority to appoint staff members to government boards. OHA, like Hezbollah, has a large pile of money, and the recognized authority to set government policy in many areas. It is clearly destabilizing for any government to allow ethnic or sectarian groups to establish and carry out official government functions.

Environmental and social paradise threatened by apartheid and ethnic cleansing

Hawaii is widely known as a paradise. We have a beautiful environment and excellent weather for enjoying it year-round.

We are also known as a social paradise – the most racially diverse and harmonious state in America, with the highest percentage of intermarriage producing the world's most beautiful children.

Every racial or ethnic group in Hawaii is a minority. All are represented at every level of government, business, labor, media, etc. Governors and U.S. Senators have been Chinese, Filipino, ethic Hawaiian, Japanese, Jewish, and White. All races are found among owners of multimillion dollar corporations, laborers who work for them, farmers and fishermen, homeless people and prison inmates. Most neighborhoods have all racial groups represented among both homeowners and renters. We live, work, play, and pray in a fully integrated multiracial society. Many

Hawaiian Apartheid

Hawaii citizens have a long list of ethnicities in their genealogies, and are very proud to recite them. It's perfectly normal for new acquaintances to ask each other: "Hey, what are you?" And it's perfectly normal to get the answer: "Chinese, Filipino, Japanese, Irish, German, and Hawaiian." But usually these days "Hawaiian" gets mentioned first, even if it's the smallest percentage of the pedigree (which it usually is).

If there were to be an ethnic Hawaiian state within the State of Hawaii, its land base could only be filled with people through an exchange of populations similar to what was done when India (mostly Hindu) broke apart to create Pakistan (mostly Muslim). With ethnic Hawaiians comprising 20% of the state's population, and demanding more than 50% of the state's land (especially if Bishop Estate were included), the best name for the concept is apartheid – which literally means "apartness." The exchange of populations might properly be described as ethnic cleansing.

If there were to be an independent nation of Hawaii, its government and laws would be dominated by the 20% of the population who have at least one drop of native blood. That dominance has already been established through more than 160 federal programs, numerous state government programs, and dozens of wealthy private institutions, all providing racially exclusive benefits to ethnic Hawaiians in addition to the benefits available to all citizens (including also the ethnic Hawaiians). Racial supremacy by ethnic Hawaiians at present is somewhat limited by the fact that under U.S. law such race-based programs are probably unconstitutional – some have come under challenge. But if Hawaii were to become an independent nation, then U.S. law could no longer protect a passive majority against a zealous minority using a theory of "indigenous rights" under "international law" to assert racial supremacy.

Sovereignty activists try to soothe these fears by pointing out that most ethnic Hawaiians are themselves racially mixed, with non-native spouses and family members they would never wish to harm. The activists point out that Hawaiian culture is noted for its spirit of inclusiveness and generosity. But let's remember what happened in Germany in the 1930s, and in other places quite recently: Bosnia, Rwanda, Zimbabwe, Fiji, Darfur, Lebanon. People of different ethnic groups lived and worked side by side, and sometimes intermarried; until one group asserted supremacy, seized control, and engaged in ethnic cleansing accompanied by mass slaughter. History shows that bad things happen in multiracial societies when one ethnic group is given a green light to pursue racial separatism or ethnic nationalism. In recent years Hawaiian sovereignty activists have revived the celebration of Kingdom holidays. Although Caucasians were among the greatest heroes of the Kingdom, today's sovereignty activists shove them aside in their celebrations.[7] This ethnic cleansing of Hawaiian history discloses a racist attitude and serves as the canary in the mineshaft – a warning that ethnic cleansing of voting rights and land ownership are likely to accompany any form of Hawaiian sovereignty.

How did the present trouble come about?

"Native Hawaiians" are a dearly beloved ethnic group perceived as poor and downtrodden. Tycoons of the Hawaiian grievance industry have played upon the public's affection and sympathy to obtain numerous affirmative action programs. Over the years those programs multiplied and became entrenched as entitlements. Powerful, wealthy institutions funded by government and philanthropic grants have grown into an Evil Empire. Hawaii's favorite ethnic group comprises 20% of the population. Politicians (wrongly) assume they will vote as a bloc. Politicians fear the consequences of angering a 20% swing-vote. Thus the Evil Empire has captured Hawaii's political establishment.

News media report and editorialize what politicians and noisy activists want to hear. Proposals for racial separatism or ethnic nationalism grab media attention, whereas proposals to protect unity and equality seem dull and are ignored. Newspapers print side-by-side articles: one favoring the Akaka bill as a way of getting more racially-earmarked money from the U.S. government, and one opposing the Akaka bill because it would damage the secessionist movement. But the argument in favor of unity and equality is not provided, even though the vast majority of Hawaii's people favor it, including probably most ethnic Hawaiians.[8] This constant publicizing of opposing views of racial separatists and ethnic nationalists, while leaving out the aloha choice of unity and equality, is repeated so often that the public has come to believe that "something must be done" and that there are only the two (bad) choices. The news media also knuckle under to the separatists because the wealthy race-based institutions spend millions of dollars in advertising for propaganda to pass the Akaka bill and for people to sign up on a racial registry. Thus the Evil Empire has captured Hawaii's media.

Hawaii's two Senators, Dan Inouye and Dan Akaka, have spent their entire Senate careers as members of the Indian Affairs Committee. Hawaii is the only state which has both of its Senators serving on that committee. In addition, Senator Inouye sometimes used his seniority to be Chairman of that committee when the Democrats were in the majority. Why would Hawaii's Senators want to serve on the Indian Affairs committee when there have never been any Indian tribes in Hawaii? The obvious answer is: filling the pork barrel. Whenever major legislation was introduced to provide housing, healthcare, or education for all of America's real Indian tribes, Inouye and Akaka made sure to insert "and Native Hawaiians" into the bills. Over the years more than 160 federally funded programs intended for real Indian tribes have brought billions of dollars into Hawaii for ethnic Hawaiians. Since this "free" money then circulates through Hawaii's economy, the business community and politicians like it. The race-based institutions are sustained and strengthened by federal dollars flowing through their coffers, while other institutions are co-opted by the money they earn providing services. Thus Hawaii's Evil Empire thrives with federal assistance and constantly pushes for more.

The Office of Hawaiian Affairs has cited in legal briefs the fact that there are over 160 federally funded race-based programs for ethnic Hawaiians.[9] OHA argues that the establishment of those programs over a period of about 30 years proves that there is a political "trust relationship" between the U.S. government and ethnic Hawaiians as a group. That claim of a political relationship is asserted in order to argue that the race-based programs are not subject to "strict scrutiny" under the 14th Amendment equal protection clause, but are subject only to a "rational basis test" appropriate to the government-to-government relationships between the U.S. on one side, and the states and the Indian tribes on the other.

OHA's assertion of a political trust relationship and legal responsibility of wardship based on a pattern of generous giving can be shown as absurd by the following analogy. On Monday while walking down the street I encounter a homeless man holding out a tin cup, and I put in a dollar. On Tuesday while walking down the street I encounter the same homeless man holding out his tin cup, and I again put in a dollar. On Wednesday the same thing happens. Then on Thursday I'm a little behind schedule, and hurry past the homeless man without giving him anything. Whereupon he chases after me and shouts "Hey, where's that dollar you owe me!" He imagines that my pattern of generosity has established a "trust relationship" where he is entitled to expect regular handouts.

How unity, equality, and aloha are defended

The fundamental principles of unity, equality, and aloha for all need to be defended.[10]

Racial separatism (Akaka bill or Plan B) is not acceptable. Ethnic nationalism (secession, or total independence) is not acceptable. The status quo is not acceptable, because it allows an Evil Empire of race-based institutions to dominate Hawaii's politics and to continue entrenching racial supremacy while pushing for legislation to strengthen it.

The unity of Hawaii and the equality of its people need to be rescued by dismantling the Evil Empire. One way to do that is to win civil rights lawsuits against the institutions. Such lawsuits might turn evil institutions into benign ones by forcing them to give up racially exclusionary policies; but if the institutions cannot be forced to desegregate then the lawsuits might abolish them completely.[11]

Another way to dismantle the Evil Empire is to cut off its money supply by persuading politicians and philanthropies to stop funding for racially discriminatory institutions. In 2006 a group in Congress actually singled out $40 million in Hawaiian racially exclusionary programs to be cut; but they were unsuccessful.[12]

A third way is to persuade politicians to change the laws, or for the people to directly change the laws through ballot initiative or referendum. Of course the legislature will never voluntarily dismantle the Evil Empire. Initiative and referendum for statute laws are not available in Hawaii, except on extremely rare occasions when the legislature chooses to place an issue on the ballot. Individual small changes to the Constitution passed by the legislature are required to be placed on the ballot and can then be ratified or rejected by a vote of the people, but the people cannot initiate a law or amendment. Fortunately the Constitution requires that once every ten years the legislature is forced to place on the ballot the question whether there should be a Constitutional Convention. In 1998 the Evil Empire spent lots of money advertising for a "no" vote and they prevailed (narrowly, and on a technicality that blank ballots should be counted as "No" votes). Perhaps the outcome will be different in 2008.

How the Evil Empire fights back: Historical grievances, victimhood statistics, and charges of racism

One way the Evil Empire fights back is to play upon public sympathy for the "plight" of an allegedly poor, downtrodden ethnic group. This argument is advanced by flaunting – actually celebrating – victimhood statistics which stereotype all members of the group as sharing the same demeaning racial profile, even when most individuals in the group have low racial blood quantum and are neither poor nor downtrodden. Another tactic is to weep often and long over historical grievances, many of which are false or grossly exaggerated. The historical grievances and victimhood statistics have even been used successfully in court, where judges relied on them to justify racial segregation at Kamehameha Schools under the guise of affirmative action to remedy past injustices or present deficits.[13]

The combination of historical grievances and victimhood statistics comes out sounding like this (including false or greatly overblown "facts" and inflammatory rhetoric). In 1778 Captain Cook arrived in Hawaii bringing with him Western diseases for which the natives had no resistance. As a result, 95% of natives died within a century. Christian missionaries came to do good and did very well (for themselves). The natives looked up to heaven to pray, and then when they looked down they saw their culture and land were both gone. Genocide and land loss were accompanied by colonization – natives were forced to assimilate to a strange new lifestyle while foreigners became dominant in the economy and political life. In 1893 the U.S. staged an armed invasion, overthrew the monarchy, imprisoned the Queen in her own Palace, and installed a puppet regime. That puppet regime made Hawaiian language illegal, further stripping the natives of their culture and making them feel like strangers in their own land. The U.S. followed an illegal procedure to unilaterally reach out and grab Hawaii through annexation in 1898, despite a protest petition signed by nearly every native and delivered to the U.S. Senate. The combination of genocide, colonization, overthrow of the monarchy, and forced annexation devastated the natives; and that devastation has continued to the present. Hawaiian natives have the lowest income and education among all ethnic groups, the worst health statistics (diabetes, breast cancer, short life span), highest rate of alcoholism, drug abuse, homelessness, and incarceration. The 1893 overthrow broke the hearts of the natives, and as a consequence their descendants today have the highest rate for heart disease. The U.S. owes huge reparations to native Hawaiians for the historical grievances, and to remedy the victimhood statistics they have caused. That's why native Hawaiians are entitled to over 160 race-based programs exclusively for them, a racially exclusionary private school system, a race-focused group of state-operated public schools – and a proposed racially exclusionary government owning huge amounts of land and money taken away from the federal and state governments.

Most of what is said in the above paragraph is false or terribly distorted. But the Hawaiian grievance industry has been pushing this propaganda aggressively for many years, assisted by the media, university, public and private schools, and the misguided Congressional apology resolution of 1993. Thus ethnic Hawaiians feel entitled to reparations, and the general public sympathizes with their "plight."

Another tactic used by the Evil Empire is to claim that civil rights activists are being racist. This book will be attacked as racism against ethnic Hawaiians. The author has sometimes been publicly accused of being anti-Hawaiian. Such inflammatory personal attacks are typical behavior of the racial separatists and ethnic nationalists. They know it's very easy for a "person of color" to hurl the "R" word against a white man; and it is nearly impossible to defend against such slander. They know it's easy to evade serious discussion of the issues by smearing an opponent.

They say "Why is it that you single out and attack Native Hawaiians, and only Native Hawaiians, when there are also other ethnic groups who have private clubs or cultural events?" Well, here's why. There is no other ethnic group in Hawaii whose leaders have over 160 racially exclusionary government programs, an agency of the state government with $400 million in assets pledged to the master race, a private school system with $8-15 billion, huge tracts of land owned in the name of the racial group, and who are seeking to establish a racially exclusionary government. The unity of Hawaii and equality under the law are not in any way threatened by the Japanese Cultural Center, the See Dai Doo Society, the Filipino Chronicle, the Narcissus Festival, St. Patrick's Day, etc. Sometimes the racial supremacists point out that the civil rights advocates attack only wealthy institutions like Kamehameha Schools while leaving alone the nearly bankrupt Lunalilo Home. It is claimed the civil rights advocates are jealous of wealthy Hawaiian institutions, want to seize control of the assets, or simply don't like seeing brown-skinned people do well. But of course the reason for not targeting Lunalilo Home is because it is truly a philanthropy not seeking political power. Queen Liliuokalani Childrens Trust is actually quite wealthy, and racially exclusionary. But until recently the QLCT, with a network of service centers, paid staff, and volunteers, has focused on its philanthropic mission. Perhaps eventually QLCT will become a target of civil rights activists, but so far it has escaped scrutiny because its wealth is not used for the purpose of seeking race-based political power.

Civil rights activists do not target ethnic Hawaiians as a racial group. The attack is certainly not against most of the individuals who have native blood as one component of their ethnicity. The attack is against racially exclusionary programs, the powerful government and private institutions supporting them, and the drive for racial separatism and ethnic nationalism.

Attitudes between ethnic Hawaiians and others

Some very courageous ethnic Hawaiians have joined hands publicly with people of all races in Hawaii to actively defend unity and equality.[14] Many more ethnic Hawaiians express support in hushed voices for fear of social, economic, or even physical retaliation by institutions and individuals who bully them into silence. However, there are also many ethnic Hawaiians who spew hate-filled rhetoric toward anyone lacking native ancestry, and especially toward whites. Newspapers frequently publish commentaries and letters asserting false or twisted historical claims using inflammatory language about "genocide", "colonization", "illegal" overthrow of the monarchy, "stolen" lands, "language made illegal", etc.

So, how should others think of ethnic Hawaiians? Should we fear them? Should we see them as enemies, hell-bent on ripping Hawaii apart and ripping the 50th star off the American flag? Should we give credence to the highly touted victimhood statistics and thereby racially profile ethnic Hawaiians as poorly educated, impoverished, diseased, drug abusers, spouse abusers, likely to be incarcerated? No doubt some are like that. Perhaps too many are like that. But most are just like everyone else, loving their families, working hard to pay the bills, getting wealthy or falling into poverty according to their efforts and abilities, and proud to be Americans.

How we should think about ethnic Hawaiians is similar to how Americans should think about Arab Muslims after September 11, 2001, or how we should have thought about Americans of Japanese ancestry after December 7, 1941. Let's remember that after the Japanese attack on Pearl Harbor many Americans feared American residents of Japanese ancestry – even native-born or naturalized. There may indeed have been a few Japanese Americans with close ties to the motherland who would have spied for Japan or tried to engage in sabotage. But the overwhelming majority of those who were incarcerated in relocation internment camps turned out to have been victims of a great injustice. Here in Hawaii most ethnic Japanese were spared such injustice and continued to be treated as the friends, neighbors, and family members they had always been. Let's think about how Americans feel today about Arab Muslims. Our news media are filled with images of hate-filled zealots cutting off heads, blowing up suicide bombs, or flying airplanes into skyscrapers. Some nations' presidents or prime ministers call for the destruction of America. Yet our hearts and minds tell us that most Muslims in America – and even the ordinary Arabs and Muslims living in rogue nations like Iran and Syria – are just like us, with loving families, generous hearts, and peaceful intentions.

It's wrong to consider a person's race or religion as his most important attribute. How should we think of ethnic Hawaiians, Japanese, or Arab Muslims? We should be careful to think of them as individuals and, as Dr. Martin Luther King said, judge them by the content of their characters rather than the color of their skins. A person's race alone tells us nothing at all about whether he is rich or poor, intelligent or stupid, upright or corrupt, egalitarian or racist, friendly or hostile, peaceful or violent.

Neither a person's character, nor his individual rights and needs, should be profiled based on race. That principle applies to avoiding prejudice, but it also applies to giving benefits or detriments based on race alone. Therefore we should give government assistance to needy people based on need alone and not race. If one racial group is really more needy than others, then it will receive the lion's share of government help when help is provided based on need alone. We should never allow creation of a government defined by race. Institutions made evil by racial exclusion or racial zealotry should be rehabilitated by forcing them to give up such policies. Powerful institutions where race is the primary defining factor, and which seek race-based political power, should be destroyed if they are unable or unwilling to be rehabilitated. Innocent people caught in dependence upon such institutions (both employees and beneficiaries) should be treated with kindness, should not be blamed for the evil of those institutions, and should he helped to escape.

Chapter 2

Mixed Metaphors

Dear reader, here are several metaphors for you to consider. Each has a different focus. All describe what's happening in Hawaii and how that threatens America. There's some repetition of concepts, but repetition facilitates understanding. (1) Evil Empire; (2) Cancer spreading; (3) Family where one beloved member is spoiled rotten, has handicaps and is a drug abuser; (4) Broken rainbow and the Aloha Spirit; (5) Boiling frog; (6) Hawaiian Jihad (aggressive religious fascism)

Evil Empire

An Evil Empire is gaining strength in Hawaii and threatening all of America. It's slowly but surely increasing its strangle-hold on Hawaii's land, money, and political power.

It is an empire because it includes dozens of powerful institutions owning vast tracts of land in Hawaii and other states, plus billions of dollars in the stock and bond markets, plus political power that forces the state legislature to do its bidding and actively lobbies Congress.

The empire is evil because it is founded on a doctrine of racial supremacy based on an ancient religion that was decisively rejected by its own adherents nearly two centuries ago. The empire is evil because it works to achieve a perverse combination of racial separatism and ethnic nationalism.

Hawaii's Evil Empire threatens the rest of America in three ways: by already taking huge amounts of money from all American taxpayers and planning to greatly increase the take; by perverting the Constitution under a new legal theory that would hasten the spread of ethnic balkanization; and by providing money and political power to fuel a secessionist movement.

Cancer spreading

A cancer is growing in the body politic of Hawaii, and threatens to spread throughout America. As with most cancers, it's hard to know exactly how it got started, and how best to destroy it.

Perhaps it got started in 1921 when Congress generously reached out to rehabilitate a downtrodden dying race by "putting Hawaiians back on the land." But the Hawaiian Homes Commission Act of 1921 spawned several dozen ghettos where only a race-based government agency can own land and only people of the favored race can get homestead leases, living under the thumb of community managers demanding patronage, political loyalty, and strict adherence to arbitrary bureaucratic regulation.

The cancer got stronger in 1978 when a State of Hawaii Constitutional Convention established a government agency, the Office of Hawaiian Affairs, founded on three pillars of racism. Trustees of the Office of Hawaiian Affairs were required by law to be elected exclusively by citizens of the favored race; trustees were required by law to be themselves members of that favored race; and assets of the agency were required by law to be spent exclusively for the benefit of members of the favored race. The first pillar was demolished by the Rice v. Cayetano lawsuit; the second pillar was demolished by the Arakaki#1 lawsuit; but the third remains standing although the Arakaki#2 lawsuit threatened to knock it down. Thus some of the cancer has been surgically removed, but we didn't get it all and so it keeps spreading. OHA now has about $400 million invested in stocks and bonds, plus an annual income of perhaps $40 million (about half from investment income and half from money given to OHA from the state treasury).

The cancer grew very strong during the past two decades when Bishop Estate (Kamehameha Schools) acquired huge amounts of cash by selling some of its land, and began aggressively intervening in state and national politics. Some influential leading members of the state legislature were on its payroll, making laws affecting KSBE's vast land holdings. KSBE has an entire division (PASE, Policy Analysis and System Evaluation) devoted to collecting victimhood statistics and publicizing them to fuel the Hawaiian grievance industry. KSBE has thousands of alumni who actively participate in alumni associations throughout the U.S. which function as lobbying agencies to influence Senators and Congressmen to support the Evil Empire. KSBE provides huge grants to selected public schools in return for considerable influence over the subject matter taught to the children – Hawaiian language immersion government-owned schools, Hawaiian culture-focus government-owned charter schools, ordinary government schools in neighborhoods where many children are ethnic Hawaiian, private schools, and various government and private colleges. KSBE provides scholarships for ethnic Hawaiian college students throughout the U.S., who then feel lifelong gratitude and engage in political activity to support the Evil Empire.

The cancer has spread to America in many important ways aside from KSBE. Congress has authorized over 160 federal programs for the exclusive benefit of citizens of the favored race. Congress has created a federal office to coordinate these programs and to ensure that federal agencies work with the Office of Hawaiian Affairs. OHA has established its own office in Washington to lobby Congress for more money and power. The Akaka bill pending in Congress since 2000 (revised many times), which was blocked by only a narrow margin in 2006, would authorize the creation of a race-based government whose members could include more than 400,000 people, of whom more than 160,000 live outside Hawaii.

Certainly the cancer got a large boost in 1993 when Congress passed an apology resolution. The resolution in its kind-heartedness was so effusive it blamed the U.S. for the entire outcome of an event where the U.S. played only a small role (sending ashore 162 Navy men as peacekeepers, who never fired a shot or took over a building, during a revolution conducted by 1500 armed local men). In its desire to show humble contrition, the apology resolution was written with flowery language containing errors of historical fact. The resolution apologized only to ethnic Hawaiians even though most of the population of the Hawaiian Kingdom, and many of its government officials, were not ethnic Hawaiians. By apologizing only to ethnic Hawaiians, the resolution now provides a primary basis for demanding race-based government handouts and for passing the Akaka bill to establish a racially exclusionary government. The resolution was worded in such a way that Hawaii's secessionist movement now cites it as a statement against interest – a voluntary confession of a crime under international law whose only remedy would be for the U.S. to withdraw its continuing belligerent military occupation of the native homeland.

Kenneth R. Conklin, Ph.D.

Family where one beloved member is spoiled rotten, has handicaps and is a drug abuser

The people of Hawaii are a close-knit family. There's one favorite family member who has a few mild handicaps (but claims many more), is spoiled rotten because we love him so much, and is a drug abuser.

Hawaii has the greatest racial diversity among the 50 states, and also the highest rate of intermarriage. Every racial group is a minority. People of every race live throughout all Hawaii's islands and neighborhoods, work in all professions and trades, earn all levels of income, belong to all the major religions, and hold all levels of political office.

For example, Hawaii's Governors and U.S. Senators have included Chinese, Filipino, ethic Hawaiian, Japanese, Jewish, and White. Many Hawaii citizens have a long list of ethnicities in their genealogies, and are very proud to recite them. It's perfectly normal for new acquaintances to ask each other: "Hey, what are you?" And it's perfectly normal to get the answer: "Chinese, Filipino, Japanese, Irish, German, and Hawaiian." But usually these days "Hawaiian" gets mentioned first, even if it's the smallest percentage of the pedigree.

As a small group of islands thousands of miles from anywhere else, with only 1.2 million people, where most people are locally born and raised, we have great love and caring for each other. The whole population gets very excited when the multiracial university volleyball team or football team scores high in national rankings; or one Filipino-American girl (Jasmine Trias) places third on the American Idol TV show; or one Korean-American teenage girl (Michelle Wie) earns high ranking in major adult golf tournaments; or one Japanese-American general (Eric Shinseki) stands strong on principle and is forced to resign because the President doesn't like to hear an inconvenient truth that more troops are needed in Iraq.

One member of our close-knit family tries to hog all the attention and often succeeds. He has a few mild handicaps; but he claims the handicaps are far worse than we acknowledge and that he has others besides. He's our favorite family member, so we lavish affection and money on him far more than anyone else. We feel he has special wisdom and some skills we greatly admire, so we try to overlook his faults and cater to his every desire.

But all too often we fall short of meeting his expectations – his sometimes outrageous demands – and when that happens he cries or screams until we give him what he wants. And then of course he wants more. Now he says the entire house really belongs to him. He'll let the rest of us stay with him but only if we obey.

He's a drug abuser too – addicted to an ever-increasing flow of government handouts, and throwing a tantrum whenever the supply is threatened. So, what's a loving family to do? Shall we enable him, feeding his habit as his demands grow larger and larger, running the family into bankruptcy along the way? Or shall we cut off the drug supply, embrace him and hold him tightly until the withdrawal symptoms subside?

Broken rainbow and the Aloha Spirit

Tourists think Diamond Head is the state icon. But for us who live in Hawaii, the rainbow is the symbol that best expresses the unity of our multicolor diversity.

Rainbows can be seen almost every day in the nearby mountains, or over the ocean. Our university sports teams are called the "Bows" or "Rainbow Warriors." TV viewers across America were moved to tears by an episode of "ER" when they heard the stunningly beautiful voice of the late Israel Kamakawiwoole accompanying himself on his ukulele while singing "Over the Rainbow." Terminally ill Dr. Mark Green of "ER" had come to Hawaii to be surrounded by beauty, and as he slowly faded out of this world, Kamakawiwoole's rainbow song played in the background.

"The Aloha Spirit" is very powerful. It is pervasive throughout the land and the people. It includes inspiration from the beauty around us, reverence for life, respect and compassion for others, random acts of kindness, and an eagerness to reach out to give help with no thought of return.

Perhaps the Aloha Spirit can be explained by using a Christian doctrine as a metaphor – the doctrine of the Trinity (although other religions also have good metaphors). God is three persons in one: Father, Son, and Holy Spirit. The Holy Spirit is not merely a dove carrying an olive branch; it is an all-knowing, all-powerful, fully-equal manifestation of God, capable of working miracles. The Holy Spirit comes through divine grace to infuse the soul of anyone who is open to receive it; inspiring faith, hope, and charity.

The Aloha Spirit is the glue which holds together Hawaii's multiracial rainbow.

But our rainbow is under attack. Powerful institutions and politicians are trying to pull it apart. Imagine how sad it would be to wake up one morning, watch the mist passing gently across the mountains, – and see the rainbow's red arc on one side of the sky while the green arc is on the other side. Or perhaps the rainbow is gone entirely, replaced by a big black cloud that hangs permanently over the land, blocking out the sun forever.

The Aloha Spirit can rescue our rainbow, but only if enough of us open our hearts to receive its grace, and use its mighty power to overcome the forces of evil.

Boiling Frog

There's a commonly heard metaphor. If a frog is thrown into a pot of boiling water, it will jump right out. But if a frog finds itself in a pot of lukewarm water which is then slowly heated to the boiling point, it will gradually grow weak and be boiled alive without struggling.

In Hawaii the Evil Empire has grown slowly and quietly. The first few institutions were not at all evil when they were founded during the Kingdom and early Territorial periods. The alii trusts were set up for truly benevolent, non-political purposes: King William Charles Lunalilo, died 1874, established a retirement home for destitute natives; Bernice Pauahi Bishop, died 1884, established schools for boys and girls to learn vocational skills as tradesmen or homemakers; ex-queen Liliuokalani, died 1917, established a program to care for orphaned or indigent children. All those trusts have survived into the present; but the only one that turned evil is Bishop Estate, which changed its corporate name to the more benign (and native-sounding) Kamehameha Schools. KSBE has grown enormously wealthy through income from its vast landholdings and sales of some lands. It has used that wealth to gain an economic and political stranglehold on the State of Hawaii, with interlocking directorates with banks, brokerage houses, and major corporations (including at one time 10% ownership of Goldman Sachs and enormous influence with Treasury Secretary Robert Rubin in the Clinton administration).

The Hawaiian Homes Commission Act of 1921 set aside 203,500 acres of land to be used for giving leases to Hawaiians of at least 50% native blood quantum, for the purpose of farming or building homes. Today the Department of Hawaiian Homelands is one of the state's largest land developers of residential housing and commercial shopping centers.

Through land swaps DHHL has also become landlord to leaseholder farmers who are not allowed to live on their farms because they lack Hawaiian native blood (including some American Indians belonging to federally recognized tribes), and whose farmland and buildings will be confiscated when the lease runs out.

One by one, more than 160 racially exclusionary federally funded programs have been established during the past 30 years, plus a large number of private ones. Alu Like was incorporated in 1975 and received its first federal funding in 1976 to provide racially exclusionary programs for vocational training. It has since expanded into areas such as a Native Hawaiian library, and a project to digitize Hawaiian language newspapers from the Kingdom and Territorial periods. Papa Ola Lokahi was created in 1988 as a Native Hawaiian health system providing direct healthcare; it also coordinates research projects to gather victimhood data for use in propaganda campaigns and in seeking additional grants. A Native Hawaiian Education Act provides federal funding for racially exclusionary programs to serve ethnic Hawaiians at all levels of schooling. Many other programs will be described in this book's chapter on racial separatism.

The NHEA includes language claiming there is a federal trust relationship with ethnic Hawaiians, and that they have the right to self-determination. Similar language is found in all federal legislation passed in recent years to benefit ethnic Hawaiians. While such language is only in a preamble which does not carry the force of law, it is nevertheless cited by Hawaiian sovereignty activists as evidence that Congress has already recognized ethnic Hawaiians as a political entity. Inserting such language that is irrelevant to the purpose of a piece of legislation violates its benevolent spirit. It undermines the unity of the State of Hawaii and the equality of its people. It turns up the heat on the pot of water, bringing the unsuspecting frog closer to the boiling point.

Hawaiian Jihad (aggressive religious fascism)

We've all had the experience of someone coming to our door, carrying a Bible and a stack of pamphlets, determined to make sure we have heard "the message." In some cases, after we make clear that we have heard the message and are not interested, the missionary becomes agitated, starts shouting, and won't take "No" for an answer. Even if we've read the Bible cover to cover many times and can battle quote-for-quote, we will never persuade the zealot that he is mistaken. Zealots KNOW they are right. Evidence to the contrary is automatically rejected, sometimes heatedly and angrily.

Hawaiian sovereignty activists are zealous. Sometimes their advocacy becomes shrill or irrational. They insist on expressing their views loudly and at length, even when it's clear there can be no hope of persuading anyone. Like all zealots they feel a strong need to "witness" for their beliefs. They feel compelled to shout their beliefs from the rooftop even if there's nobody listening. Spreading the message is a moral imperative for religious zealots both because their church requires it and because "witnessing" is an offering to please God.

Like other zealots, Hawaiian jihadists build their own monuments. During the 1993 centennial mourning the revolution that overthrew the Hawaiian monarchy, the zealots erected a rock pile at Iolani Palace. The "ahu" (altar) is composed of rocks brought there by fellow zealots from various islands and neighborhoods, symbolizing the coming together of all Hawaiians to rebuild a sovereign nation on the grounds of its former national capitol. Since then the rock pile has been a place for prayers and ceremonies. When the rock pile was vandalized in 2006, zealots quickly spread word by cell phone and reassembled it within a single day. Hawaiian zealots have repeatedly carried huge Hawaiian flags to the cold and windy summit of Mauna Kea specifically to place the Hawaiian flag higher than all the American flags throughout Hawaii. On August 6, 2005, following a court decision threatening Kamehameha School's racially exclusionary admissions policy, a crowd of twenty thousand red-shirted zealots (including Hawaii's Governor) marched from the Royal Mausoleum to Iolani Palace, where many anti-American signs were on display.

Zealots around the world vandalize and seek to destroy opposing expressions. A few years ago the Taliban in Afghanistan blew up two Buddha images despite pleas from world leaders of all faiths. The images were 175 and 120 feet tall, carved by chipping away a mountainside more than 1500 years ago. Hawaiian zealots behave similarly, although on a smaller scale. Books in the libraries and bookstores which challenge their view of history are routinely stolen or vandalized. The only guest professor to teach a course with an opposing viewpoint encountered threats of violence against the program director who dared to make arrangements, and against the elderly students who had specifically invited him.

When a celebration was held in August 2006 on the official holiday commemorating the admission of Hawaii to the U.S. as a state – at the former capitol building of the Territory and State of Hawaii where the transition to statehood occurred – a group of Hawaiian sovereignty zealots disrupted and prevented the celebration. Children in a high school band, seated and waiting to play, were threatened both up close and also from a megaphone a few yards away, causing their parents to remove them. Zealots simply walked up to event organizers and would-be speakers, shouting in their faces.

Hawaiian zealots sometimes behave like a dog running through the neighborhood lifting its leg at every fire hydrant, claiming territory by leaving a scent mark. A small group of zealots traveled to Boston and used the tourist attraction Tea Party ship to stage their own protest demanding Hawaiian independence – they had a Boston "Ti Party", throwing Hawaiian ti leaves over the side of the Tea Party ship. They traveled to Washington D.C. and staged a "march" to the nation's Capitol with about 50 people – one observer derisively called it "The Million Malo March" (using the name for the Hawaiian male loin-cloth as a reference to the African-American "Million Man March" which truly had a huge turnout).

Hawaiian zealots feel compelled to enter every open venue of discussion, but to exclude opposing views from their own turf. Forums at the university typically have several presenters all supporting different aspects of the same theory, but no opponents. In internet discussion groups open to the public, any essay from an opposing view will be viciously and repeatedly attacked, often with personal comments directed at the author. Sometimes an opposing essay will be attacked by "slicing and dicing" – singling out large numbers of small phrases or short passages and attacking them at length with irrelevant or silly comments to divert attention from the main focus.

Tourists are sometimes attacked and beaten by young men who regard tourism as an industry that desecrates sacred places and is hostile to "native" interests – an attitude which has been encouraged in writing by Haunani-Kay Trask, the former Chair (and still professor) of the Center for Hawaiian Studies.

A man who calls himself "reverend" (although never ordained and never the pastor of a church) has repeatedly committed virtual violence by reminding listeners that "Hawaiians are a warrior people" and by threatening that there will be violence unless Hawaiian sovereignty demands are met. This "reverend" served for many years as the Chairman of the Hawaii Advisory Committee to the U.S. Commission on Civil Rights, even during the period when he gave speeches and published articles threatening that there would be violence if civil rights activists continued to oppose demands for racially exclusionary government handouts. He is a strong supporter of the Akaka bill, and views it as an economic and political engine to move toward total secession of Hawaii from the United States.

The Hawaiian jihad resembles fascism in possessing a religious theory that supports racial supremacy. According to this theory, the gods gave birth to the Hawaiian islands as living beings, and later gave birth to the primordial ancestor of all ethnic Hawaiians. Therefore any person with a drop of Hawaiian native blood is descended from the gods and is a brother to the land. Outsiders lacking a drop of the magic blood are forever outside that family. Outsiders have no standing and the best they can hope for is to be guests in the Hawaiian homeland. In order to exercise their god-given right to control the land, ethnic Hawaiians are entitled to political power based on race. Sometimes the activists cover up their racism by calling it genealogy, not race – but in practice it's the same thing. This religious theory is taught as fact in both government and private schools: especially The University of Hawaii Center for Hawaiian Studies, Kamehameha Schools, the Hawaiian-culture-focus public charter schools, the Hawaiian language immersion public (K-12) and private (nursery) schools, and the ordinary public schools where Kamehameha pays one-fifth of operating costs in return for major influence over what the children learn.

In addition to a religious theory that race provides an entitlement to political supremacy, there are other similarities to fascism. The zealotry already described leads to an astonishing level of intellectual, social, and political activity. There are mass marches through the streets where everyone wears red shirts with the slogan "Ku i ka pono" (rise up for justice). There are threats of violence, and even death threats, against any who disagree.

As with other forms of fascism, the Hawaiian jihad elevates group rights far above individual rights. The religious theory includes a concept of group consciousness. "Hawaiian epistemology" claims that anyone with a drop of Hawaiian native blood has inborn special ways of knowing allowing him to access ancient wisdom from the ancestors and to see the natural environment through special lenses. Every individual is intimately connected with the entire sequence of his genealogy, so that each action done today is empowered by (and reflects back on) his ancestors and future descendants, who are all spiritually present at every moment. A popular book on "Polynesian" voyaging says that today's leaders were able to learn how to navigate by the stars by accessing racial memories even after several centuries when skills were lost (they actually got trained by a Micronesian master navigator and by using the projector at Bishop Museum's planetarium). There's talk of a "deep culture" underlying the more superficial customs of everyday life. There's a belief that "indigenous" people have a special kind of group intellectual property rights – informal but nevertheless binding group patents and copyrights to ancient knowledge (such as drugs derived from indigenous plants), and forms of cultural expression (such as hula).

The color of the red shirts worn in mass marches was chosen for several reasons. Just before the first big red-shirt march there was a rare phenomenon of nature. Large schools of a species of red fish (aweoweo) were seen in the shallow ocean waters – a hoailona (sign from heaven) traditionally associated with major change (such as the death of a high chief). Thus the mass of people wearing red shirts and marching in unison down the street resembled the schools of aweoweo swimming through the reef. Red is also the color of the ever-popular fire goddess Pele, and of Ku (god of war). Red is also the color of the blood that unites the ethnic Hawaiians into a single family descended from the gods. Red is the color "ula" in Ilioulaokalani (red dog in the sky, referring to an ominous cloud) – the name of the activist group previously formed by a red-shirt organizer who is also a hula master, to defend ethnic Hawaiian gathering "rights." On an even more ominous note: the Wilcox Rebellion of 1889, in which the Palace bungalow was blown up and several men died, featured Robert Wilcox's army of 80 men all wearing red Garibaldi shirts. Thus the whole red-shirt concept is filled with fascist symbolism signifying a combination of political power, warlike zealotry, racial solidarity, empowerment by the gods, and mass movement where the individual person is nothing more than one fish in a large school moving in unison.

Sovereignty activists like to say that in ancient times the land owned the people rather than the people owning land. The land was controlled collectively. A konohiki (land czar) dictated how each resource should be used in a coordinated way to serve the greater good and maintain "pono" (balance and righteousness) among the gods, the land, and the people. Resources included forests, streams, reefs, fishponds, taro patches, irrigation ditches, and even the people themselves – all organized by the konohiki into a unified organic ecological system, where the people belonged to the land. Today's sovereignty activists hope to revive that style of land management, using expressions like "sustainable land use" or "public trust doctrine" or "ahupuaa concept." All these forms of group knowledge and group rights are based on the religious theory that anyone with a drop of native blood is a descendant of the gods and a brother to the land, as members of a family which outsiders can never belong to.

If someone previously quiet begins asking too many questions, or makes a few comments the sovereignty activists don't like, the activists pursue a sequence of escalating interventions. Family members are often fairly easy for the zealots to control, through a combination of charming and shaming. Strangers or newcomers are harder to handle. First the zealots take aside the challenger, speaking quietly with him to help him understand the message. They assume the challenger simply needs to "hear the facts" or "learn the history." Since the challenger clearly doesn't understand, he needs to be "educated." The challenger is told to be quiet, to listen and learn, so that eventually he will understand. But what if it becomes clear that the challenger really does know the facts and history, has heard the message and does understand it; but nevertheless disagrees? Only one conclusion is possible. The challenger has an evil heart – he has heard the message and knows the truth but stubbornly and maliciously persists in his wickedness. Therefore the zealot has a moral right – perhaps even a moral obligation – to treat the challenger like a religious heretic or like the Devil. Hawaiian sovereignty zealots launch personal attacks against the character of an incorrigible challenger, trying to sabotage his work and reputation; perhaps engaging in identity theft or vandalism against his property; and perhaps turning verbal attacks into physical ones.

A further example of intolerance for opposing views is provided by Haunani Apoliona, who is Chair of the Office of Hawaiian Affairs. In June 2006 the Hawaiian jihadists suffered a major loss in U.S. Senate, when the Akaka bill failed to obtain the 60 votes needed on a cloture motion to bring the bill to the floor. One reason for that failure was a strong campaign against the bill by conservative think tanks, conservative commentators, and civil rights groups at both the state and national level. Haunani Apoliona was so shocked by that defeat that she used her editorials in the OHA monthly newspaper for August, September, and October to write a trilogy entitled "Nutgrass Network Conspiracy." Apoliona ranted and raved about a vast anti-Hawaiian conspiracy, providing names of numerous institutions that had helped defeat the Akaka bill – Aloha For All, Heritage Foundation, Grassroot Institute of Hawaii, Citizens Equal Rights Alliance, etc. Apoliona thought she was naming a rogues gallery of villains, when in fact she was naming a pantheon of heroes. Apoliona thinks it's perfectly fine for OHA to spend millions of dollars of government money hiring lobbyists, paying for TV and newspaper ads, and paying for dozens of its own people to travel repeatedly to Washington (first-class), but she gets very upset at civil rights groups and private individuals traveling at their own expense and for an idealistic purpose, to oppose a selfish racist bill.

Chapter 3

Racial Separatism in Hawaii, Past and Present

Summary

Caucasians were full partners in the Hawaiian Kingdom from its founding until its overthrow. There was no racial separatism until the Kalakaua and Liliuokalani reigns. Kalakaua became King in 1874. His personal corruption, lavish lifestyle, and unstable government cabinets provoked subjects (citizens) and foreign businessmen to take action. Mass meetings and armed militias, mostly Caucasian, imposed a Constitution on Kalakaua in 1887 that reduced him to a figurehead. In 1891 Kalakaua died and his sister Liliuokalani took the throne. The corruption continued. In January 1893 the Queen began a coup to overthrow the Constitution that had been forced on her brother and to unilaterally proclaim a new Constitution giving herself near-dictatorial powers. The same groups who had forced Kalakaua to sign the Reform (bayonet) Constitution in 1887 mobilized again and staged a revolution overthrowing the monarchy.

Ethnic Hawaiians during 1874-1902 united for racial pride and to protect the monarchy. After the Reform Constitution of 1887 several ethnic Hawaiian political parties tried to restore monarchial power. After the overthrow of 1893 they attempted a racially-driven counter-revolution to put the ex-queen back on the throne. When that failed they struggled mightily to prevent Hawaii's annexation to the United States. After annexation the ethnic Hawaiian splinter groups merged to form the Home Rule Party and were successful in electing firebrand Robert Wilcox to be Hawaii's first Territorial Delegate to Congress. Wilcox was a racial demagogue and had led the 1895 failed counter-revolution. His poor performance as Territorial Delegate, and the party's disrespect to Prince Jonah Kuhio Kalanaianaole (heir-apparent to the throne), caused the Prince to resign from the Home Rule Party. Kuhio formed an alliance with Caucasian businessmen and joined the Republican Party. Kuhio, elected in 1902, served as Territorial Delegate in Congress for two decades.

Ethnic Hawaiians had a large voting majority and dominated the Hawaii Legislature throughout the first half of the Territorial period. But their power slowly declined because more Americans from the mainland came to live in Hawaii, and many more Asians immigrated to Hawaii. People of Asian ancestry born in Hawaii were U.S. citizens and grew old enough to vote. Anti-Asian U.S. laws eventually were changed, allowing Asians to immigrate and then to become naturalized citizens and vote. Thus ethnic Hawaiians slowly became an ever-smaller minority of voters, leveling off at about 20%.

The decline of ethnic Hawaiian political power, and the rise of Black pride and Black political assertiveness on the mainland, prompted ethnic Hawaiians to start their own movement for pride and power. During the last thirty years ethnic Hawaiians have revived or reinvented elements of their ancient religion and culture, together with Hawaiian language, and used them to build political solidarity. There is now a very aggressive racial separatist movement in Hawaii, similar to the separatist demagoguery of the early Malcolm X, the Black Panthers, Elijah Muhammad and Louis Farrakhan.

But ethnic Hawaiians have what mainland Blacks do not – wealthy and powerful government and private agencies collaborating with each other, dominating the media and the political establishment. This consortium, referred to as Hawaii's Evil Empire, has grown so strong that it is pushing a bill through Congress (The Akaka bill) to authorize creation of a racially exclusionary government empowered to negotiate with the federal and state governments to partition Hawaii along racial lines, thus creating an apartheid regime. The state government agency "Office of Hawaiian Affairs" has spent many millions of dollars lobbying and advertising for the Akaka bill. OHA has also spent millions in advertising and travel expenses, both in Hawaii and on the mainland, to get people to sign up on a racial registry (at the end of 2006 the "Kau Inoa" registry had nearly 60,000 names). OHA has devised a Plan B to create a state-recognized tribal government in the absence of the Akaka bill, and in preparation for eventual passage of the bill.

Caucasians were full partners in the Hawaiian Kingdom (government and culture)

Before Captain Cook's arrival in 1778, all residents of Hawaii were what today would be called "pure Hawaiian." There was no racial separatism. Of course there never were any people who sprang up originally from the land of the Hawaiian islands. The "pure Hawaiians" were a genetic mix of several waves of immigration during a period from perhaps 400 to 1400 AD. The first immigrants may have come from the Marquesas, although there are legends of an earlier race of "Menehune." The warrior culture, alii social system, and human sacrifice were all apparently brought in by conquerors from Tahiti, perhaps 1300-1400 AD. It's unclear whether the Tahitians exterminated the Marquesans, enslaved them, or intermarried with them peacefully. Today's ethnic Hawaiians are less entitled to call themselves "indigenous" than the white people of Europe, especially those British people descended from the Celts, Angles, and Saxons. The Norman conquest of England took place centuries earlier than the Tahitian conquest of Hawaii.

Following Captain Cook's arrival there were several decades of intense warfare among competing native warlords. Kamehameha was the first person able to kill all his enemies and take over all the Hawaiian islands under a single ruler. He accomplished that only because he made friends with British naval officers and businessmen. Kamehameha acquired technology previously unknown in Hawaii, such as metal knives, guns, cannons, and large warships. Kamehameha also acquired the services of two British sailors. Isaac Davis and John Young were initially kidnapped but soon decided to stay voluntarily, training Kamehameha's warriors in techniques and strategy for using the new technology.

Caucasians were full partners and important leaders of the Hawaiian Kingdom throughout its history. There was neither racial separatism nor assertion of "indigenous rights."

Kamehameha was so grateful to John Young that he gave Young land and a house immediately next to the great heiau Puukohola, and appointed Young to be Governor of Kamehameha's home island (Hawaii Island).[15] John Young's tomb is today in Mauna Ala, the Royal Mausoleum, marked by a raised flat stone monument resembling a small ancient heiau and accompanied by a pair of puloulou (taboo sticks); he is joined in Mauna Ala by the tombs of monarchs Kamehameha II, III, IV, V, Kalakaua, and Liliuokalani.

Hawaiian Apartheid

Also in Mauna Ala is the tomb of white man Charles Reed Bishop, husband of Princess Bernice Pauahi Bishop. The princess donated her land to create Bishop Estate and to launch Kamehameha Schools. Charles Bishop later donated more money than her land was worth to finance both Kamehameha Schools and the Bishop Museum.[16] All five original trustees of Bishop Estate, appointed by the princess, were Caucasian; and over the years most trustees continued to be Caucasian or Asian. The same is true of the directors of Bishop Museum, until political correctness finally produced a majority of ethnic Hawaiian directors in 2006. Bishop Museum's President and CEO resigned in 2006 and the racial zealots will push hard to be sure his successor is ethnic Hawaiian.

Throughout the Kingdom period, most cabinet ministers and executive department heads were Caucasian, along with nearly all the judges and perhaps one-fourth to one-third of the members of the Legislature (both Nobles and Representatives, both appointed and elected). Two of the greatest heroes of the Kingdom were Caucasians. Rev. Dr. Gerrit Judd was the closest advisor to Kauikeaouli Kamehameha III, always walking next to the King in formal processions and ahead of the native chiefs. Gerrit Judd and William Richards were the heroes of the Kingdom in 1843, in two events that were so important they led to the establishment of two national holidays.[17]

When a rogue British naval captain seized control of Hawaii and forced Kamehameha III to cede sovereignty to him, Judd wrote an appeal to the British government which resulted in the return of sovereignty to the King a few months later. Judd risked his life, writing the appeal in secret, at night, using the coffin of the recently deceased Queen Kaahumanu as his writing desk, and passing the document secretly to an American sailor for delivery to the British. When British Admiral Thomas sailed into Honolulu harbor with a proclamation restoring sovereignty to the King, Judd and the King led a huge procession to Kawaiahao Church where Judd read the English-language proclamation out loud in fluent Hawaiian; and the King then delivered his famous one-liner which has been handed down as our state motto today: "Ua mau ke ea o ka aina i ka pono" (generally translated as "The life of the land is perpetuated in righteousness"). Thus was established Ka La Hoihoi Ea (Sovereignty Restoration Day, July 31, 1843). Judd was also a medical doctor who saved many native lives (including reportedly that of the King himself); and who created a human anatomy textbook in Hawaiian language, using it to teach medicine to natives.

William Richards was a missionary, who became a close advisor to the King. In 1839 he helped the King write a Declaration of the Rights of Man. The first two sentences of that document use powerful, beautiful language to assert the very opposite of racial separatism: "God hath made of one blood all nations of men to dwell on the earth, in unity and blessedness. God has also bestowed certain rights alike on all men and all chiefs, and all people of all lands." In 1840 Richards helped the King write Hawaii's first Constitution, modeled after the U.S. Constitution, including the 1839 Declaration as its preamble.

In 1842-1843 Richards, together with a young native chief (Haalilio), traveled on a mission to achieve diplomatic recognition. They went to the U.S., England, and France. Richards was entrusted with blank parchments with the King's signature and Royal Seal already in place, and he was authorized to make whatever deal he thought best. Haalilio died before the mission was finished, but Richards brought back a joint declaration by England and France in which those two nations promised each other that neither would try to take over Hawaii. Thus was established Ka La Kuokoa (Independence Day, November 28, 1843).

The role of Caucasians in Hawaii was not limited to government work. In 1819, shortly after the death of Kamehameha The Great, his son Liholiho Kamehameha II abolished the old religion that had been the basis for Hawaiian culture for centuries. A short civil war broke out as diehard followers of the old religion tried to save it, but Liholiho's forces were victorious.

Several years before the old religion was abolished a small group of native young men got on a ship going to America. One of them was the son and heir-apparent of the King of Kauai. Another of them, Opukahaia, was a commoner who had seen his civilian parents and a younger brother (a small child) killed in one of Kamehameha's wars. The Hawaiians made their way to Connecticut, to Yale University, where they studied Christianity. Opukahaia (also spelled Obookiah) became fluent in English, was a great public speaker, and became a fervent Christian. One day he was sitting on the steps of the Yale library weeping, and was asked why. He begged and pleaded with the faculty to please send missionaries to Hawaii to raise up his people out of their heathen ways.[18]

And so a boatload of Calvinist missionaries set sail from Boston to Hawaii. Opukahaia had died back at Yale, but the remaining native men returned with the missionaries, and on the long voyage taught them to speak Hawaiian fluently and helped them begin inventing a written version of Hawaiian. The ship arrived in Hawaii in 1820 at exactly the right historical moment, just a few months after the old religion had been overthrown. The missionaries were amazed to hear that news, and gave thanks to God for that miracle of timing.

The missionaries brought more than Christianity and medicine. They created a written Hawaiian language and taught it to the people. They brought a printing press and printed the Bible in Hawaiian, using it to teach reading. In a few years thousands of natives had converted to Christianity, including important high chiefs and the King. The people eagerly learned how to read and write. Hawaii soon had the highest literacy rate in the world. Daily newspapers began to be published, some in Hawaiian and some in English (both natives and whites became increasingly bilingual).

By 1848 twelve boatloads of Calvinist missionaries had come to Hawaii from New England. Some were medical doctors in addition to being ordained ministers. The missionaries and their wives rendered great service and were dearly beloved by the native commoners and most of the chiefs. A grateful King showed his appreciation by proclaiming an official national Thanksgiving holiday in 1849 (fourteen years before Abraham Lincoln proclaimed it a national holiday in America!).[19] The new holiday was celebrated by the King, high chiefs, missionaries, and American residents of Honolulu in a service at the great coral church (Kawaiahao), after which everyone went across the street to the missionaries' housing complex for a luau. Kawaiahao Church itself is a monument to the loving cooperation between natives and whites in service to a lofty ideal. The church was constructed in the 1820s with 14,000 huge rectangular blocks of coral, harvested by natives using hand tools in the shallow offshore reef, dragged to the site, carved, and assembled under the instructions of the missionaries.

American companies came to dominate the economy of Hawaii through the whaling industry and the sugar plantations. Tens of thousands of Japanese and Chinese, and thousands of Portuguese, came to Hawaii to work on the sugar plantations. By 1892 (the year before the monarchy was overthrown) only 40% of Hawaii's people had any Hawaiian native blood. 95% of the Kingdom's government schools were using English as the language for teaching all the subjects, because the Kingdom government realized English was the pathway to success; and most native parents cooperated by speaking only English to their children at home.[20]

The reason for this lengthy discussion of history is to show that Caucasians were full partners in the Hawaiian Kingdom, right from the beginning. There was never a unified Hawaii until Kamehameha used Western technology and Caucasian military advisors to take over all the islands by 1810. In gratitude Kamehameha appointed John Young to be governor of his home island. American missionaries arrived in 1820 bringing Christianity and written language, both of which were eagerly embraced by the natives. Caucasians were the closest advisors to Kamehameha III, helping him write the Kingdom's first Constitution. Caucasians were heroes of the Kingdom, helping restore sovereignty in 1843 after a rogue British takeover, and helping gain diplomatic recognition of Hawaii's status as a nation. Caucasians held most of the cabinet positions, nearly all the judgeships, and a substantial number of Legislative seats (both Nobles and Representatives, both appointed and elected) throughout the Kingdom period.

Racial separatism in the politics of 1874 to 1902

There was no desire for racial separatism in the Kingdom, until the Kalakaua and Liliuokalani reigns. By that time American and European business interests had come to dominate Hawaii's economy. They had a strong need for good government and economic stability; which clashed with Kalakaua's lavish lifestyle, the corruption rampant in both Kalakaua's and Liliuokalani's governments, and their frequent turnover of cabinets.

Kalakaua became King through corruption tinged with racism. King Lunalilo who died in 1874 had failed to name a successor, so it was up to the Legislature to elect the next monarch. Kalakaua ran against dowager Queen Emma (wife of Alexander Liholiho Kamehameha IV). The campaign was conducted in public meetings and in the Hawaiian language newspapers. Kalakaua made a racial appeal by having his own genealogy embellished and published – Emma was one-fourth Caucasian, being granddaughter of John Young. Kalakaua also gave liquor and monetary bribes to the legislators. When the 39-6 vote electing Kalakaua was announced from the balcony of the legislature building, a riot broke out in the street below. The crowd stormed into the building, and a Representative was thrown out an upper floor window later dying from the fall. Peace was restored only when 150 American sailors and 80 British sailors came ashore and put an end to the rioting.[21]

Kalakaua was a very big spender. He ordered the building of Iolani Palace, completed in 1882 at a cost of $360,000 – an enormous sum. For comparison, Bernice Pauahi Bishop's estate probated around 1884 had a value of only about $300,000 including 400,000 acres of land. While the Palace was under construction Kalakaua spent another huge sum, taking a ten-month trip around the world in 1881 – the first monarch in world history ever to do that. After furnishing the Palace luxuriously, he then staged a massive coronation ceremony (even though he had been King for many years already). This lavish lifestyle contrasted sharply with the extreme poverty of many natives whom he never tried to help, and the low wages and poor living conditions of the indentured Asian and Portuguese sugar plantation workers.

In 1887 Kalakaua took $71,000 from rice plantation owner Tong Kee in return for a promise to give him an exclusive opium license; but shortly thereafter the license was sold for $80,000 to a merchant, Chun Lung. Kalakaua refused to give Tong Kee his money back. Even a lawsuit and public exposure of the scandal in the newspapers failed to get Tong Kee his money back. Finally the return of the money was made one of the requirements imposed on Kalakaua in the revolution of 1887 that established the so-called "Bayonet Constitution."[22] During his reign from 1875 to 1891, his government was so unstable there were 26 different cabinets in 16 years.

Liliuokalani's reign of less than two years was also filled with corruption and instability. The final overthrow of the monarchy in 1893 was precipitated by Liliuokalani's publicly announced intention to unilaterally proclaim a new Constitution, violating the existing Constitution she had sworn to uphold. Her new Constitution would have restored strong powers to the monarch, including undoing the reforms of the Constitution of 1887. It was also reported that the proposed Constitution would have limited the right to vote to ethnic Hawaiians only; but we will never know because Liliuokalani ordered all copies destroyed when the revolution took place.[23]

The Morgan Report (U.S. Senate Committee on Foreign Affairs, 1894)[24] has numerous sworn testimonies describing how the Queen bribed the Legislature to support the dismissal of her cabinet a few days before the Legislature's term ended; and the appointment of a new cabinet favorable to her lottery, distillery, and opium bills. The Morgan Report testimonies describe corruption related to the passage of those bills; the closing of the Legislature; and then the immediate attempt to proclaim a new Constitution restoring royal prerogatives. Her final cabinet ministers refused to support her attempt to proclaim her new Constitution, despite the fact that she had appointed them only a few days previously. In the throne room she threatened them with bodily harm so angrily and severely that some of them ran away as fast as they could to a downtown law office a few blocks away.

Liliuokalani was clearly a racial partisan. In speeches and writings during her reign, and also long after the revolution, she used the phrase "my people" to refer not to the entirety of the multiracial populace who were truly the monarch's people, nor even to the multiracial subjects of her Kingdom who had voting rights, but rather to her racial group. For example, here is a now-famous quote from Liliuokalani's diary entry for Sunday September 2 1900 (following Annexation and the Organic Act): "Tho' for a moment it [the overthrow] cost me a pang of pain for my people it was only momentary, for the present has a hope for the future of my people." In May and June of 2003 the accuracy of that quote was a subject of great controversy in the Honolulu media, not because of the ex-queen's racism, but because the quote indicates her easy acceptance of an event which today's ethnic Hawaiians claim was so traumatic to their entire race that the effects are still felt to this day as shown in the (alleged) victimhood statistics so aggressively flaunted by the Hawaiian grievance industry. The highly respected Bishop Museum archivist DeSoto Brown, himself ethnic Hawaiian, at first publicly expressed doubt about the quote's accuracy; but shortly thereafter he published in Honolulu Weekly the fact that he had searched the State Archives and had found the quoted sentence in Liliuokalani's own handwriting. Liliuokalani's use of "my people" as a racial reference, when it should be a reference to a multiracial political group, is well known and therefore was not the focus of the controversy.

In the 1880s and 1890s ethnic Hawaiians felt it was a matter of racial pride to support the monarch, and resented the passing of economic and political power to the Caucasians. Several splinter political parties were formed which were almost entirely ethnic Hawaiian. The Reform (Bayonet) Constitution of 1887 imposed severe restrictions on the King, reducing him to a figurehead under the control of his cabinet and the Legislature. The King agreed to sign that Constitution only after a mass meeting of about 1500 people, mostly Caucasian and many armed. The overthrow of the monarchy in 1893 was done by mostly Caucasians (of American and Portuguese ancestry). The attempted counter-revolution in January 1895, led by Robert Wilcox, was done mostly by ethnic Hawaiians. Two ethnic Hawaiian political groups, from 1893 to 1898, led the resistance to annexation, gathering 21,269 signatures on a petition opposing annexation and allegedly 17,000 signatures on a different petition (now lost) demanding restoration of the monarchy.

After annexation was completed in 1898, the ethnic Hawaiian resistance groups merged to form the Home Rule political party. Their plan was to use their racial voting majority in the Territory to elect ethnic Hawaiians to office and to write laws favorable to their race. The Home Rule Party nominated firebrand revolutionary Robert Wilcox for Territorial Delegate to Congress. Since ethnic Hawaiians were the majority of voters, the Home Rule Party easily won and Wilcox served as Delegate from 1900 to 1902.

Wilcox did a poor job in Congress, and the Home Rule Party was splintered by internal quarreling. Prince Jonah Kuhio Kalanianaole, heir-apparent to the throne, was abused and disrespected by the radicals at the Home Rule Party political convention. Kuhio resigned, and made a deal with Caucasian businessmen to run as the candidate of the Republican Party in 1902 for Territorial Delegate. He won, and served in Congress for two decades, introducing the first bill for Hawaii statehood in 1919 and securing passage of the Hawaiian Homes Commission Act in 1921.[25]

Racial separatism in the alii trusts, and Department of Hawaiian Homelands

In Hawaii the Evil Empire has grown slowly and quietly. The first few institutions were not at all evil and not aggressively separatist when they were founded during the Kingdom and early Territorial periods. The alii trusts were set up for truly benevolent, non-political purposes. King William Charles Lunalilo (died 1874) established a retirement home for destitute natives. Princess Bernice Pauahi Bishop (died 1884) established schools for boys and girls to learn vocational skills as tradesmen or homemakers. Ex-queen Liliuokalani (died 1917) established a program to care for orphaned and indigent children. All those trusts have survived into the present. The only one that turned evil is Bishop Estate, which recently changed its corporate name to the more benign (and native-sounding) Kamehameha Schools. First, let's look briefly at Lunalilo Homes, Queen Liliuokalani Childrens Centers, and the Department of Hawaiian Homelands. Kamehameha Schools will be dealt with after that.

King William Charles Lunalilo left substantial land holdings in trust when he died in 1874, to support a retirement home for destitute native Hawaiian elders. As Lunalilo's will had specified, the trustees sold most of the land to raise cash for operating expenses and investments. The market crash of 1929 and other bad investments cost the Lunalilo Trust huge losses, and it has been struggling for many decades. Lunalilo Home was recently renovated, and no longer restricts itself to clients who are destitute. It serves only a few dozen nursing home residents, who are still required to be ethnic Hawaiian. It also has small adult daycare and meals-on-wheels outreach programs, which bring in a little revenue and are not racially exclusionary. It has not been a factor in today's political battles.

The Queen Liliuokalani Childrens Trust was established in the will of the ex-queen, who died in 1917. Through a small network of widely scattered "Queen Liliuokalani Childrens Centers" the trust provides help to about nine thousand needy ethnic Hawaiian children and their families each year. Some of that help is in the form of family counseling for alcoholism, drug abuse, child neglect, child abuse, anger management, dispute resolution, etc. Some of the family counseling is done using the Hawaiian culture-based technique of hooponopono which includes prayer and mediation by a trusted community or family elder.

There was political controversy surrounding the founding of QLCT, and again quite recently. Ex-queen Liliuokalani had tried for many years to get money from the U.S. government as compensation for the ceding to the U.S. of the former Kingdom's crown lands. She filed a lawsuit in 1909 against the U.S., claiming the crown lands had belonged to her personally and she should receive compensation for them. But the U.S. Court of Claims ruled in 1910 that she had never owned the lands personally.[26]

For about ten years before the Court of Claims decision she had been trying to get Congress to pass a bill to give her compensation. She relied on Hawaii's Territorial Delegate Jonah Kuhio Kalanianaole to push her legislation. She gave Kuhio a parcel of her land in Waikiki as a sort of informal bribe to spur his work on her behalf. But Kuhio greedily wanted all her Waikiki property. In 1915 Kuhio filed a lawsuit to nullify Liliuokalani's will on the grounds that she was mentally incompetent, and to name himself as her guardian (and trustee of her estate). The court ruled against Kuhio in 1916, and the QLCT was saved.[27]

In 2002 QLCT came into public controversy regarding a bill in the Honolulu City Council to make it easier for owners of leasehold condominium apartments to force the landowner to sell them the land under their building. A law already in place allowed apartment owners to petition the City to condemn the land at fair market value, allowing the apartment owners to pay for the land and convert their leases to fee-simple. Several owners of apartments in Foster Towers (on the beach alongside Kapiolani Park in Waikiki) had tried to buy their land, but QLCT refused. The percentage of apartment owners who were living in their apartments who wanted to purchase their land was not sufficient to require the City to begin condemnation, and so there was an attempt to pass a revision in the law easing the requirements to force condemnation. QLCT waged a huge political campaign to defeat the legislation, with great help from Kamehameha Schools. Along the way there was a mass rally at Iolani Palace, including a highly inflammatory racist speech by University of Hawaii Professor Haunani-Kay Trask.[28] City Council hearings were packed by ethnic Hawaiians. There were TV programs and newspaper ads; and speeches about how the land is sacred to ethnic Hawaiians (even when they lease it for a huge apartment building?). The bill to ease requirements for forced lease-to-fee conversion was defeated. Later the entire law was repealed that had allowed condominium apartment owners to force landowners to sell. Thus QLCT used racial demagoguery and political activism to hold onto land in Waikiki, citing claims of land being sacred, deprivation of rights caused by the overthrow of the monarchy, etc. Meanwhile the truly benevolent work of the QLCT continued. However, that benevolence is soured by being restricted to ethnic Hawaiian children.

In 1921 Congress passed the Hawaiian Homes Commission Act. That was the first time the federal government passed legislation to provide racially exclusionary benefits to ethnic Hawaiians. In a way, HHCA can be thought of as an alii trust, because it was the greatest accomplishment and legacy of Prince Jonah Kuhio Kalanaianaole (heir apparent to the throne) during his two decades of service as Hawaii's Territorial Delegate. But unlike Lunalilo Home, Queen Liliuokalani Childrens Centers, and Kamehameha Schools, all of which were entirely based on private property bequeathed through a will or trust, the HHCA was government legislation to set aside government lands and to administer them through a government agency.

The HHCA set aside 203,500 acres of land to be used for giving leases to Hawaiians of at least 50% native blood quantum, for the purpose of farming or building homes. The language in that legislation is very demeaning to ethnic Hawaiians, identifying them as a dying race incapable of taking care of themselves. Hawaiians were not to be trusted with outright grants of land which they would probably then sell and squander the money.

One reason the HHCA was regrettable is that it put an end to a very good non-racial homesteading law already in place in Hawaii, and replaced it with racial exclusion. On the surface it seems like an act of benevolence to provide land for a poor, downtrodden, dying race to help them have homes and farms. However, Kuhio had been a racial partisan throughout his public career, and was politically astute enough to realize that the racially exclusionary HHCA would provide a nucleus for further growth of race-based political power and racial separatism.

Kuhio had conspired with Robert Wilcox in the bloody attempted counter-revolution of 1895. Kuhio was convicted of misprision of [conspiracy in] treason and sentenced to a fine of $1,000 and one year in prison. In the late 1890s he went into voluntary exile, serving in the British military in the Boer War. His quest for excitement found him doing something very politically incorrect. Indeed, it's amazing that today's sovereignty activists turn a blind eye to Kuhio's hypocrisy. In the Boer war Kuhio was helping one white colonial power fight another white colonial power to control the far-away land of a dark-skinned indigenous people. He was especially irresponsible in doing this at the same time his own people in Hawaii were struggling to oppose annexation. He finally returned to Hawaii and joined the racist Home Rule Party until they disrespected him at their party convention. Since it was clear he could not win the nomination in a political party controlled by Wilcox, Kuhio broke away and joined the Republican Party in his own self-interest for seeking political power.

The Department of Hawaiian Homelands is the State of Hawaii agency that administers the HHCA. DHHL is one of the state's largest land developers of residential housing and commercial shopping centers. DHHL manages several dozen voluntary racial ghettos known as Hawaiian Homelands. It has the strong support of the Governor for an aggressive program to build segregated housing developments where home "owners" have 99-year land leases. Those leases come with many strings attached. One of the most evil strings is that when an ethnic Hawaiian homeowner dies and the spouse has no native blood, that spouse must leave and sell the house to an ethnic Hawaiian with at least 50% blood quantum who is on the waiting list and preapproved by DHHL. Through land swaps DHHL has also become landlord to leaseholder farmers who are not allowed to live on their farms because they lack Hawaiian native blood (including some American Indians belonging to federally recognized tribes). The non-native leaseholders will have their farms and buildings confiscated when the lease runs out.

One especially poignant situation came to media attention in 2004 in Waiahole, Oahu, and continued to be controversial for a couple of years. Homeowners and farmers living in a multiracial community had long-term leases on state land that was not part of DHHL. But DHHL made a deal with the state housing department for a land swap that would have transferred ownership of that entire area to DHHL. As a result, when the leases expire in a few years, everyone who lacks a family member with 50% native blood quantum would be forced to move out. The community staged a protest at a hearing in the state legislature. For several hours in a packed room, people of all races, including ethnic Hawaiians, spoke with tears in their eyes about their loving relationships with their neighbors and their love for the land which they farm with their own hands. They pleaded with the legislators to rescind the land swap. DHHL Chairman Micah Kane sat sullenly through the testimony, which was broadcast for several hours on local cable TV. These are some of the heart-wrenching consequences of imposing racial requirements on who can live in a community. For once, at least, outraged people of all races stood up publicly to fight back against racial separatism.

The Department of Hawaiian Homelands has always had a very large backlog of 50%ers on its waiting list to receive a homestead lease. All other separatist programs require only one drop of native blood, but this one requires 50%. Some 50%ers strongly oppose the Akaka bill for fear that it will open the door to hundreds of thousands more people demanding homestead leases, after the new akaka tribe pressures Congress to remove the HHCA blood quantum.

Often there are sob stories about granny dying without ever getting a lease after waiting for 30 or 40 years. But as with so many aspects of the Hawaiian grievance industry, weeping over the waiting list is largely overblown. In "Honolulu Magazine" of January, 2007, Micah Kane said *"There are about 20,000 names on the list. We estimate that one out of every two has a home right now. There isn't any urgency for them to get a home from us. Another 25 percent we're statutorily required to keep on our list, but we don't have any communication with them."* So, half the people on the waiting list already have homes, which means that for them DHHL is nothing more than a way to cash out the equity from the land under the house they already own. by selling that house and replacing it with another house on land they rent for one dollar. And another quarter of those on the waiting list don't care enough about it to maintain contact with DHHL.

In addition, the waiting list has actually grown significantly even though the Lingle administration has granted a record number of leases. That's because all the publicity about people getting land for free attracts an even larger number of additional people to sign up. In an article in the Honolulu Advertiser of February 11, 2007, Gordon Pang quoted Micah

Kane and another DHHL spokesman as follows: *"Today the residential waiting list stands at its peak — more than 19,000. The number of applications has even grown as more people have found out about DHHL's successes, Kane said. At the beginning of 2003 there were 17,392 applications, but despite issuing more than 2,200 leases, the waiting list at the end of 2006 had climbed to 19,068. [Lloyd Yonenaka, a DHHL spokesman] said that what's more important than the raw numbers is that, at this point, those on the list 10 years or more have had at least one or two opportunities at a home or lot, while those on the list for two decades may have seen half a dozen."*[29] People do not stay on the waiting list for decades due to lack of offers of a lease. They stay on the list because they turn down leases for places where they don't want to go. Contrary to the old saying, these beggars ARE choosers. Success in achieving racial separatism breeds an even greater demand for it, all at the expense of the non-ethnic-Hawaiians.

Kamehameha Schools (Bishop Estate)

Bishop Estate was founded by Princess Bernice Pauahi Bishop, a descendant of Kamehameha the Great. King Lot Kamehameha V had offered to name her his successor, but she declined (After Lot's death the Legislature then elected the next monarch, Lunalilo). When Pauahi's will was probated in 1884, the estate owned about 11% of all the lands of Hawaii, valued at $300,000 – substantially less than the cost of Iolani Palace whose construction was completed two years previously. In 1887 Kamehameha School for Boys was opened (using English as the language of instruction). The estate's value was mostly in land, with not much cash; and Pauahi's Caucasian husband Charles Reed Bishop eventually donated more money than the estate's probated value.

Kamehameha Schools, formerly known as Bishop Estate, now has assets somewhere between $8-15 billion, and is the largest private landowner in Hawaii. Theoretically, its sole reason for existence is to operate forever a small network of private schools. KSBE has grown enormously wealthy through income from its vast landholdings and sales of some lands. It used that wealth to gain an economic and political stranglehold on the State of Hawaii, including interlocking directorates with banks and brokerage houses. At one time KSBE owned 10% of Goldman Sachs, giving them great influence with Treasury Secretary Robert Rubin in the Clinton administration.

Hawaiian Apartheid

During the 1990s the five trustees of KSBE were giving themselves over a million dollars apiece as compensation for their services, and had members of the Legislature on their payroll. One state senator used his KSBE credit card to charge $20,000 in expenses at Las Vegas strip clubs. The U.S. Internal Revenue Service stepped in, threatening to remove KSBE's tax exempt status. Eventually all five trustees were forced to resign, but the scandal remained largely hidden and none of the trustees was forced to repay the personal attorney fees they had charged to the "charitable trust" they had treated as their personal fiefdom. A best-selling book about the scandal, "Broken Trust: Greed, Mismanagement & Political Manipulation at America's Largest Charitable Trust" was published in 2006. It was written by Hawaii's only professor of trust law, Randall W. Roth, and a retired federal judge, Samuel P. King (ethnic Hawaiian), both of whom had been instrumental in bringing the scandals to public attention a few years previously. The book has no footnotes but the authors created a large and growing website providing extensive documentation.[30]

The trustees of this tax-exempt charitable trust have maintained a race-based admissions policy for 120 years.[31] They give "preference" to children who have at least one drop of Hawaiian native blood; but the preference ends up as an absolute racial requirement because there are always more ethnic Hawaiian applicants than the number of seats available. Pauahi's will imposes the racial preference only in cases of orphans and indigents, but the trustees have exercised their discretion to apply the racial preference to all applicants. By a current policy of the trustees, 15% of the children are admitted because they meet the regular admissions requirements and are either (1) below the school's lower middle class definition of "poverty" or (2) are "orphans" in the sense of having at least one parent dead or absent from their lives. These are not the complete orphans and destitute indigents Pauahi had in mind; today they need be only semi-half-orphans (with only one parent absent but not necessarily dead), or somewhat hard-scrabble.

For four decades prior to 2002 there were zero non-ethnic-Hawaiians admitted. For seven decades before that there were only exceedingly rare exceptions, mostly for children of Caucasians employed as teachers at the schools. In 2002 school officials announced that one white boy with no native ancestry had been admitted to the brand new Maui campus after there were not enough qualified ethnic Hawaiians to fill every opening. A major uproar among parents and thousands of alumni produced a pledge from the trustees to modify admissions procedures to zealously defend the exclusion of non-ethnic-Hawaiians.

In 2003 two lawsuits were filed seeking to force the admission of two well-qualified white applicants. One of those applicants had been accidentally admitted (his first name sounded Hawaiian) and then had his admission rescinded at the last minute when it was discovered that his mother had been adopted as a child into an ethnic Hawaiian family but did not herself have native blood. The judge ordered that student to be admitted temporarily pending the outcome of the lawsuit. Kamehameha then promptly settled that lawsuit by agreeing to let the boy attend the school for all 6 years remaining through graduation, thereby getting a settled dismissal of a lawsuit that otherwise might have desegregated the school.

The other case, involving a child whose name is being kept secret, was not settled. U.S. District Court Judge Alan Kay ruled on November 17, 2003 in favor of Kamehameha and dismissed the lawsuit. An appeal was filed in the 9th Circuit Court in January 2004, with oral arguments on November 4, 2004. The appeals-court decision was handed down on August 2, 2005. By a 2-1 vote, the panel of judges ruled that the racially exclusionary policy is contrary to law. In response 20,000 red-shirted supporters of apartheid (including the Governor) staged a protest march and rally at Iolani Palace.[32] In February 2006 the 9th Circuit Court voted to grant Kamehameha Schools' request to have an en banc review of the 3-judge decision by a panel of 15 judges. On December 5, 2006 the en-banc panel voted 8-7 to allow Kamehameha to maintain its racially discriminatory admissions policy on the grounds that the schools provide affirmative action to remedy the deficits of poor, downtrodden natives and that non-natives have plenty of opportunities to attend other schools. That decision is being appealed to the U.S. Supreme Court.

The zealousness with which Hawaiian activists have defended Kamehameha's racially exclusionary admissions policy has increased dramatically in recent years. This dramatically increasing zealousness clearly shows a growing surge toward all-out racial separatism. That's why it's important to emphasize that Kamehameha Schools' racially exclusionary admissions policy is not required by Pauahi's will. Today's policy is voluntarily maintained by the trustees under tremendous pressure from alumni and racial separatist zealots (some of whom have no Hawaiian blood!). Indeed, Pauahi established the school for the purpose of fostering assimilation rather than separatism. She specified that the language of instruction should be English (not Hawaiian). She specified that the curriculum should be the standard European/American subjects (not hula, taro, and fishponds). All of the five trustees she personally named to run her estate were Caucasians.

Hawaiian Apartheid

A webpage created in 2000 cites from Pauahi's will to show that the will does not impose an admission requirement for Hawaiian native ancestry, and that even the so-called "preference" applies only to orphans and indigents.[33] But whenever this author or other commentators tried to point out that Pauahi's will did not require any racial preference except for orphans and indigents, and certainly did not impose any racial requirement across the board, the Kamehameha trustees and their public relations staff immediately responded that the will does indeed include such requirements. Finally a panel of three federal judges agreed unanimously that the will is not racially exclusionary and that the preference is only for orphans and indigents. That opinion was handed down on July 2, 2005.[34] Although that opinion was later overturned by an 8-7 vote of an en banc panel, the en-banc ruling did not in any way affect or overturn the interpretation of the 3-judge panel that the will does not require even a mere racial preference, outside the category of orphans and indigents. Here's what the judges said:

"Pauahi's will contains several instructions pertaining to the administration of the Kamehameha Schools, none of which establish race as an admissions criteria." (pages 5-6) *"... She further instructs that a portion of the trust's annual income should be devoted 'to the support and education of orphans, and others in indigent circumstances, giving the preference to Hawaiians of pure or part aboriginal blood.' Pauahi Bishop Will at 18. While this racial preference is expressly listed as a criterion for the administration of estate resources charitably directed to orphans and indigents, the Will is notably devoid of any mention of race as a criterion for admission into the Kamehameha Schools. As the Schools' 1885 Prospectus observed: 'The noble minded Hawaiian chiefess who endowed the Kamehameha Schools, put no limitations of race or condition on her general bequest. Instruction will be given only in English language, but The Schools will be opened to all nationalities.'"* (page 6). Footnote #2 on page 6 adds: *"Similarly, in a February 11, 1897 letter, Charles Bishop noted: 'There is nothing in the will of Mrs. Bishop excluding white boys or girls from the Schools . . . .' In a February 20, 1901 letter he further stated: 'According to the reading of Clause 13 on Page 8 of the Will as published, the preference to Hawaiians of pure or part aboriginal blood, applies only to education of orphans and others in indigent circumstances.'"* And again, on page 40 in summarizing the decision, the judges wrote: *"[14] We emphasize that our ruling today is a narrow one. We conclude only that the plaintiff-appellant has met his burden of establishing the invalidity of the racially exclusionary affirmative action plan in*

place at the Kamehameha Schools, as that plan currently operates as an absolute bar to admission for those of the non-preferred race. Nothing in our decision, however, implicates the validity of the Pauahi Bishop Will, as we do not read that document to require the use of race as an admissions prerequisite."

Racial discrimination is not the only thing troubling to civil rights activists about Kamehameha Schools. The KSBE trust fund has grown to a value somewhere between eight and fifteen billion dollars, broadening its scope and exercising great political power in service to the Evil Empire in ways never envisioned by Pauahi's benevolent intentions.

An entire division (PASE) is dedicated to analyzing data for the purpose of showing that ethnic Hawaiians are poor and downtrodden. These "studies" are then publicized as propaganda to gain sympathy for the "plight" of ethnic Hawaiians; supporting demands for race-based government handouts, for racial separatism, and for the Akaka bill. Thousands of alumni throughout all 50 states are organized to lobby Congress for those demands. Through interlocking directorates KSBE heavily influences banks, brokerage houses, news media, etc. KSBE awards college scholarships to thousands of ethnic Hawaiians for use throughout the U.S., and of course the recipients are forever grateful as they move up their corporate and academic ladders to positions of power and influence. KSBE has partnership arrangements with numerous ordinary state government schools in neighborhoods with large numbers of ethnic Hawaiian children, providing 20% of operating budget in return for enormous influence over faculty and curriculum. KSBE awards large grants to government charter schools where Hawaiian culture is the focus and where 90% of the children are ethnic Hawaiian; and to government Hawaiian language immersion schools. Thus KSBE is a powerful engine driving racial separatism and instilling racist attitudes.

Office of Hawaiian Affairs

In 1978 a State of Hawaii Constitutional Convention was held for the purpose of making a large number of wide-ranging amendments to the fundamental law of Hawaii. All the proposed amendments were ratified by the voters. One of the amendments established the Office of Hawaiian Affairs. That amendment was approved by the smallest percentage among all the amendments. It would have been defeated except for the fact that a rule in place at that time required that ballots left blank on that issue by a voter should be counted as "yes" votes (the rule in place today for Constitutional amendments is opposite). A lawsuit[35] nullified the racial restrictions in the setup of OHA, on the grounds that the voters had not been properly informed about the proposal and thus did not know what it was they were approving. But the Legislature resolved the matter. In 2006 OHA had assets of about $400 million, plus annual income of about $40 million (half from investment income and half from a combination of legislative appropriations and state revenues from government lands). All the money is set aside by law exclusively for ethnic Hawaiians. The vast bulk of OHA's assets (all principal and income deriving from ceded land revenues) is required to be set aside for those eligible to benefit from the HHCA (i.e., 50% native blood quantum), but OHA has clever ways of getting around that restriction.

As set forth in the new Constitution of 1978, OHA was founded on three pillars of racism.

(1) The Constitution specified that only ethnic Hawaiians would be allowed to vote for OHA trustees. Thus, citizens of Hawaii were singled out by race every time they exercised their most fundamental democratic right. The voter registration form contained a special affidavit whereby ethnic Hawaiians swore under oath that they have Hawaiian native blood and wish to vote for OHA trustees. When pollbooks were printed, a special column labeled "OHA" had an "X" next to the name of every voter who had signed that affidavit. Voters stepped up to the pollbook to show their photo ID. Those who had the "X" next to their name were asked to orally confirm their racial identity (to guard against clerical error in the Office of Elections) and were then given a special OHA ballot in addition to the regular ballot given to all voters. In March 1996, after 16 years of passively tolerating this racism, one brave Caucasian man filed a lawsuit against it. The U.S. District Court in Honolulu upheld the race-based voting scheme; and then the 9th Circuit Court of Appeals also upheld it. But in February 2000 the U.S. Supreme Court handed down its decision in Rice v. Cayetano, 528 U.S. 495 (2000), voting 7-2 that the racial restriction violates the 15th Amendment to the U.S. Constitution (The right to vote "shall not be denied or abridged" on account of race). Thus the first pillar of racism on which OHA was founded had been toppled.[36]

(2) The Constitution specified that OHA trustees were required by law to be ethnic Hawaiian. Thus, anyone trying become a candidate was denied the right to run for this statewide office unless he was registered specifi-

cally as an ethnic Hawaiian voter. Following the Rice v. Cayetano decision, a Caucasian who wanted to run for OHA trustee logically concluded there should no longer be a problem in doing so. He went to the Office of Elections to get nominating papers; but when a clerk checked to verify that he was a registered voter, the clerk then challenged him, saying "You can run for any other office; but since you are not Hawaiian you cannot run for OHA." The would-be candidate said "Rice v. Cayetano." The clerk (and her supervisors) said "Rice v. Cayetano only says everyone can VOTE for OHA trustees regardless of race but it does not say everyone can RUN for OHA trustee." The would-be candidate, and a multiracial group of supporters, then filed a lawsuit (known informally as Arakaki#1). The U.S. District Court in Honolulu ruled in favor of the plaintiffs. The State of Hawaii appealed to the 9th Circuit Court, which also ruled in favor of the plaintiffs. Thus the second pillar of racism on which OHA was founded had been toppled.[37]

(3) The Constitution specified that the assets of OHA must be spent exclusively for the benefit of ethnic Hawaiians. This third pillar of OHA's racism has proved more difficult to topple. Three lawsuits have been filed against it over the past several years. The Barrett and Carroll lawsuits were dismissed on grounds that the plaintiffs lacked "standing." The Arakaki#2 lawsuit at the U.S. District Court in Honolulu was initially whittled down to a small portion on grounds of "standing" and then the remaining portion was dismissed on grounds that the court lacks authority to rule on a "political question." Plaintiffs appealed to the 9th Circuit Court, which overturned the political question ruling and affirmed that plaintiffs do have standing as taxpayers. Defendants appealed to the U.S. Supreme Court, in light of a new Supreme Court ruling in another case (DaimlerChrysler) regarding taxpayer standing, and the Supreme Court sent the case back to the 9th Circuit for further proceedings regarding the issue of taxpayer standing in light of DaimlerChrysler. The 9th Circuit then overruled its previous decision, now ruling the plaintiffs do not have standing as taxpayers. The case now goes back to the Honolulu district court where most observers expect it will be dismissed.[38]

In addition to financial assets, OHA now owns large tracts of land. In 2005 OHA acquired ownership of a 40-square-mile rain forest, Wao Kele o Puna, in the Puna district of Hawaii Island (where a geothermal power plant was tried and was protested by zealots complaining about violating the sacred land of the fire goddess Pele). Most of the money to acquire the land was paid by a consortium of public and private groups, with a small percentage from OHA; and then the deed was simply handed over to OHA. In 2006 OHA acquired ownership of the entire Waimea Valley on the north shore of Oahu, where formerly there was a nature park operated as a tourist attraction by the same company that owned Sea Life Park. Most of the money to acquire the valley was paid by a consortium of public and private groups, with a small percentage from OHA; and then the deed was simply handed over to OHA. Why did these consortiums hand over the deeds to OHA rather than to the state Department of Land and Natural Resources or city Parks Department? Presumably because ethnic Hawaiians are regarded as the rightful stewards of their ancestral homeland, and as a racial group that has a genealogical relationship with the land according to a Hawaiian creation legend.

Under the Constitution of 1978, OHA has authority to provide advocacy for ethnic Hawaiians as a racial group. OHA interprets that very broadly, as giving it the right to spend millions of dollars on advertising for the Akaka bill and for signing up tens of thousands of people on a racial registry expected to become a membership roll for a phony new Indian tribe. OHA by law appoints staff members who sit as voting members of important state government boards and commissions. Its trustees and staff members also sit on the boards of major banks, corporations, and law firms. An ethnic Hawaiian state Supreme Court justice wrote a controversial decision granting ethnic Hawaiians the right to trespass on private land to gather food and cultural materials; later he resigned from the Court to become the attorney representing OHA in several important lawsuits.[39]

Ceded lands[40]

When OHA was founded following the Constitutional Convention of 1978, the question arose how OHA should be funded. Most state government agencies are operated with money appropriated by the Legislature out of general funds. But instead of following that normal method, the Legislature decided to provide a dedicated funding source consisting of 20% of the state's revenues from its government owned ceded lands. The reason that funding method was selected illustrates how overblown grievances based on historical falsehoods combine with compassion and affection for Hawaii's favorite ethnic group, to produce enormous problems for the state.

In the early days of the Kingdom the King personally owned all the lands of Hawaii by right of conquest, and had the power to confiscate and keep or redistribute any lands he wished. In the Mahele of 1848 King Kauikeaouli Kamehameha III created private property deeds. He kept some land for himself (the crown lands); gave some land to the government for schools, roads, harbors, etc.; and gave some land to various high chiefs on condition that they respect the rights of tenants living on those lands. The crown lands were initially regarded as the King's own lands, but as time went by it became clear (and was enacted into law) that the crown lands were owned by the government to provide revenue to support the King only in his official capacity as head of state. When a King died the crown lands were always passed to the next King rather than to the dead King's private heirs, even when the monarchy passed to a different family (as in the transition from Lot Kamehameha V to Lunalilo, and again from Lunalilo to Kalakaua). By the time the monarchy was overthrown the crown lands were virtually indistinguishable from government lands, as shown by the decision of the Court of Claims in 1910, previously cited.

The Annexation Act, Organic Act, and Statehood Act all treated the government and crown lands under the single category of ceded lands. They are called "ceded" lands because control of those lands was ceded by the Republic of Hawaii to the U.S. government at the time of annexation (1898), to be held as a trust on behalf of all Hawaii's people with the revenue to be used "for education and other public purposes." When statehood was achieved (1959) the ceded lands were returned to the control of the new State of Hawaii, except for national parks and military bases. Thus the ceded lands today are held by the government for the benefit of all Hawaii's people, just as was true during the Kingdom.

Ethnic Hawaiian zealots claim that "ceded" means "stolen." They claim that both the government and crown lands rightfully belong to ethnic Hawaiians as a racial group, and that the overthrow of the monarchy and annexation to the United States were illegal acts which resulted in taking the ceded lands away from them without compensation. OHA was established as a government institution of, by, and for ethnic Hawaiians, where only members of that racial group could vote for trustees, run for trustee, and receive benefits. So the legislators felt that fairness and justice required them to fund OHA by using a portion of the revenues from the ceded lands. Also, using ceded land revenues rather than direct appropriation of tax dollars provided a way to hide the amount of money being transferred to a racially exclusionary purpose, and avoid the annual scrutiny and accountability of the budget process.

The Statehood Act said that ceded land revenues could be spent on any one or more of five purposes. One of those purposes was public education, and for the first 20 years of statehood that's where all the ceded land revenues were spent (which benefitted ethnic Hawaiians along with everyone else). But one of the five purposes was "the betterment of Native Hawaiians." It seemed logical that one of five reasons equals 20%; and also ethnic Hawaiians were roughly 20% of Hawaii's population. That's why the legislature decided to permanently allocate 20% of ceded land revenues to OHA for the exclusive benefit of Hawaii's favorite race (even while ethnic Hawaiians also continued to benefit from all the rest of the revenue and from tax appropriations).

One problem is that no exact inventory of ceded lands has ever been compiled. Thus OHA and other zealots constantly demand that millions of dollars be appropriated to do an exhaustive study of the history of the crown and government lands from the Kingdom period right up until this moment, so that an exact figure can be determined for OHA's 20% share of ceded land revenues. Of course, another reason for demanding such an inventory is to make it easier for a future separatist government to pinpoint the lands it will demand from the state.

A more serious problem is that OHA now has legal standing to interfere with decisions the state government makes regarding the sale, lease, or use of the ceded lands. The theory is that because OHA is entitled to 20% of ceded land revenues, therefore any decision how the ceded lands are used will have an impact on OHA's dedicated income source. Thus OHA believes it should have the right (or perhaps also ethnic Hawaiian individuals should have the right) to say how the ceded lands are used, and can sue the state to prevent the sale of ceded lands. This is a huge problem because 95% of all the government-owned lands in Hawaii are ceded lands. If the Akaka bill passes, the new government of the phony tribe will also have standing, under that theory, to attack the federal government's use of the military bases.

In one especially bizarre lawsuit OHA claimed a right to 20% of the revenue produced from a tourist duty-free shop on private land in Waikiki because of the fact that purchases made there are delivered at the airport and because of the fact that a portion of the airport runway sits on ceded land. A judge actually ruled in OHA's favor; but on appeal the state Supreme Court, after many years, finally overturned that decision on technicalities.[41] An unhappy OHA continues to sponsor bills in the legislature to "clarify" that OHA is entitled to airport revenues. Similarly OHA has sued for revenue from a state-owned hospital which sits on ceded lands — even though the hospital is heavily subsidized by the government and operates at a loss, OHA claims it is entitled to 20% of all the revenue received by the hospital from payments by patients and insurance companies. The City and County of Honolulu recently approved a plan to construct a mass transit system at a cost of several billion dollars, that will run for many miles. No doubt some of the track will run through ceded lands. One wonders whether OHA will demand 20% of all the money paid by riders and all the money earned from leases and rents in the train stations and nearby commercial establishments.

Over 160 racially exclusionary federally funded programs[42]

Alu Like was incorporated in 1975 and received its first federal funding in 1976 to provide racially exclusionary programs for vocational training. It has since expanded into areas such as an ethnic Hawaiian library, and a project to digitize Hawaiian language newspapers from the Kingdom and Territorial periods. Papa Ola Lokahi was created by an act of Congress in 1988 as an ethnic Hawaiian health system providing direct healthcare. POL also coordinates research projects to gather victimhood data purporting to show that ethnic Hawaiians have the worst disease and mortality statistics, for use in propaganda campaigns and in helping other ethnic Hawaiian institutions seeking federal or philanthropic grants.

The Native Hawaiian Legal Corporation is group of ethnic Hawaiian lawyers who receive state government tax dollars which they use to provide legal representation to ethnic Hawaiian individuals and institutions for litigation on issues such as land title or water rights. In effect, the government is providing money taken from taxpayers of all races to help ethnic Hawaiians fight legal battles against everyone else including the government.

The Native Hawaiian Education Act is a federal law that provides grants for educating ethnic Hawaiians at all levels. The University of Hawaii Department of Business Administration had a young ethnic Hawaiian faculty member who got a multimillion dollar grant over a period of years to establish the Native Hawaiian Leadership Project. Ethnic Hawaiian college students at the undergraduate and graduate level, and also young professors, throughout all 50 states, could get grants to pay for tuition, books, travel to academic conferences, etc. Another program, Na Pua Noeau, was headquartered at various college campuses to provide resources and enrichment programs for gifted and talented ethnic Hawaiian children.

In a recent incarnation, as part of the No Child Left Behind PL 107-110 (2001-2002), the Native Hawaiian Education Act included frightening Hawaiian sovereignty political language in its "findings" (preamble); for example TITLE VII, Part B, Sec. 7202: *"Congress does not extend services to Native Hawaiians because of their race, but because of their unique status as the indigenous people of a once sovereign nation as to whom the United States has established a trust relationship; ... the political status of Native Hawaiians is comparable to that of American Indians and Alaska Natives; and ... the aboriginal, indigenous people of the United States have (i) a continuing right to autonomy in their internal affairs; and (ii) an ongoing right of self-determination and self-governance that has never been extinguished. ... The political relationship between the United States and the Native Hawaiian people has been recognized and reaffirmed by the United States."*

While such language is only in a preamble which does not carry the force of law, it is nevertheless cited by Hawaiian sovereignty activists. For example it was cited in the Arakaki#2 lawsuit as evidence that Congress has already recognized ethnic Hawaiians as a political entity and not merely a racial group; and therefore funding for OHA is a "political question" not subject to adjudication by the courts under the 14th Amendment equal protection clause. Inserting such language that is irrelevant to the purpose of a piece of legislation violates its benevolent spirit. It undermines the unity of the State of Hawaii and the equality of its people. Its purpose is to protect the Evil Empire against lawsuits and to help it grow stronger. It's very easy to insert such language into the preambles of legislation, because Senators and Congressmen generally don't bother reading the preambles and never debate or fight over them.

Racial separatism in Hawaii's "Public" schools

From preschool through Ph.D., a racial separatist educational system has been assembled from a combination of federal and state government grants and private philanthropy. Those ethnic-Hawaiian-oriented programs operated by Hawaii's public schools must by law be open to all races; but in practice 90-95% of the students are ethnic Hawaiian.

Punana Leo is a private preschool program for Hawaiian language immersion so that children who might normally grow up speaking English will now grow up speaking Hawaiian. The K-12 public schools have a similar Hawaiian language immersion program, where all the school subjects are taught through Hawaiian language. Sometimes there is just one language immersion classroom in an English-language school; occasionally there is an entire school that is language immersion.

Readers should bear in mind that it is not necessary for anyone to speak Hawaiian in order to go through daily life. Everyone who speaks Hawaiian also speaks English; and for almost every Hawaiian-speaker English is their primary language. The language immersion program was started for the benevolent purpose of rescuing a beautiful dying language. Hawaii's people enthusiastically supported it for the same reason they adopted the endangered native nene goose as the state bird – an expression of sympathy and support. However, the language immersion program is also using unsuspecting children as political pawns, forcing them to learn a language that has little practical use but great potential for building racial pride and unifying a racial group in pursuit of political sovereignty.

In 2000 the State of Hawaii passed a law allowing charter schools to be established with government money. A charter school can start from scratch with no building, and rent space; or a charter school can be created by converting an existing public school if parents and staff approve. The law authorizes only a limited number of charter schools, and allows them to adopt their own curriculum and teaching methods independent of most government regulation. Half the charter schools were created by ethnic Hawaiian groups, and their curricula are focused on Hawaiian culture, Hawaiian language, environmental activism, and political activism. Once again a law passed with benevolent intentions has been abused by racial separatists, as will be shown below.

Kanu O Ka Aina is the leader in the consortium of Hawaiian-focus charter schools known as Ka Lei Naauao. The founder and CEO, Ku Kahakalau, speaks out constantly about how her wonderful school has outstanding attendance and enthusiastic students. She likes to say her students are doing far better than regular public school students; and points out that in 2006 her school was one of the few public schools identified as making "adequate yearly progress." However, it earned that label only because the law allows a school to be classified that way if it shows a 10% improvement in test scores from the previous year (and her scores were so dismal it was easy to make a 10% improvement). She has a small enrollment and gets huge grants from Kamehameha Schools to supplement the tax appropriations, so it's astonishing her students' performance is so poor. Perhaps they spend more time memorizing Hawaiian chants, planting taro, doing the hula, making videotapes, and learning a twisted version of Hawaiian history; than learning mathematics and reading.

The Kanu O Ka Aina website included the following language in 2002.[43] The wording has been toned down slightly since then so the public will not be too frightened, but the school's philosophy remains the same. Remember this is a "public" school open to all races, and imagine how children with no native ancestry would feel in such a place.

"The name "Kanu o ka 'Aina" evolved from of a Hawaiian proverb that refers to natives of the land from generations back as "kalo kanu o ka 'aina" literally "taro planted on the land". This name was chosen because this model wants to give native Hawaiians of all ages the opportunity and the choice to remain natives of their kulaiwi and to perpetuate Hawai'i's native language, culture and traditions into the future. In addition, Kanu wants to empower Hawai'i's native people, who are direct descendants of earthmother Papa and skyfather Wakea, to once again assume our rightful stewardship over our archipelago. ... The purpose of Kanu is to provide students of Hawaiian ancestry residing in the Hamakua and Kohala area of Hawai'i Island with an equal opportunity to quality education that addresses their distinctive cultural learning styles and allows them to successfully walk in two worlds. ... Kanu wants to encourage Hawaiian students to become politically conscious, and individually and collectively tackle the problem of Hawaiian oppression by the United States and our subjugation to American law and a Western way of life. In that vein, Kanu has the potential of significantly contributing to the Hawaiian sovereignty effort. ... Utilizing problem-posing as an instructional technique, Kanu hopes to make our students realize that the occupation of Hawai'i by the United States of America is not fatal and unalterable, but merely limiting – and therefore challenging. Additionally, Kanu wants to empower our students to accept this challenge and find solutions to this and the many other dilemma, that face Hawai'i's native people in their homeland today. By actively participating in finding solutions to native problems, it is envisioned that Kanu students will become an intricate part of the process of native liberation from American domination that nearly caused the demise of our native people and our way of life."

In 2002 Ku Kahakalau, the head of Kanu O Ka Aina school, on behalf of her consortium of 12 such ethnic Hawaiian-focus "public" charter schools, began pushing a bill through the legislature to liberate the consortium from the grasp of the State Department of Education. The consortium would become its own independent (racially separate) tax-supported school system with the power to certify its own teachers; set its own standards for curriculum, student progress, and teacher certification; and authorize the creation of additional schools for the consortium. The legislation she proposed included provisions that a majority of board members for each school and for the consortium must be ethnic Hawaiian.[44]

The bill for a racial separatist ethnic nationalist tax supported school system did not pass, but continues to be reintroduced in modified form each year. Meanwhile the Governor has been trying to break up the highly centralized state public school system (the only one in America) into local school districts with locally elected school boards to promote innovation and accountability. That concept would seem to dovetail nicely with the proposal by Kanu O Ka Aina. Each of the regular school districts would encompass one entire island, or a portion of one island; but the Kanu proposal calls for a non-contiguous school district comprised of all the schools in Hawaii that meet the racial and ideological requirements of the separatist movement.

University of Hawaii

The University of Hawaii flagship campus at Manoa is dominated by a pernicious racial supremacist ideology. It's like an octopus, whose head is the Center for Hawaiian Studies (CHS). Its tentacles reach into every academic department which services substantial numbers of CHS students. These cognate departments enjoy lucrative collaborative projects and consulting contracts for academic research, field studies, and community activities.

For example, Kamehameha School owns real estate which includes an ancient Hawaiian fishpond or taro patch system; a community group would like to restore the fishpond or taro patches and gets permission from Kamehameha; then CHS might offer a course on historical, cultural, and environmental aspects of fishponds, taro patches, and ahupuaa, including field trips and hands-on restoration work. Professors in cognate departments might attract CHS students into their related courses, or use fishpond and taro patch restoration work as field activities for their own students in departments like biology, biochemistry, anthropology, sociology, political science, urban and regional planning, ethnic studies, religion, etc.

Hawaiian Apartheid

The medical school established a program to take advantage of federal grants to study breast cancer, diabetes, and general healthcare in the ethnic Hawaiian population; naturally that will require collaboration with CHS specialists in Hawaiian culture and social work. The law school hosts many Hawaiian sovereignty activists seeking to become attorneys; and law professors for many years have enjoyed huge consulting fees from work done for the Office of Hawaiian Affairs, the Department of Hawaiian Homelands, and Kamehameha School. Professors publish papers attacking the Rice v. Cayetano decision and its progeny, thereby gaining academic prestige, promotions, and credit toward meeting their "community service" obligations.[45] A proposal to give federal recognition to a phony Hawaiian Indian tribe, if successful, would feed this octopus tremendous power and wealth. The Law School recently received a multimillion dollar federal grant to establish a center for Native Hawaiian law. It will focus on Hawaiian Kingdom law, plus today's theories of indigenous rights; and it will examine how the laws of America and Hawaii can be used to support and defend racial separatism and ethnic nationalism.

The Center for Hawaiian Studies controls a building paid for by the taxpayers, including a large auditorium for mass meetings where every lecture or panel discussion takes place against a backdrop of a red-colored political call to "resist." The faculty, with high salaries, assistants and secretaries paid by taxpayers, indoctrinates a new generation of activists into the party line, rewarding zealous freedom-fighters with race-based tuition waivers, scholarships, good grades, and degrees. CHS students swell the enrollments of classes in cognate departments taught by professors who actively promote the CHS party line. Professors of History or Political Science who might be inclined to be politically neutral or academically rigorous (if any such exist in these departments!) dare not act responsibly, for fear of low enrollments, loss of government grants, and loss of jobs.

Evan Dobelle, newly hired as President of the University of Hawaii, began work in Summer 2000 (shortly after the Rice v. Cayetano decision). He was hired at an annual salary of $442,000 plus use of the Presidential Mansion and other perks. One of his first official events was to be keynote speaker at the first annual convention of the newly created Council for Native Hawaiian Advancement. In his speech he promised to harness UH as a tool in service to Hawaiian ethnic nationalism. He followed up by providing unprecedented levels of funding to CHS even while core liberal arts departments were suffering cutbacks and budget restrictions. The newly hired Dobelle promptly hired Peter Englert to become the new Chancellor of the UH flagship Manoa campus, at a salary of $254,000. Englert was then an administrator at Victoria University in Wellington, New Zealand. What made Englert's appointment to UH notable was his strong support from the Maori of New Zealand, who ceremonially handed him over to the ethnic Hawaiians upon his arrival to begin duty on August 1, 2002.

In Fall 2002 the author of this book was invited by students to teach a short course (six 2-hour sessions) about Hawaiian sovereignty through the University of Hawaii Center for Lifelong Learning. As soon as the CLL catalog was published, the program director received very frightening threats at her office both in person and by telephone. When she discussed the threats with the elderly students who had signed up for the course, they all dropped out. The course was cancelled. University officials had zero concern or interest in trying to protect academic freedom. Then the Honolulu Advertiser published a news report about the matter, followed by an editorial that academic freedom should be protected. University officials still did nothing to provide protection or to encourage reinstatement of the course. But the very brave program director moved the course classroom to an undisclosed location (which participants humorously referred to as "the bunker"); all the previously registered students signed up again plus a few new ones; and the course went forward very successfully. A large webpage provides documentation for the contents of this paragraph, and also includes some statements from other UH personnel whose property was damaged and who received threats of bodily harm on account of their views on Hawaiian sovereignty. The University of Hawaii is a hostile work environment for anyone who does not follow the CHS party line.[46]

The UH Manoa Center for Hawaiian Studies has miniature clones on the campus of every government community college, and also at Hawaii's private colleges. The drive for racial separatism is illustrated in a small way by what happened at Windward Community College in Kaneohe. A federal grant was obtained through the Native Hawaiian Education Act, allowing the school to enhance a focus on Hawaiian Studies and to buy computers for use by ethnic Hawaiian students. The chancellor did not want to have computers with signs pasted on them "for Hawaiians only," but some of the ethnic Hawaiian students zealously demanded the computers be racially dedicated, pointing to the funding source in NHEA. At the same time an old house in an isolated corner of the campus was undergoing renovations for use as classroom and office space. That house was set aside to become the Center for Hawaiian Studies, where it was likely that most of the students using the new computers would be ethnic Hawaiian. Ironically the old house has always been painted white, and is known on campus as "The White House."

Sandwich Isles Communications

One of the more bizarre and powerful examples of racial separatism is a company named Sandwich Isles Communications. That company was created to win a contract to provide high-speed fiberoptic cable wiring to interconnect all the DHHL Hawaiian Homelands widely scattered on six islands. The contract is worth $500 million, paid for mostly by $400 million federal dollars from the U.S. Department of Agriculture Rural Utilities Service. Every phone line in America pays a tax of several dimes per month to USDARUS to subsidize telephone companies to provide service to remote areas that otherwise would be uneconomical. No matter that cellular phones or CB or ham radio would be cheaper – this program is part of a federal bureaucracy going back to earlier times. All 69 Homelands are being interconnected – even those which are in remote corners of the islands, where nobody lives and where nobody is ever likely to live. SIC is also providing fiberoptic service to Hawaiian Homelands in suburban Honolulu which already have excellent phone and TV hookups – its contract is to provide fiberoptic cable to every Hawaiian Homeland whether they need it or not.

Sandwich Isles Communications was sole bidder in a sweetheart deal with DHHL. Clayton Hee, who was Chairman of the Office of Hawaiian Affairs, helped broker the deal between DHHL and his brother Al Hee, who was president of SIC. The Chief Executive Officer of SIC, who will also profit handsomely, is retired Vice Admiral Robert Kihune, chairman of the Board of Trustees of Kamehameha Schools. One feature of the $500 million project is that SIC gets a guaranteed profit not based services actually provided to customers but rather based on how much money is invested digging trenches for cables. So it doesn't matter whether very many customers actually use the service, it only matters that SIC gets a profit for every foot of cable trenches it digs, including along the ocean floor between islands and trenches to remote places where nobody lives. SIC is "serving" the Hawaiian Homelands and only the Hawaiian Homelands, thus fulfilling the dreams of racial separatists. This outrageous boondoggle earned the admiration of Forbes Magazine, which published an article "Dreaming & Scheming Hawaiian Style" in the issue of October 28, 2002. SIC is a prime example of ethnic Hawaiians controlling wealthy, powerful government and private institutions exclusively for the benefit of ethnic Hawaiians and conspiring with each other to make enormous fortunes off the taxes paid by people of all races across all of America.

A Tale of Two Islands: Kahoolawe and Niihau

There are eight major Hawaiian islands. The story of racial separatism already existing in Hawaii would not be complete without briefly mentioning the special situations of two of those eight: Kahoolawe and Niihau.

In the 1820s Kahoolawe was used as a prison colony for the Kingdom of Hawaii. In 1858 a lease was given for cattle grazing, and in 1918 the island was leased to Kahoolawe Ranch. Following the bombing of Pearl Harbor in 1941 and the declaration of martial law in Hawaii, the U.S. Navy took control of the entire island and used it as a bombing target for U.S. and foreign military forces to practice their skills.[47]

In January 1976 ethnic Hawaiian protesters formed a group called the Protect Kahoolawe Ohana and briefly occupied the island to force a temporary cessation of the bombing. They repeatedly went back for more short occupations. A lawsuit forced the Navy to reduce the number of bombings, to begin cleanup, and to do an archeological assessment. In 1990 President Bush ordered a permanent end to the bombing. In 1993 the state legislature established the Kahoolawe Island Reserve Commission to manage the island. In 1994 the federal government returned ownership of Kahoolawe to the state, but kept control of access to the island for ten more years to do cleanup. Congress appropriated $400 million to clean up debris and unexploded shells. When the money was gone parts of the island were still not cleaned at all. Most of it was cleaned only to a shallow depth, leaving the possibility that unexploded ordnance deeper in the ground might slowly work its way to the surface causing injury or death to someone walking there. In 2004 the Navy completely departed.

There have been no permanent residents on Kahoolawe for many decades. There were no known sacred ceremonies performed there in recorded history (up until the past few years!), and especially since the old religion was overthrown in 1819 and the prison colony and cattle grazing were established. Nevertheless, modern reinventions of ancient legends say Kahoolawe is an altered name of Kohemalamalama, which means the sacred (or shining) female genitalia, possibly having some connection to one of the sisters of the fire goddess Pele. Another reinvented ancient name for Kahoolawe is Kanaloa (the god). Hawaiian zealots like to use claims that lands are sacred as a way of demanding race-based political control of those lands. Every parcel of land in Hawaii no doubt has some ancient legend associated with it that could be dredged up or reinvented to suit the needs of the activists.

Most people in Hawaii believe that Kahoolawe now belongs to ethnic Hawaiians and has been set aside to be given to the future Akaka tribe. Language in the Hawaii Revised Statutes tantalizingly suggests this, but there are loopholes. The island was returned from the federal government to the state by deed dated May 7, 1994 pursuant to Title X of Public Law 103-139. Neither the statute nor the deed imposed a requirement that the island be in any way dedicated to ethnic Hawaiian use. The State of Hawaii in HRS section 6K-9, anticipating the federal transfer, stipulated that "[u]pon its return to the State, the resources and waters of Kaho'olawe shall be held in trust as part of the public land trust; provided that the State shall transfer management and control of the island and its waters to the sovereign native Hawaiian entity upon its recognition by the United States and the State of Hawaii." At that time there was no "sovereign native Hawaiian entity" and as yet there is none.

HRS section 6K-3 provides that the island shall be used "solely and exclusively" for (1) preservation and practice of all rights customarily and traditionally exercised by native Hawaiians for cultural, spiritual, and subsistence purposes; (2) preservation and protection of its archaeological, historical, and environmental resources; (3) rehabilitation, revegetation, habitat restoration, and preservation; and (4) education. Only one of these uses even mentions persons of Hawaiian native blood, and the use of an initial lower-case "n" in the term "native Hawaiian" implies (perhaps inadvertently) that only those with 50% Hawaiian "blood" are referred to. There is no requirement that the educational use of the island be limited to "Native Hawaiians" as defined in the Akaka bill.

Indeed, since the Kahoolawe Island Reserve Commission designated by HRS chapter 6K to administer the island is a state agency established by state statute, the decision in Rice v. Cayetano, 528 U.S. 495 (2000), might indicate that any preference or special treatment for "native Hawaiians" (or for "Native Hawaiians" as defined in the Akaka bill) would be vulnerable to Constitutional challenge. The claim that Kahoolawe belongs to ethnic Hawaiians is based on the language passed by the state legislature anticipating the return of the island from federal control. That language, just like the allocation of 20% of ceded land revenue to OHA, was passed by the legislature and can be rescinded at any time by the legislature. But in practice, from 1993 to the present, the Kahoolawe Island Reserve Commission controls access to the island. The members of KIRC are appointed by the Governor, and all of them are ethnic Hawaiians. The chairman of KIRC is Sol Kahoohalahala, who gave up a seat in the legislature to accept that position, presumably because he sees a bright future for the island under ownership of the anticipated Akaka tribe. Perhaps a casino will be built there!

Niihau is a small island of about 70 square miles located 17 miles to the west of Kauai. In 1864 a Caucasian woman, Elizabeth Sinclair, purchased the island from King Lot kamehameha V for $10,000 in gold. Today her descendants, the Robinson family, still own the island, worth perhaps $100 million. It is known as the "Forbidden Island" because outside access has been strictly controlled by the owners for 150 years. Its population in Census 2000 was 160, all of whom were ethnic Hawaiians, probably of high native blood quantum, except for the Robinson family. Housing conditions are primitive, with no electricity except from generators and no indoor plumbing. Because of the island's isolation for so many decades, and the fact that nearly all residents are native Hawaiian, the Hawaiian language is the dominant language of everyday use. It is a dialect of Hawaiian which was always strikingly different from what was spoken on other islands and remains distinctly different today.

On one hand some Hawaiian sovereignty activists look to Niihau as an inspiring example of a place that is closer to possessing Hawaiian sovereignty than anywhere else. Hawaiian language is dominant; nearly all residents are native Hawaiians of high blood quantum; the subsistence lifestyle is close to the earth. Niihau is also a shining light to the independence zealots because it was the only precinct which voted against statehood in 1959.

On the other hand the island is owned by a Caucasian family who exercise dictatorial control, requiring their permission if a resident wants to have a friend or family member come for a visit. The residents seem pleased to have access restricted since it guarantees the continuity of their lifestyle. The residents also seem to support the Robinson family's resistance to government bureaucratic regulation of the school system and the natural environment (endangered species act, and fishing regulations); while some sovereignty activists on the main islands deplore the residents' lack of political correctness. The upper grades travel to school on Kauai. In recent years there was a dispute between one faction of parents who wanted the Hawaiian language immersion school to include English lessons and some subject mater instruction in English, while the other faction wanted all Hawaiian for all subjects. For a while there were two separate schools for the two factions, each with low enrollment and therefore very expensive for the government to operate. OHA provided a grant to tide them over, and counseling/mediation/hooponopono to settle their dispute.

Racial separatism gone wild – The Akaka bill to create an apartheid government and fuel a secessionist movement

A bill in Congress since 2000, informally known as the Akaka bill, has had various names and many different versions. When first introduced in the 106th Congress on July 20, 2000 it was the Native Hawaiian Recognition bill. During the 109th Congress, ending in December 2006, it was the Native Hawaiian Government Reorganization bill.

The large number of major changes in the bill seems surprising in view of the fact that Senators Inouye and Akaka have both served for many years on the Indian Affairs Committee (Inouye was Chairman for quite a while) where they undoubtedly have developed great expertise from handling so many other tribal recognitions. Yet their handling of the bill seems amateurish. One explanation is that there are strong political currents pulling in conflicting directions. Another explanation is that Hawaii's two Senators are doing their best to make sure the bill gives maximum power to ethnic Hawaiians at the expense of the other residents of Hawaii and America. Over the years the bill was repeatedly amended with stronger and stronger language to prevent tribal gambling. In 2005 an amended bill was drafted, but never seriously pushed forward until 2007, that would allegedly prohibit the Akaka tribe from interfering with military lands. Senators Akaka and Inouye have served so long on the Indian Affairs Committee they clearly know how to write a bill that will actually take care of various problems. But on gambling, military bases, and other topics our two Senators have repeatedly told other Senators and the general public "Don't worry, be happy" and then were forced to amend the bill, and amend it again because even the amendments did not satisfy the concerns of knowledgeable people.

Here's the basic concept of the Akaka bill.

Congress would go on record that ethnic Hawaiians are the indigenous people of Hawaii; and that the United States has a longstanding trust relationship with ethnic Hawaiians as a group. Ethnic Hawaiians would be assisted in assembling a roster of ethnic Hawaiians who come forward and are certified by a committee of genealogists as being racially Hawaiian; i.e., having at least one ancestor who lived in Hawaii before Captain Cook's arrival in 1778; or having an ethnic Hawaiian ancestor living in Hawaii before the monarchy was overthrown in 1893; or being descended from at least one person who would have been eligible for a homestead lease under the Hawaiian Homes Commission Act of 1921 (i.e., someone who lived in 1921 and had at least 50% native blood). Eventually the people on the roster could choose a committee to write a governing document (Constitution) and decide on a process to choose a governing entity (tribal council). When the Secretary of Interior confirms that the governing document is acceptable and the governing entity has been properly chosen, then the U.S. automatically recognizes the governing entity. The governing entity is thereby authorized to negotiate with federal and state governments for the transfer of money, land, and lawmaking authority.

Ethnic Hawaiians who choose not to sign up for the tribe are left out of the process, but might nevertheless be affected by and subjected to decisions made by the tribe. Certainly the tribe will be perceived as speaking on behalf of all ethnic Hawaiians, and government benefits will be channeled through the tribal council. Thus ethnic Hawaiians will feel pressure to join the tribe or risk losing government handouts. Ethnic Hawaiians who oppose the whole idea have no way to block the tribe from being formed, even if the opponents are a majority of ethnic Hawaiians. There is no minimum percentage of ethnic Hawaiians who must sign up for the tribe in order to authorize creation of the tribe. Certainly the rest of Hawaii's people have no voice at all regarding whether the tribe gets created. If the Akaka bill passes Congress, there is no doubt the Akaka tribe will be created even if most ethnic Hawaiians and most of Hawaii's people oppose it.

When the tribal council negotiates one or more deals with the state or federal governments, those deals can be ratified by the tribal council and the state legislature and Congress, without ever asking for a vote of the tribal members or the people of Hawaii. Supporters of the bill point out that any deal requiring a change in the state Constitution would require a vote by the people to ratify the Constitutional amendments. But it seems possible (and likely!) that major transfers of money, land, and lawmaking authority could be accomplished without amending the state Constitution. Already huge tracts of land and hundreds of millions of dollars have been simply handed over to OHA without any ratification by the people. The State of Hawaii legislature authorized the governing council of a political subdivision (the City and County of Honolulu) to raise the excise tax to collect several billion dollars to finance the construction of a mass transit system, and that decision did not need to be ratified by the people of Hawaii nor by the people of Honolulu. If the Akaka bill passes Congress, the Akaka tribe will be created and it will negotiate a very favorable deal with docile and compliant state legislators who regard ethnic Hawaiians as a 20% swing vote they dare not disappoint.

Ever since the Akaka bill was first introduced on July 20, 2000 Hawaii residents have been bombarded by waves of advertising on TV, radio, and newspapers, paid for by OHA. Some of those ads featured sweet little girls, or distinguished men, looking humble and somewhat downcast, softly pleading "Recognize me." But the Akaka bill is not simply about recognizing ethnic Hawaiians as being indigenous or as being worthy people. It is about money, land, political power and racial separatism. Some of the ads featured glistening colored lines connecting ethnic Hawaiians throughout the world. But the Akaka bill is not merely about improving communications. Some ads featured a single stick being broken in half but a bundle of sticks wrapped together being too strong to break, implying that ethnic Hawaiians need to come together in unity or else their culture and economic handouts will be broken. The Akaka bill is indeed about pulling together a widely disparate group of fully assimilated individuals and making them into a collective where group rights are more important than individual rights. The Akaka bill is all about protecting race-based government handouts and building political power to demand more, even at the expense of carving up Hawaii and creating an apartheid regime. The Akaka bill is not about recognizing a small homogeneous Indian tribe living communally on a remote reservation. It's about pulling fully assimilated individuals out of their widely scattered lifestyles and residences in order to lump them together and subject them to domination by zealous advocates of racial separatism. Passing the bill is like driving over a cliff while wearing a blindfold – there's no turning back and no way to predict what will happen afterward.

OHA's Plan B

The Akaka bill failed to survive a cloture vote in the Senate on June 8, 2006, following several hours of heated floor debate over a two-day period.[48] OHA's secret "Plan B" memo became known to some members of the media and public on June 22. On June 23 the actual document was published on the internet and was described in a news report printed in the Hilo and Kona newspapers. On June 24 the Honolulu Advertiser finally caught up. It was unclear whether the OHA planning document, marked "confidential," was released in the "normal" way or was leaked either intentionally or unintentionally.[49]

As outlined in the memo, OHA on its own initiative and at its own expense will follow the procedures set forth in the Akaka bill, even though the bill has not been passed by Congress. The steps include the following. Outreach and advertising to enlarge the racial registry "Kau Inoa" (by the end of 2006 almost 60,000 had already signed up). Make use of Indian tribe computer software to organize the verification of ancestry for the names on the racial registry. Assemble an apportionment advisory board and decide how to apportion districts for an election (both in Hawaii and on the mainland; and perhaps in foreign nations). Conduct an election of delegates to a Constitutional Convention. The con-con writes a governing document. The governing document is ratified by a vote among the members of the racial registry whose ages and genealogy have been verified. The governing document begins to be implemented, with transitional coordination among OHA, the new governing entity, and the State of Hawaii. The new governing entity and the Governor of Hawaii together decide whether and how to pursue federal recognition. It is intended that the entire process will be finished by the end of 2007

Essentially, this process is an end-run around the Rice v. Cayetano Supreme Court ruling. That ruling forced the State of Hawaii to let people of all races vote for OHA trustees. The followup Arakaki#1 ruling forced the State of Hawaii to allow people of all races to run for and serve as OHA trustees. The racial separatists absolutely hate the fact that OHA is no longer an institution of and by ethnic Hawaiians alone (although the racial restriction on who can receive benefits remains in place due to legal technicalities and delays). What forced desegregation is the fact that OHA is an agency of the state government. During the years between 2000 and 2005 there were various proposals in the state legislature to create a racially exclusionary private trust (along the lines of Kamehameha Schools) and transfer OHA's assets into that trust (and perhaps also to transfer the Hawaiian Homelands). But those concepts never gathered much support.

The new OHA Plan B would create a state-recognized Indian tribe similar to those found in other states. OHA's Plan B essentially re-creates the old OHA as it was before Rice v. Cayetano, but as a private club rather than a state agency. In some ways, members of the club would be like people who own apartments in a condominium association, where the association has rules which members must obey.

The Hawaiian racially exclusionary private club or condominium association would have more than 400,000 potential members. The State of Hawaii would "donate" to this "private" club huge "grants" of money, plus perhaps half the land in Hawaii, plus the authority to pass laws governing its members and excluding non-members.

It seems likely that the voters of Hawaii will never have a chance to decide whether to allow those transfers of money, land, and legal authority. State laws can easily be changed by a friendly and compliant legislature, without Constitutional amendment or voter referendum. For example, state law could be changed to reflect national Indian law so that in cases of a divorce between a member of the Hawaiian tribe and a non-member, child custody disputes would be resolved with a presumption in favor of the tribal member (Indians raising non-Indians is politically incorrect because the dying Indian culture needs to be preserved in the public interest).

OHA will fade into history after spawning this new clone, and the clone will grow to become more powerful and more racially exclusionary than OHA ever was. If the Akaka bill eventually passes, then Plan B will have prepared the way because the Native Hawaiian Governing Entity described in the Akaka bill will be ready and waiting to "hit the ground running." If the Akaka bill fails, racial separatism will nevertheless move forward aggressively. Either way Hawaii's gathering storm is poised to become a hurricane.

Degrees of separatism: Four models for the relationship between "indigenous" people and everyone else

For reasons discussed elsewhere (see Chapter 8), it is doubtful whether ethnic Hawaiians should be classified as an "indigenous" people. They may not be descended from the first people to settle in Hawaii. Their length of residence in Hawaii is less than the length of residence of other indigenous peoples in other places (including the white people of Britain). They no longer maintain an indigenous subsistence lifestyle, depending on intimate daily contact with the land for food, clothing, shelter, and animist religious practices. They do not need special protection as an endangered species incapable of fending off threats to their unique way of life. They are not a compact homogeneous group living a communal lifestyle separate and apart from a surrounding non-indigenous population.

In Hawaii the word "indigenous" is a buzzword synonym for "ethnic Hawaiian." The label "indigenous" automatically arouses compassion for a poor, downtrodden people; and carries feelings of awe or mysteriousness that compel deference to special needs. Thus calling ethnic Hawaiians "indigenous" automatically conveys a gentle but firm demand for special legal status and government handouts. The Akaka bill rests on a claim (false) that the U.S. Constitution empowers Congress to establish a political relationship with any indigenous people, whether or not they were ever organized as a tribe; and a claim (false) that ethnic Hawaiians are an indigenous people.

A symposium has been proposed for January 2008, to be held at Brigham Young University at Laie Hawaii – Indigenous Peoples: Sovereign Nations, Constituent Governments, Private Clubs or Individual Citizens.

Those four categories identify four possible degrees of racial separatism for ethnic Hawaiians by analogy to the political relationships between indigenous people and the rest of the world. However, there's no reason to limit these four categories to indigenous people. The symposium will focus on indigenous people only because the symposium's bias is that ethnic Hawaiians are an indigenous people and should be able to have the same degree of separatism other indigenous people sometimes have.

Here is my own brief description of the concepts I imagine the symposium organizers have in mind. (1) Perhaps an indigenous people can be its own nation-state, comparable to small ethnically monochrome independent nations like Tonga, or to ethnically mixed societies where the dominant group is indigenous, like Fiji. (2) Perhaps an indigenous people can be a "nation within a nation" such as American Indian tribes, or the Maori of Aotearoa (New Zealand). (3) Perhaps an indigenous people can achieve some degree of separatism by organizing themselves as a private club, somewhat like the Japanese Cultural Center or the See Dai Doo society. State-recognized Indian tribes like the one proposed for Akaka Plan B are in a murky gray area between options two and three, legally operating like a private club but hoping someday to become a recognized nation-within-a-nation. (4) Perhaps indigenous people are merely individual citizens of a multiethnic society, practicing their culture and religion in the same way as all other ethnic groups. That's not such a bad outcome. In many parts of the world ethnic and religious minorities are oppressed, persecuted, and exterminated.

Now let's examine those same four categories but no longer limited to indigenous people. By doing that we'll see that the four categories are simply one way to classify the degrees of separatism among the subgroups of any nation's or continent's population.

(1) The continent of North America is divided into three sovereign nation-states: Canada, the United States, and Mexico. (2) The United States is divided into 50 separate states, and nearly 600 Indian tribes, each of which has the authority to make laws governing important aspects of life within its own territory – such aspects as marriage, divorce, child custody, inheritance, state or tribal taxes, drivers licenses and car registrations, state highways, universities. Each state also has political subdivisions (counties and municipalities) which regulate zoning, local roads, local school systems (except that in Hawaii all public schools are owned, operated, and paid for solely by the state). (3) There are private clubs whose members are defined by race, ethnicity, gender, age, profession, attendance at a particular school (past or present), ownership of property, etc. Japanese American Citizens League, League of Women Voters, American Association of Retired People, American Bar Association, University of Illinois Alumni Association, Foster Towers Condominium Association, etc. (4) Every person is an individual with rights (voting) and responsibilities (taxes, fees, and dues) pertaining to every level of membership.

In the course of history, entropy is at work. The usual pattern is that entities move down in their degree of separatism rather than up. One nation gets overrun by another, losing its sovereignty. If the people of the overrun nation are lucky, their new overlords allow them to maintain a degree of regional or local autonomy. That's what happened to the Armenians (very little autonomy) and Kurds (substantial autonomy in Iraq but little autonomy in Turkey), and to the American Indians (legally recognized political autonomy growing stronger). If the overrun people are unlucky, their new overlords deny them any political status and they must do the best they can by joining private organizations. Immigrants to a nation often try to hold onto their ethnic heritage by joining such clubs. Finally, people "on the loose" in a society may join private clubs for whatever reason they choose; and one such reason is to learn, maintain, or celebrate an ethnic or indigenous heritage.

When a level one group is overrun or falls apart, level two groups are formed. When a level two group becomes assimilated through the passage of time, some individuals continue to identify strongly with their heritage and form level three clubs, while other individuals fall away, become disillusioned or uncaring, or even spurn their heritage in order to blend in and "pass for" an ordinary member of the dominant society.

Every society allows level four individuals to join level three private clubs. But most societies do not like to allow level three clubs to become level two politically recognized entities, because that is a pathway to balkanization and to eventually splitting up one nation into two or more splinter nations. The United States fought a civil war to prevent a level one nation from splintering into two level one nations. The Soviet Union splintered into many level one nations, some of which then reached out to each other to reunify at least partially.

Should any group playing identity politics be allowed to exercise self-determination to create its own separatist government? In the United States in 1860, why should the northern states not have allowed the southern states to split away and form a separate nation? In today's Russia, why not allow the Chechens to secede? In today's South Africa after apartheid, why should the new government not have allowed the Caucasians to form their own nation-within-a-nation, as they requested? In all of these examples the group seeking political autonomy had a far more distinctively separate way of life and economy than ethnic Hawaiians.

At present ethnic Hawaiians exist at level four as individuals scattered throughout a multiracial Hawaii and scattered throughout the United States (and world). Some of them come together in level three private clubs such as Kamehameha Schools, the Hawaiian Civic Clubs, hula groups, etc. It's hard to know whether Akaka Plan B is at level three-plus or at level two-minus. But any private club at level three which has pretensions to massive landholdings and political law-making authority is certainly straining very hard to become a level two group and will not rest until it achieves that status. And any group which ever moves up from level three to level two must surely have aspirations to rise to level one. A struggle against entropy requires great energy and perseverance; and success generates more energy. Thus the racial separatist movement in Hawaii, while apparently demanding only level two status as an Indian tribe, will surely then strive mightily for level one status as the independent nation Hawaii once was.

The symposium planned at BYUH for January 2008 is clearly intended to bolster the Akaka bill (level 2) and, as a fallback, Akaka Plan B (level 2-minus or 3-plus). Senator Akaka has been invited and has tentatively accepted. Academicians from Pacific island nations and indigenous peoples' organizations will present fancy theories to explain why indigenous peoples are entitled to nationhood. It's doubtful whether anyone presenting a paper at the symposium would recommend in favor of level three or four, because those will be perceived as loser's choices. Who would ever say "I'm happy with what I have and want nothing more." What kind of intellectual arguments could be devised to make that a proposition worthy of time at the symposium? Who would ever stand in front of such a group to explain why ethnic Hawaiians are not indigenous? The symposium is a set-up; another arrow in Senator Akaka's quiver.

Chapter 4

Ethnic Nationalism

Hawaiian ethnic nationalism, secession, and multiplicity of sovereignty theories

The title of this chapter, "Ethnic Nationalism," will be criticized immediately as being inaccurate. Zealots proposing an independent nation of Hawaii will claim it's not about an ethnic group but about a multiracial nation. And of course they are correct – until the rest of the story makes it clear that the multiracial nation they envision will have racial supremacy for ethnic Hawaiians guaranteed by law under a theory of "indigenous rights." People with no native blood, although presently an 80% majority, would be merely along for the ride, with varying levels of rights depending on their ancestors' long-ago political status or birthplace. The secessionist Confederate States of America was multiracial, but that did not stop it from being ethnic nationalist with Caucasians having racial supremacy by law over Negro slaves. South Africa under apartheid was multiracial, but a small racial minority was able to maintain absolute control over a large majority even without the institution of slavery.

The subtitle word "secession" will also be criticized. The zealots claim there never was a legitimate cession in the first place, so there is no need for a se-cession. They claim that under international law Hawaii has continuously remained the same independent nation it formerly was. They say an illegal overthrow of the monarchy by the U.S., and installation of a U.S. puppet regime, resulted in a unilateral takeover of Hawaii by the U.S. and a belligerent military occupation which has lasted ever since 1893. So instead of using the word "secession" they prefer to use expressions like "de-occupation" or "U.S. withdrawal."

There are many different sovereignty groups already claiming to be the one true government of the Nation of Hawaii. There are also some loose-knit groups whose organizers do not claim to be head-of-state – they merely coordinate political activities (and highly politicized cultural activities) to keep alive a "deep culture" or "living nation." Each "nation" group has its own spin on history and international law. Each of the various "Kingdoms" has its own egotistical "King" or "Regent Pro Tem" proudly claiming to be humble – some claim they already own all the lands of Hawaii; and a few of them actually do own or lease land for small communities. The more loose-knit groups simply have frequent meetings and occasional public events, without pretensions to actually possess political authority as yet.

The various groups have different sets of words to describe their beliefs, or different definitions for some of the same words, so there's no way to talk about the issues without having arguments over semantics. Semantic differences are not merely technical or trivial – they go to the core of disagreements over what happened historically, and how to go about making things right. For example, was Hawaii ever colonized by the U.S., and does it remain so? Then Hawaii could make use of a decolonization process at the United Nations already used successfully, or currently underway, for several "non-self-governing" colonial territories. But if Hawaii was always an independent nation and now finds itself under a prolonged belligerent military occupation, then the process for decolonization is inappropriate. Trying to implement a decolonization strategy might backfire and damage lawsuits in the "World Court" or petitions to the United Nations Security Council demanding withdrawal of the prolonged occupation. Highly zealous and knowledgeable participants engage in progressively combative semantic quarrels with each other, getting all tied up in knots.

Race is the core

Most Hawaiian independence leaders believe race is the core. They don't come right out and say that, but if someone can get them to sit still long enough to probe the depths of their beliefs, their racism becomes increasingly clear. They believe, quite simply, that ethnic Hawaiians were Hawaii's first people; that life was good before Captain Cook arrived; that the coming of Caucasians and Asians was unfortunate and is really just a blip on the radar screen of Hawaiian history. "Hawaii for the Hawaiians." End of story. Some of the independence leaders make loud noises about the fact that the Kingdom of Hawaii had non-natives as full-fledged subjects (citizens). They proclaim that fact in order to solicit support from non-ethnic-Hawaiians by seeming to promise racial equality; but they also believe in a theory of "indigenous rights" that would make second-class citizens out of everyone lacking Hawaiian native ancestry.

The most highly respected independence leader, an elderly medical doctor with a soft voice and smiling demeanor (Dr. Kekuni Blaisdell), says "We are 'Kanaka Maoli'," speaking those Hawaiian words with puffed up chest and growling throat. He explains his view by saying that when Captain Cook first greeted the Hawaiian natives, he asked them "Who are you?" And the natives responded "We are Kanaka Maoli – the real people. And who [the hell] are you?" Blaisdell and his close associates have several non-ethnic Hawaiians who have worked at their sides for many long years. One man of entirely Chinese descent, who is also a medical doctor, had an ancestor who became naturalized as a subject of the Kingdom. Another man is of entirely Japanese ancestry and his family has lived in Hawaii for several generations. Both have been entrusted with organizing meetings and political rallies, doing environmental work and political advocacy, etc. The Chinese doctor has a huge Hawaiian flag which he is proud to display at political rallies; and in parades he carries his flag at the front – of the group of non-ethnic Hawaiians whose place is at the rear of the parade! These two men are treated as subservient to the ethnic Hawaiians (including many of lesser ability and accomplishment), and they humbly accept their second-class status. Humility is one of the cardinal "Hawaiian values." So long as these non-ethnic-Hawaiians "know their place" they are welcome to assist the "real people."

Four levels of political and economic rights depending on race and long-ago circumstances

Because of semantic difficulties and significant conceptual disagreements, there's no way the many sovereignty issues and proposals can be discussed that would meet everyone's approval. But let's do the best we can anyway, and not allow the Liliputians to tie our tongues with cords of semantic obfuscation or political correctness.

Let's consider how voting rights and land ownership would look in Hawaii after independence has become established. Some of these concepts are taken from a 1996 masters thesis by Anthony Castanha, who interviewed Hawaiian sovereignty leaders to discover their views on voting and property rights for non-ethnic-Hawaiians in a restored Hawaiian nation.[50] Some of the concepts come from long years of listening to radio and television programs featuring independence activist Hayden Burgess, alias Poka Laenui, whose website contains articles discussing some but not all of these issues.[51] There would be four different levels of rights and participation.

(1) Resident aliens. All residents of an independent Hawaii would have fundamental human rights, perhaps comparable to the rights enjoyed by foreigners in America. They have the right to security of life and property, the right to due process of law, the right to speak freely, etc. People who remain at this level would have rights comparable to recent immigrants to America who get permanent resident status and "green card" work permits; except that the right to buy and sell property would be restricted to specific areas. Everyone who was living in Hawaii at the time independence was restored will qualify at least for this minimum level and will be allowed to stay (unless expelled for treason or serious crimes), along with those who immigrate afterward. Non-ethnic Hawaiians living in Hawaii at the time independence is restored, who choose to remain at this level and do not become naturalized citizens, will probably be given a limited period of years during which they must sell all their real estate; and they might (or might not) be forced eventually to move into areas where foreigners are allowed to live.

(2) Naturalized citizens. The residents of Hawaii with no native blood, who presently comprise 80% of the population, will be allowed to stay on at least as resident aliens, and also can become naturalized citizens if they wish. Being born in the Kingdom automatically conferred the status of Hawaiian subject regardless of race. However, that rule does not apply to people born and raised in Hawaii after January 17, 1893, because ever since then Hawaii has been under belligerent foreign occupation and unable to control immigration. Thus, at least 3/4 of today's citizens of Hawaii will suddenly find themselves treated as resident aliens unless they acquire certain knowledge, passes certain tests, and take an oath of loyalty to the Nation of Hawaii. Required knowledge and skills might include a minimum level of fluency in Hawaiian language, and a knowledge of Hawaiian history as that history is revised by government officials to be "politically correct." Anyone born in Hawaii to a visitor or resident alien, and growing up here, would be treated as a resident alien eligible for naturalization upon reaching adulthood. Anyone born and raised in Hawaii as a child of a naturalized citizen is presumably a naturalized citizen, at least

until adulthood, at which time he might (or might not) be required to pass the naturalization tests and take the loyalty oath or else devolve to resident alien status (independence proposals are unclear on this point, so this issue would need to be decided after independence by enacting a law).

(3) Non-ethnic-Hawaiian Citizens of Kingdom descent. The Kingdom of Hawaii was a multiracial nation. Only 40% of its people had any native blood at the time the monarchy was overthrown in 1893. Most of the rest were contract laborers of Japanese and Chinese descent, and there were also a few thousand Caucasians of American or European ancestry including Portuguese contract laborers. Most of the contract laborers expected to remain in Hawaii only a few years and then return home; but many ended up staying, getting married, and making babies. Only a handful of Japanese became naturalized subjects of the Kingdom, and only a few thousand Chinese and Caucasians did that. A website of the "Hawaiian Kingdom" contains a registry of naturalized Kingdom subjects. The final Kingdom census in 1890 counted 48,117 Kingdom subjects. 40,622 of them were ethnic Hawaiians, and 7,495 were naturalized or Hawaii-born Kingdom subjects with no native ancestry.[52]

Every baby born in Hawaii was automatically a subject of the Hawaiian Kingdom by right of birth, regardless of the status of his parents (except for children of foreign diplomats). Thus there were many thousands of Hawaiian Kingdom subjects with no native blood, before the monarchy was overthrown in 1893. It is unclear whether the "Hawaiian Kingdom" census of 1890, reported above, included local-born babies of Asian sugar plantation workers – the babies would have been Kingdom subjects even though their parents were not.

All male Kingdom subjects had full voting and property rights (upon reaching adulthood) and were equal to ethnic Hawaiians in every way, regardless of race. There were a few laws at various times which discriminated against the natives in the interest of protecting them; for example, a law prohibiting the sale of alcohol to natives.[53] But there were no laws giving natives superior rights over Hawaii-born non-native subjects. There was never a difference between native-born vs. naturalized subjects. The Constitution of 1864 imposed property and income requirements for voting. Those requirements were race-neutral but had a greater impact upon ethnic Hawaiians because more Hawaiians than Caucasians were landless and living in poverty.

Today's sovereignty activists like to blame Caucasians for imposing the racial restrictions on voting rights found in the "Bayonet Constitution" of 1887. However Kalakaua was King before that event, and remained King until he died four years later. Was he King or not? Did the imposition of the new Constitution constitute a genuine revolution so the Kingdom ended in 1887, or was the King still head of government and therefore responsible for the new Constitution? He signed the new Constitution to hold onto power, when he could have stood on principle and suffered the consequences. There is no evidence he made any objection at all to the stripping of Asian voting rights. On the contrary, anyone who thinks ethnic Hawaiians "owned" the Kingdom must agree that ethnic Hawaiians had more to gain than Caucasians by stripping Asian voting rights, since Asians greatly outnumbered ethnic Hawaiians, who in turn outnumbered Caucasians.

If Hawaii once again becomes an independent nation, the descendants of non-ethnic-Hawaiian subjects of the Kingdom would have the same voting and property rights as the descendants of the ethnic Hawaiian subjects; with some very important exceptions to be noted below. It's unclear whether non-ethnic-Hawaiian descendants of Kingdom subjects would be expected to pass the citizenship tests and take the loyalty oath. If they would indeed be expected to do that, then they would be treated essentially the same as resident aliens waiting to be naturalized. That seems very unfair, and needs further discussion (next).

There are two basic reasons put forth by the sovereignty activists to explain why today's ethnic Hawaiians should have special rights in an independent Hawaii over and above the rights of everyone else. One reason is essentially racial – the theory of indigenous rights (see below). The other reason is political – the theory that sovereignty, citizenship, voting rights and property rights can all be inherited in a bundle. If the reason is truly political and not racial, then non-ethnic Hawaiian descendants of Kingdom subjects must be treated identically as ethnic Hawaiians.

Today most ethnic Hawaiian advocates for Hawaii independence are proud to say they will welcome non-ethnic-Hawaiian descendants of Kingdom subjects as equals (except for the "catch 22" of indigenous rights). They endorse the theory that even though the Kingdom government has been ineffective and went into limbo since 1893, it is still the rightful government of Hawaii. Therefore its laws remain in place. But if all that is true, then non-ethnic-Hawaiian descendants of Kingdom subjects must be treated equally with ethnic Hawaiians, and should not need to pass any tests or take any loyalty oath in order to have full voting and property rights. Most of today's advocates for independence say it's about a (multiracial) nation, not about a race. But insisting on a theory of indigenous rights destroys any pretensions to racial equality.

(4) Ethnic Hawaiians and indigenous rights. Most independence activists say that people with no native ancestry should have voting rights and property rights. That's where the activists want the conversation to end. If pressed they will acknowledge that ethnic Hawaiians would have unchallenged full voting rights and property rights in an independent Hawaii because of their special status as the indigenous people, while others would have only limited rights. Ethnic Hawaiians would have special lands set aside exclusively for them, while also enjoying full access and ownership rights to all the remaining lands. Ethnic Hawaiians would have exclusive voting rights on certain topics, such as immigration and land-use policy; while also enjoying full voting rights on all other topics. They would not need to pass any tests or take any loyalty oath, because of their birthright. All persons lacking native blood would be relegated to second-class citizenship, including non-ethnic-Hawaiian (therefore non-indigenous) descendants of Kingdom subjects.

It's interesting to note that the Akaka bill, and OHA Plan B, envision a similar scenario (except that Hawaii as a U.S. state is unable to limit immigration). Both the Akaka bill and OHA plan B would set aside huge tracts of land exclusively for ethnic Hawaiians, and establish racially exclusionary membership and voting in tribal government; while allowing ethnic Hawaiians to continue participating fully in all the other public lands of the State of Hawaii and in voting for state and federal officials.

Details of the political system for an independent Hawaii are unclear. Different independence activists envision different institutional arrangements, but all are agreed on racial supremacy. "Ka Lahui", a sovereignty organization which once claimed 20,000 members, created a Constitution and ran its organization allowing non-ethnic-Hawaiians to become citizens – but only "honorary" citizens without voting rights. Ka Lahui was noted for holding "treason" trials and expelling citizens (both ethnic and non-ethnic Hawaiians) who publicly disagreed with its doctrines. The "Nation of Hawaii" under charismatic leader Dennis "Bumpy" Kanahele allows all citizens regardless of race to have voting rights. However, Kanahele's Constitution[54] says ethnic Hawaiians are guaranteed a majority in the legislature. The head of state, all the judges, and all members of the age-defined councils of kupuna (elders), makua (parent generation), and opio (youth) – all must be ethnic Hawaiian. Every independence proposal which has sufficient structure to be clear includes racial supremacy for ethnic Hawaiians and second-class citizenship for everyone else.

It's important to note that "indigenous rights" played no part in the Hawaiian Kingdom. Perhaps that's because there were far more ethnic Hawaiians than Caucasians in the Kingdom, while the even greater majority of Asians had no political power and were seen as merely short-term contract laborers. Also, "international law" was much less developed at that time, and had not yet invented the concept of indigeneity.

Nation-states have standing and rights internationally; but indigenous people are under the authority of the nation-states where they live. For one nation to complain about the way indigenous people are treated in another nation would be seen as interference in that nation's internal affairs, until quite recently. A Draft Declaration on the Rights of Indigenous People(s) has been floating around the United Nations for about two decades.[55] It has never been officially adopted because the nation-states correctly view it as an attack on their sovereignty and territorial integrity. How, exactly, would the following provision be implemented without allowing indigenous people to secede if that's what they want? "Article 3: Indigenous peoples have the right of self-determination. By virtue of that right they freely determine their political status and freely pursue their economic, social and cultural development."

If the Kingdom has maintained its continuity (although ineffectively in limbo), then why would today's Asians and Caucasians born in Hawaii not be Kingdom subjects fully equal to ethnic Hawaiians?

Suppose we agree the overthrow of the monarchy was illegal because it was the result of an armed invasion by the U.S. Suppose we agree the Republic of Hawaii was merely a U.S. puppet regime with no legitimacy to speak on behalf of the Hawaiian nation. Suppose we agree the Treaty of Annexation was illegal both because the Republic had no legitimacy or standing to offer it and because the U.S. failed to ratify it by 2/3 vote of the Senate as the U.S. Constitution requires (It was ratified by a joint resolution with a vote of 42-21 in the Senate [but some abstentions] and 209-91 in the House). Suppose we agree the statehood vote of 1959 was illegal because Hawaii was under U.S. belligerent military occupation at the time (an agreement forced under duress is null) and because the ballot failed to offer the option of independence (allegedly a requirement of the United Nations). Therefore, suppose for the sake of argument we agree that the Kingdom of Hawaii has continued to exist from the 1800s until now.

Kingdom law said that any male born in Hawaii (except children of foreign diplomats) was a subject of the Hawaiian Kingdom and would have full voting rights upon reaching adulthood. Since Kingdom law is still the rightful law of Hawaii, therefore there are hundreds of thousands of Asians and Caucasians now living in Hawaii who have no native blood but who have rights fully equal to ethnic Hawaiians. Ethnic Hawaiians would therefore be a minority of voters in a reinstated independent Hawaii.

Hawaiian ethnic nationalists have difficulty reconciling their views on history with their views on the status of Asians. The sovereignty activists don't like the Bayonet Constitution of 1887 because it was forced on the King by (mostly) Caucasians. It stripped the King of most of his powers, making him into little more than a figurehead somewhat like today's Queen of England. However, that Constitution stripped Asians of voting rights, and it was the last Constitution of the Kingdom before the monarchy was overthrown. Therefore some clever Hawaiian ethnic nationalists who want to have maximum political power for themselves in a democratic system (and assuming the continuity of Kingdom law) reluctantly embrace the 1887 Constitution in order to be able to legally exclude today's Asians from voting rights.

Non-ethnic-Hawaiians are 80% of Hawaii's current population. Subtract U.S. military personnel, and everyone not born in Hawaii, and there is still a huge majority of non-ethnic-Hawaiians. The ethnic nationalists do not like that at all, especially if they deny the legitimacy of the 1887 Constitution and therefore must allow Asians to vote. Even if the 1887 Constitution is embraced and Asians are excluded, ethnic Hawaiians today would still be a minority, because there are significantly more Caucasians than ethnic Hawaiians. Thus, regardless of the status of the 1887 Constitution, ethnic nationalists need some sort of rationale to deny voting rights to all who are not descendants of Kingdom subjects from before 1893.

Here's the rationale to guarantee an ethnic Hawaiian majority. Following the 1893 U.S. invasion, puppet regime, and continuing belligerent military occupation, the rightful government has been forcibly prevented from exercising its authority. In particular, Hawaii has been unable to control immigration. All persons who immigrated to Hawaii after January 17, 1893 came as illegal aliens under the authority of a hostile foreign occupying power. They are therefore agents of that foreign power, and their children born in Hawaii have the same status as children of foreign diplomats (i.e., they are not subjects of the Kingdom and they have no voting rights).

"International law," as well as common sense, does not allow an occupying power to flood the population of the occupied country with the occupier's own people and thereby establish a voting majority. In Tibet a massive Chinese military invasion caused many Tibetans, including the Dalai Lama, to flee to exile in India; and the Chinese then flooded Tibet with Chinese families and ordered Chinese soldiers to rape Tibetan women to begin a process of destroying the Tibetan genealogy. Hawaiian sovereignty zealots have claimed America's occupation of Hawaii is similar to China's occupation of Tibet.

This rationale for stripping the great majority of Hawaii's people of voting rights would clearly be frightening to most of today's citizens of Hawaii, if they were aware of it.

The sovereignty activists have figured out a way to minimize and deflect this concern by saying that once ethnic Hawaiians have seized control of Hawaii there would be various options for protecting the rights of ethnic Asians and Caucasians – options which have actually been pursued to protect the rights of ethnic Russians in the Eastern European nations that emerged from behind the Iron Curtain after the collapse of the Soviet Union. The trouble is that it would be up to ethnic Hawaiians alone to decide whether to adopt any of these options. The history of racial exclusion in today's powerful ethnic Hawaiian institutions does not bode well.

During World War 2 Nazi Germany invaded and conquered several European nations. Slowly the "Allied" powers invaded those nations and kicked out the Germans. The U.S., France, and Britain helped rebuild the nations they liberated, and gave back their independence. But the Soviet Union did not. The USSR kept tight control of the nations it "liberated," installing puppet regimes backed up by huge numbers of Soviet troops permanently stationed there (just as the U.S. has maintained a puppet regime in Hawaii backed up by tens of thousands of troops and dozens of military bases). The Soviet occupation of eastern Europe lasted for 50 years (the U.S. occupation of Hawaii has lasted only a little over twice that long), until the Soviet Union collapsed (the U.S. has not yet collapsed, but Hawaiian sovereignty activists keep gleefully pointing out that the U.S. is looking more shaky every year).

During the five decades of Soviet occupation, large numbers of ethnic Russians migrated to Eastern Europe, especially the Baltic nations of Latvia, Lithuania, and Estonia (just as tens of thousands of Americans moved to Hawaii, and even more Asians moved to Hawaii while the American occupation prevented Hawaiians from controlling immigration). Huge numbers of ethnic Russians now live in the Baltic nations, some for several generations (just like Japanese, Chinese, Filipinos and Euro-Americans in Hawaii). Ethnic Russians comprise one-fourth to one-third of the populations of these countries. Some of them are hated and despised by the natives of those nations, because they (actually their grandparents) were installed there against the wishes of the natives under belligerent occupation.

What now should become of the ethnic Russians living in the Baltic nations following the collapse of the Soviet Union and the restoration of full independence? Most of them were born and raised in the nation they now call home. Many of them own farms and businesses. Some of them have learned the local language and customs. But do they really belong there? The three Baltic nations have each followed different paths for dealing with this problem. Perhaps the Russians were ordered to go "home" (to a Russia they had never seen). Perhaps the Russians were allowed to stay as resident aliens. Perhaps the Russians were allowed to become naturalized citizens by passing tests and swearing an oath of allegiance. It is not the purpose of this book to describe those solutions nor to trace whether they worked out well or poorly. However, in no case were the ethnic Russians allowed to participate in voting to decide what the solution would be. That decision was for the native Latvians, Lithuanians, and Estonians to make.

In Hawaii some Caucasian families have eight generations of residence. Some Chinese and Japanese have six generations; some Filipinos have four or perhaps five generations. According to Hawaiian sovereignty activists, none of the Asian or Euro-American ethnic groups have an absolute right to stay in an independent Hawaii except for a relatively few who are descendants of naturalized or native-born subjects of the Hawaiian Kingdom. There will be gut-wrenching uncertainty and fear if Hawaii gains independence. Caucasians who already consider themselves Americans and who speak English could escape to the U.S. if they choose not to swear allegiance to the new (ethnic) Hawaiian nation. But third, fourth, and fifth generation Japanese, Chinese, and Filipinos, who speak only English and consider themselves Americans, could theoretically be forced to "return" to their ancestral "homelands" in Asia where neither they nor their parents nor their grandparents have ever lived and whose language they do not speak.

Hawaiian ethnic nationalists say they would never do anything to harm non-ethnic Hawaiians, especially since some of their own family members or spouses are in that category. And yet there are over 160 federal programs in Hawaii, and many state and private institutions, which zealously guard racial exclusion. In recent years Hawaiian sovereignty activists have revived the celebration of Kingdom holidays. Although Caucasians were among the greatest heroes of the Kingdom, today's sovereignty activists shove them aside in their celebrations. This ethnic cleansing of Hawaiian history[56] discloses a racist attitude and serves as the canary in the mine shaft – a warning that ethnic cleansing of voting rights and land ownership are likely to accompany any form of Hawaiian sovereignty.

The situation in Fiji is also a cautionary tale.

Fiji and Hawaii both have large numbers of Asians descended from contract laborers brought in to work on the sugar plantations. Since Fiji and India were both colonies of Britain, the British imported their Asian contract laborers for Fiji from India. Hawaii was an independent nation. King Kalakaua wanted to help the sugar plantations increase their work force to generate lots of money to feed his insatiably lavish lifestyle. But he also wanted the imported laborers to be a "cognate race" whose dark skin would blend well with ethnic Hawaiians and whose genealogies might trace back to common origins in Asia. Kalakaua furthermore wanted his laborers to come from independent nations that were under a monarchial system just like Hawaii rather than from a colony under Caucasian dominance. So the King imported his Asian sugar plantation laborers from China and Japan rather than India. (It's interesting to speculate that if Emma had defeated Kalakaua in the election of 1874, Kalakaua would never have gone to Japan. Hawaii would have grown closer to Britain and would have imported plantation workers from India just like Fiji did, rather than from Japan).

By the 1990s the Asian Fijians had become about 45% of Fiji's population. The Asian Fijians were mostly native-born and living in Fiji for several generations (just like Hawaii's Chinese, Japanese, and Filipinos). The Asian Fijians dominated the economy as professionals and business owners, while the natives owned nearly all the land but often had poor skills and low incomes.

The concept of racial supremacy for ethnic Hawaiians in an independent Hawaii closely resembles the reality of racial supremacy for ethnic Fijians written into the laws of Fiji. The Fijian racial supremacy laws were defended by several military coups during the past 20 years. These were violent overthrows of democratically elected governments where Asians had acquired powerful leadership positions and were threatening to change the laws to provide greater equality.[57]

For example, the new constitution imposed in 1990 following the racial supremacy military coup of 1887 specified that Asian Fijians could have only 27 seats in the 71 member parliament (substantially less than their 45% of the population would warrant), and that Asians could vote only for candidates for the Asian seats but not for candidates for the Native Fijian seats.

The system in place in Fiji resembles what Hawaiian ethnic nationalists are striving for. It's also the sort of system likely to develop over time in Hawaii if the Akaka bill passes or if Akaka Plan B moves forward. A Fiji-style racial voting system actually existed in Hawaii until the Rice v. Cayetano decision of 2000. Hawaii voters were asked to identify their race when getting their ballots on election day. People with no native ancestry were refused the right to vote for candidates in the general elections for seats on the state government Office of Hawaiian Affairs that controls a portion of state government revenues and expenditures and has special power over some government lands, boards, and commissions.

In the Fiji elections of 2000 a democratically elected government emerged whose new Prime Minister was Mahendra Chaudhry – it was the first time in Fiji's history that an Asian Fijian was Prime Minister. All hell broke loose. Elements of the Fiji military staged a(nother) coup, taking over the legislature, arresting Asian Fijians, and appointing a new Native Fijian government. The military singled out areas where large numbers of Asians lived, for violent rampages. That situation was understandably frightening to all Asian Fijians, who realized they would never be allowed full equality as citizens of their nation. Racial tensions escalated, causing Asian Fijians to fear for their lives and property. Many left Fiji. Tourism is a major economic engine in Fiji just as in Hawaii, and the economy went into a tailspin. In the tourist capital Nadi, on Fiji's western coast, banners were erected – even on some homes of indigenous Fijians – denouncing Speight (the native coup leader). The slogans included: "Mr.

President give us our government back" and "We want Chaudhry. Go to hell Speight"

Intimidation and racial tension took their toll. Thousands of Asian Fijians left their country forever. Since they were among Fiji's leading professionals and business owners the quality of life and the economy declined. When the 2006 elections were held, only 37% of Fiji's people were Asians, and the natives easily won. They began pushing a bill in the legislature to pardon the coup plotters from 2000 in the name of "peace and reconciliation." That bill had been proposed for several years, but the election victory boosted the confidence level of the racial radicals to believe they could further trample everyone's rights. After months of rising tensions between the military and the government, another military coup took place toward the end of 2006. This time the coup was mostly about government corruption rather than race; but the continuing instability is having a severe impact on the economy as well as the sense of security people need for happiness.

Decolonization – Is Hawaii legitimately the 50th state?

The first half of this chapter has been devoted to a theory that Hawaii is under a prolonged belligerent military occupation by the U.S.; and the U.S. should withdraw thereby leaving Hawaii free and independent. But there's also a theory that Hawaii is a colony of the U.S. comparable to the way Massachusetts and Virginia were once colonies of England. The theory says that both in America and in Hawaii, a land containing only indigenous people was "discovered" and invaded by Europeans. New diseases decimated the native populations. Superior technology enabled the Caucasians to take control of the land and economy, sending home huge profits gained through exploiting native lands.

By the early 1900s there were dozens of European colonies in Africa, the Middle East, the Americas, and the Pacific; controlled by Britain, France, Belgium, Holland, Italy, Germany, and others. The United States also established a few colonies.

Following World War 2 the United Nations was created, and began a process of decolonization which continues today. Dozens of newly independent sovereign nation-states emerged either through bloody revolutions or through peaceful decolonization. India broke free from Britain; then Pakistan broke free from India; and then Bangladesh broke free from

Pakistan. Algeria, Tunisia, and Morocco broke free from France. Ethiopia broke free from Italy. The Congo got liberated from Belgium.

In the Spanish-American War the U.S. acquired several colonies previously owned by Spain. The Philippines have since been given total independence, while Puerto Rico remains an American colony. Eastern Samoa, formerly a colony of Germany, became independent after World War 2; while Western Samoa remains a colony of the U.S. Alaska, formerly colonized by Russia, was purchased from Russia by the United States and remained a U.S. colony until achieving statehood in 1959.

The Territory of Hawaii was established by the Organic Act of 1900 following the annexation of 1898. But was the Territory of Hawaii really a colony like Puerto Rico or Alaska? Hawaii had been an independent nation, whose government offered a treaty of annexation which the U.S. accepted. Alaska and Puerto Rico had never been independent nations. The fate of those colonies was decided by the foreign nations that occupied, bought, and sold them. Alaska had been a colony of Russia which the U.S. purchased. Puerto Rico and Guam had been colonies of Spain which the U.S. won through warfare. Hawaiian sovereignty zealots who favor the decolonization model get quite excited whenever the status of Puerto Rico or Guam is discussed, because they imagine that Hawaii has the same claim to independence under United Nations decolonization procedures.[58]

From 1946 until the statehood vote of 1959 Hawaii was officially treated by the United Nations as a colony of the U.S. eligible to be decolonized. Here are the titles and dates of the six most important United Nations documents related to the listing and de-listing of Hawaii on the list of "non-self-governing territories" as found on the website of ethnic nationalist zealot Hayden Burgess, alias Poka Laenui, at http://www.opihi.com:

United Nations Charter, chapter XI, Article 73, Declaration Regarding Non-Self-Governing Territories, 1945.

United Nations General Assembly, Resolution 66 (I), List of Non-Self-Governing Territories, December 14, 1946.

United Nations General Assembly, Resolution 742 (VIII), Factors which should be taken into account in deciding whether a Territory is or is not a Territory whose people have not yet attained a full measure of self-government, November 27, 1953.

United Nations General Assembly, Resolution 1469 (XIV), Cessation of the transmission of information under Article 73e of the Charter in respect of Alaska and Hawaii, December 12, 1959.

United Nations General Assembly, Resolution 1514 (XV), Declaration on the granting of independence to colonial countries and peoples, December 14, 1960.

United Nations General Assembly, Resolution 1541 (XV), Principles which should guide Members in determining whether or not an obligation exists to transmit the information called for under Article 73e of the Charter, December 15, 1960.

According to Hayden Burgess (Poka Laenui), the United States perpetrated a fraud on the United Nations. The U.S. notified the U.N. that the statehood vote of June 1959 (94% voted "yes"), and the final certification of Hawaii's admission to the U.S. as a state in August 1959, had resulted in incorporating Hawaii as an integral part of the U.S. and therefore Hawaii should be removed from the list of non-self-governing territories. The U.N. then did in fact remove Hawaii (and also Alaska) from that list in December 1959. Burgess (Laenui) claims that this notification about statehood was a fraud, because the ballot for the statehood vote did not offer the option of independence. And somehow the real experts on international law at the U.N. (unlike amateur Burgess) got fooled by this fraud. And somehow they have remained fooled all these nearly fifty years since then, despite his repeatedly calling it to their attention.

Burgess (Laenui) claims the U.N. requires three choices on the ballot: full integration (statehood), free association (treaty granting military and diplomatic control in return for protection and financial assistance), or total independence. However, none of the documents he provides include any language delineating a requirement for those three choices. The two documents he refers to as his strongest arguments are the last two, resolutions 1514 and 1541. But those were passed in December 1960, 18 months after Hawaii's statehood vote and a full year after Hawaii was formally removed from the list of non-self-governing territories. As an attorney he should know that new laws cannot be applied ex-post-facto to undo actions previously taken; and even so those two 1960 resolutions do not set forth his theory that three choices must be offered on the ballot. He has never shown that it is illegal under "international law" – even now 50 years later – to simply ask people "Do you want to become a permanent part of our nation?" without simultaneously asking them "Do you want to become your own nation?"

Burgess and other Hawaiian nationalist zealots go further. They claim that international law imposes strict requirements on the circumstances that must prevail for a status vote on sovereignty to be valid. They say all military forces of the occupying power must be withdrawn for a substantial period of time before the vote is taken (to avoid intimidation or control of the outcome), and there must be a period in which the population of the occupied territory is thoroughly educated (propagandized) on the meaning and consequences of the choices, and the vote must be conducted under auspices of the United Nations or a neutral third party. Thus even if all three choices had been on the ballot in 1959, the vote would still have been "illegal."

In 2001 Burgess wrote Senate Resolution 98 for the Hawaii Legislature which asked the U.S. Congress and the United Nations to: "Review the actions taken in 1959 relevant to Hawaii's Statehood within the Union of the United States of America, the fact that, in affording the people the opportunity for self-governance, no choices were given for independence or free association, but only for integration within the United States of America; and Consider the implications for the continuing right of self-determination for the native Hawaiian people and for the people of Hawaii, as both a matter of domestic law and international law; BE IT FURTHER RESOLVED that certified copies of this Concurrent Resolution be transmitted to the President of the United States, the Majority Leader of the United States Senate, the Speaker of the United States House of Representatives, the Secretary General of the United Nations, and the United Nations' Special Committee on the Situation with Regard to the Implementation of the Declaration on the Granting of Independence to Colonial Countries and Peoples."[59]

The Senate of the State of Hawaii actually passed that resolution, and certified copies of it were actually sent to the places specified. Thus the State of Hawaii is on record as saying to the United Nations, in effect: We the people of Hawaii are being held captive against our will and we ask you to help liberate us. Were the Senators merely being nice to a daffy zealot with good lobbying skills, or did they seriously mean it? The written recommendations of the Senate committee that held hearings on the resolution show that they clearly understood its importance and possible consequences.[60] In 2002 the House and Senate failed to even hold hearings on a resolution (HR11, SR22) calling on the Governor to hold an active celebration of the official Statehood Day holiday, because Hawaiian ethnic nationalist zealots objected to it.[61] In 2003 a nearly identical Statehood Day celebration resolution (SR144) did receive a committee hearing in the Senate, but the committee then killed the resolution by refusing to vote on it.

In August 2006, a group of patriotic citizens of Hawaii acted on their own initiative to hold a Statehood Day celebration at Iolani Palace, which was used as the Capitol of the Republic of Hawaii, Territory of Hawaii, and State of Hawaii until a new Capitol building was completed in 1968. The Palace was where the Territorial and State Legislatures met, where the Governor had his office, and where the transition to statehood was made official and huge celebrations took place. The 2006 Statehood Day celebration was disrupted and prevented by Hawaiian ethnic nationalist wannabe terrorists. They threatened members of a high school band causing parents to remove the children; they played loud music on a sound system; they used a megaphone to shout threats, and walked right up to would-be speakers and celebrants to stand nose-to-nose yelling in their faces. A few days later the Governor and the incoming head of the group that controls Iolani Palace held a meeting to figure out how to stop the Parks Department from granting permits that would allow "inappropriate" events there. Clearly the powers-that-be have sided with the protesters rather than with the celebration of Statehood Day, because of a feeling that Iolani Palace is sacred to the memory of the Kingdom of Hawaii. It is politically incorrect to allow the United States flag to be used there or to celebrate the transition to statehood which took place there in 1959.[62]

Passage of the ethnic nationalist resolution in 2001 questioning the legitimacy of Hawaii statehood, failure of the Statehood Day celebration resolution in the following two years, ethnic terrorists being allowed to destroy a statehood day celebration, and subsequent actions of government officials condoning their hooliganism on grounds of political correctness; all seem to indicate that the nuts have taken over the insane asylum. These are things to remember as we imagine the Governor and Legislature "negotiating" with a Native Hawaiian Governing Entity under auspices of either the Akaka bill or Akaka Plan B.

Using the expression "the nuts have taken over the insane asylum" might cause readers to wonder whether all the fuss is merely about a few delusional individuals whose extreme zealousness grabs attention. It must be noted that the Hawaiian ethnic nationalists have leaders who are highly educated and hold positions of responsibility in the community. Several of them are medical doctors either in practice serving patients or working as researchers. Many are attorneys licensed to practice law, including some younger ones who graduated from law school and passed the rigorous bar exam quite recently. Many hold Ph.D.s (usually from the University of Hawaii), or are in the late stages of completing that degree, usually in Political Science, Anthropology, Ethnic Studies, etc.

It must also be noted that these ethnic nationalist zealots do not merely shout slogans, hold signs, and participate in red-shirt marches. Some of those with professional degrees and plenty of money travel around the world actively lobbying other nations, and the United Nations.

One of them organized a highly publicized "hearing" at the "World Court" in the Hague which produced a document signed by three internationally respected barristers which, he says, affirms that the sovereignty of an independent nation of Hawaii continues until today and that Hawaii is under belligerent U.S. military occupation (see Chapter 9). He also has submitted documents to the U.N. Security Council calling for U.S. withdrawal from Hawaii.

Several of the zealots who are professionals holding advanced degrees have traveled to various meetings of the Pacific island nations where they were able to meet informally with diplomats to seek reinscription of Hawaii on the United Nations list of non-self-governing territories in need of decolonization. It was through this sort of activity that the French territory of New Caledonia actually did get reinscribed on that list due to repeated requests from the Kanak and Socialist National Liberation Front and despite strong objections from France. Reinscription on the list forced an agreement from France to "liberate" New Caledonia gradually over a period of many years.

Attorney Mililani Trask, who served as elected trustee of the Office of Hawaiian Affairs, also served a partially overlapping three year term as U.S. representative to the United Nations Permanent Forum on Indigenous Issues established by UNESCO in 2000. In that quasi-official capacity Trask led groups of Hawaiian ethnic nationalists to meetings in New York, Geneva, and elsewhere. There are also high-status Hawaii residents with no native ancestry who have actively participated in Hawaiian nationalist events – for example Niklaus Schweizer, Professor of German at the University of Hawaii, who has diplomatic status as honorary consul in Honolulu for Switzerland.

Ethnic nationalists are gradually trying to contact representatives of nations which formerly had treaty relations with the Kingdom of Hawaii to solicit their help in gaining diplomatic recognition and perhaps financial help. Some of those Kingdom treaty partners are today unfriendly toward the U.S., raising the possibility of deals to commit espionage or even sabotage against U.S. military bases in Hawaii so strongly hated by the activists. (See Chapter 7)

Tax evasion on grounds that Hawaii is not really part of the United States[63]

Many people try to avoid or evade paying income taxes.

Avoiding taxes is perfectly legal when accomplished by taking legitimate deductions; or by scheduling income or charitable contributions in such a way as to minimize taxes; or by investing in tax-exempt municipal bonds or drilling for oil and gas.

But evading taxes is illegal. One way some people justify tax evasion is by saying that they are part of a sovereign nation or political entity. It is correct that enrolled members of federally recognized Indian tribes, and corporations they own, can legally avoid many federal or state taxes on income earned on tribal reservations. Non-Indians also sometimes organize themselves into fortified private communities behind barbed wire, where they claim to be sovereign. Some people also claim to have individual sovereignty after "dissolving" all their "contracts" with governments (renouncing citizenship, canceling social security numbers, etc.).

Hawaiian sovereignty activists, both those favoring Indian tribe status and those favoring total independence, agree unanimously that the overthrow of the monarchy in 1893 was illegal. They agree that the overthrow was the result of an armed U.S. invasion (162 U.S. troops came ashore from a boat in Honolulu harbor to help preserve lives and property during the revolution staged by about 1500 armed local militiamen). The U.S. in 1993 passed a centennial commemorative apology resolution for the U.S. actions of 1893, which sovereignty activists regard as a confession to a crime.

The logical conclusion is that Hawaii is not legitimately a part of the United States. Therefore citizens (subjects) of (the still-living Kingdom of) Hawaii should not owe any income taxes to the United States. In addition, if the State of Hawaii is perceived as an illegal U.S. puppet regime, then state income taxes also would not be owed. Even people who acknowledge that they are U.S. citizens and are not descendants of Hawaiian Kingdom subjects would be entitled to take large deductions from their U.S. income taxes on the theory that income earned in Hawaii comes under the foreign-earned tax credit because it is income earned outside the United States.

Kenneth R. Conklin, Ph.D.

Some people who evade income tax do so as a result of sincere belief in such theories. Many others who evade taxes merely for personal gain will cynically refer to such theories to rationalize or justify their selfishness. Regardless of motivation, tax evasion is illegal. It forces honest taxpayers to pay higher taxes to provide government services (including services provided to the tax evaders!), it undermines public morale, and it is a direct challenge to the legitimacy of the governments whose taxes are evaded.

Ethnic nationalist zealot Hayden Burgess, alias Poka Laenui, has repeatedly stated on his weekly radio program (running for many years) that he has not paid federal or state income taxes for many years. By proclaiming that loudly and repeatedly on the radio, he taunts the IRS and, in effect, encourages thousands of others to evade taxes on the same theory. A TV station reported on November 5, 2003 that 30 Honolulu bus drivers were under investigation for tax evasion on the theory of Hawaiian sovereignty; and Burgess gleefully reported that news on his radio program.

A Honolulu tax preparation business, RB Tax Service, had owners and employees who filed fraudulent tax returns for themselves and on behalf of thousands of clients, claiming the foreign-earned income tax exemption on the grounds that Hawaii is not part of the United States – this story was followed by the Honolulu Star-Bulletin as prosecutions unfolded over several years. Along the way a former Bishop Estate trustee (Lokelani Lindsey) became entangled with Richard Basuel of RB Tax Services. A document filed with the U.S. District Court in Honolulu became public, in which Lindsey herself asserted Hawaiian independence arguments.

A federal tax fugitive was given sanctuary in the (leased) compound of the Nation of Hawaii in Waimanalo. Dennis "Bumpy" Kanahele, head of state, barred federal officials from entering the compound to arrest the fugitive. Kanahele was charged with obstructing justice and harboring a fugitive, and served four months in jail and four months under house arrest. He was later pardoned by a sympathetic outgoing Governor, perhaps to help Kanahele engage in various activities (such as forming an ethnic Hawaiian bank) that would be prohibited to a convicted felon.

On September 17, 2004 John Philip Souza (no relation to the famous composer), alias "Pilipo," was found guilty in a jury trial on four counts of theft and false statements in his State of Hawaii income tax filings for 1999 and 2000. Mr. Souza claims that the Kingdom of Hawaii was illegally overthrown in 1893, and therefore the State of Hawaii is not legitimate and lacks jurisdiction to compel him to pay taxes. He further claims that he is a subject (citizen) of the still-living Kingdom of Hawaii.[64]

Souza's assertion of these claims is especially interesting because he has no Hawaiian native ancestry. He points out that under Kingdom law (which be says still remains in effect), all persons born in Hawaii (including himself) are native-born subjects of the Kingdom. Although we have seen earlier in this chapter that Hawaiian ethnic nationalists now assert arguments to vitiate the claim that today's non-ethnic-Hawaiians born in Hawaii are subjects of the allegedly still-living nation, nevertheless those same activists were very supportive of "Pilipo"'s rationale for not paying taxes, and he was welcomed as a brother (albeit an adopted one). In effect the ethnic nationalists are treating Souza as a resident alien whose actions are tantamount to swearing an oath of loyalty to the nation of Hawaii and therefore entitle him to be treated as a non-native subject of the still-living Kingdom.

Mr. Souza was imprisoned for about 80 days while awaiting trial because of his refusal to cooperate with court procedure, describing himself as a "political prisoner" while ethnic nationalists raised money for his legal defense and to support his family. A public campaign encouraged ethnic nationalist zealots to send letters to the judge as part of the customary pre-sentencing report. The author of this book also sent a letter asking for maximum possible fine and jail time to set a public example for deterrence and because attempts to undermine the sovereignty of the government need to be taken seriously. On December 28, 2004, Pilipo was sentenced by Judge Michael Wilson to one year in prison (minus time served), plus five years probation, plus several thousands of dollars in fines and the forfeiture of about $10,000 in bail.

On December 1, 2004 a feature article about this case, "The Kingdom Has Come", was published in "MidWeek" newspaper pages 10 and 61. The timing of the article might have been an attempt to influence sentencing. MidWeek is mailed free of charge to every household on O'ahu every week on Monday, Tuesday, or Wednesday; and includes feature articles, commentary, and advertising circulars for all the major supermarkets. Unfortunately most articles, including this one, are not available on the newspaper's small website. The December 1 article was about 46 column-inches long, not including a 7x5 inch photograph of six people in front of a decorated 'Iolani Palace. The group "Ke Aupuni O Hawaii Nei" claims to be the revived Kingdom of Hawaii, and issues its own passports (small photo). The large photo shows six people, but the caption names seven, left to right! The caption on the large photo, with Iolani Palace in the background, identifies Leon Siu as foreign minister; Kealoha Aiu, minister of interior; Lydia Amona, kupuna council; William Koomelani Amona, kupuna council [and attorney for Pilipo]; Kimo Turner, minister of finance; Aran Ardaiz, attorney general; and Pilipo Souza, kupuna council. The article was very respectful toward the group, more or less portraying them as patriots fighting for the rights of the Kingdom of Hawaii by not paying income taxes, not having State of Hawaii license plates and drivers' licenses, etc.

The Akaka bill as a pathway to secession

A velvet revolution is underway in Hawaii. Activists wanting to rip the 50th star off the flag have been pushing nonviolently for Hawaiian independence for many years. The apology resolution of 1993 gave great impetus to both the secessionist movement and to demands for race-based group rights, communal land tenure, and megabucks in reparations – despite assurances from Senator Inouye on the floor of the Senate that the apology bill would not be used in that way.

The Akaka bill now under consideration would be a major boost to the secessionist movement – indeed, supporters of the Akaka bill, including Senator Akaka himself, go as far as they can go to support secession without actually committing treason.[65] The Hawaii Advisory Committee to the U.S. Commission on Civil Rights, supported by left-leaning national commissioners at that time, relied heavily on the apology resolution to write a major report based on hearings they held in Honolulu in 2000. The HAC reported to USCCR that the civil rights of ethnic Hawaiians are violated by the Supreme Court decision in Rice v. Cayetano, and that the Akaka bill should be supported as a way to protect those rights during a transitional period in which ethnic Hawaiians have a perfect right to force the secession of Hawaii from the United States. Excerpts are provided at the end of this section.

The desire to be an independent nation is logically and emotionally contrary to the concept of having a tribal government that would be subjected to the plenary power of the U.S. Congress and the Department of Interior. The Akaka bill would make ethnic Hawaiians wards of the federal government, not citizens of an independent nation. It appears this conflict between these two positions is irreconcilable. Activists for independence have bitterly opposed the Akaka bill. All ethnic Hawaiians have great nostalgia for their history from before the coming of Caucasians and Asians, and for their history as the internationally recognized Kingdom of Hawaii. This nostalgia is being intensified by highly-funded TV programs and cultural events intended to build racial pride; and resentment toward whites who allegedly stole their land, suppressed their culture and language, and ultimately stole their nation.

Most activists for sovereignty (including Akaka bill supporters) have their hearts set on eventual independence. So there is some guilt being laid onto Akaka bill supporters that they might be "selling Manhattan for $24 worth of beads." The loud voice of independence activists opposing the Akaka bill has been heard throughout Hawaii and all the way to Washington. It's hard for Akaka bill supporters to convince Washington politicians to vote for the bill when large numbers of ethnic Hawaiians loudly oppose it (they are, after all, allegedly the "beneficiaries" of the bill).

However, independence is seen by most sovereigntists as an impossible dream, or at least a long way off; and in the meantime why not accept U.S. government handouts? Huge, powerful institutions want the federal dollars to keep flowing to them, but those noisy independence activists pose a threat to passing the Akaka bill. That's why Akaka supporters are now reaching out to acknowledge and even celebrate the desire for independence, while some independence activists are now saying it's OK to pass the Akaka bill as a temporary guarantee of federal money and political power even while continuing to seek independence. Both independence activists and Akaka bill supporters say the U.S. owes huge reparations to ethnic Hawaiians as damages for the U.S. role in the overthrow and for the annexation of Hawaii despite protests at the time – so why not get a down-payment on some of those reparations during the transitional period before full independence?

The Akaka bill should not be seen as a way to strengthen the ties of Hawaii to the United States, to make ethnic Hawaiians more patriotic toward America, to dampen demands for independence, or to promote racial reconciliation. On the contrary, the Akaka bill facilitates and enables the Hawaiian independence movement by giving money and political power to race-based institutions harboring people who see themselves as primarily Hawaiians and only secondarily (or not at all) as Americans.

Here are some shocking highlights from the June 2001 report of the Hawaii Advisory Committee to the U.S. Conmnission on Civil Rights, clearly showing that the Akaka bill is supported as a pathway to secession.[66]

"Conclusions and Recommendations"

"1. The federal government should accelerate efforts to formalize the political relationship between Native Hawaiians and the United States. This recommendation can be accomplished through the formal and direct recognition by Congress of the United States' responsibilities toward Native Hawaiians, by virtue of the unique political history between the United States and the former Kingdom of Hawaii....[T]he Advisory Committee requests that the U.S. Commission on Civil Rights urge Congress to pass legislation formally recognizing the political status of Native Hawaiians."

"4. International solutions should be explored as alternatives to the recognition of a Native Hawaiian governing entity.

"The Hawaii Advisory Committee recognizes that the sentiment for an international resolution to restore a sovereign Hawaiian entity is beyond the immediate scope and power of the U.S. Commission on Civil Rights. Nevertheless, that limitation does not preclude the United States from exploring such alternatives as a part of the reconciliation process that the United States committed to pursue in the 1993 Apology Resolution. ... Accordingly, the United States should give due consideration to re-inscribing Hawai'i on the United Nations' list of non-self-governing territories, among other possibilities. ...

"The Hawaii Advisory Committee is fully cognizant of the concern expressed by some that international resolution would necessarily involve secession, a drastic endeavor over which this nation purportedly fought a civil war. However, this view ignores the troubled and racist roots of our nation's history. The Civil War was at its core a conflict over the issue of slavery. Moreover, the Civil War Amendments and Civil Rights Acts, upon which the plaintiff in Rice based his claims, were supposed to effect a reconstruction of American society through equality for African Americans.

"The principle of self-determination necessarily contemplates the potential choice of forms of governance that may not be authorized by existing domestic law.[420] Whether such a structure is politically or legally possible under the law is secondary, however, to the expression of one's desire for self-determination. The important proposition is that those who would choose to swear their allegiance to a restored sovereign Hawaiian entity be given that choice after a full and free debate with those who might prefer some form of association with the United States (including, perhaps, the status quo)....

"Those supervising the reconciliation process should provide for an open, free, and democratic plebiscite on all potential options by which Native Hawaiians might express their inherent right to self-determination. The process should allow for international oversight by nonaligned observers of international repute. After a period for organization of that government, the federal government should engage in negotiations with the sovereign Hawaiian entity.

"The Hawaii Advisory Committee believes that these deliberations should take into consideration and protect, or otherwise accommodate, the rights of non-Native Hawaiians. Thereafter, the federal government should provide financial assistance for the educational effort that may be necessary to reconcile conflicts raised by the choices made by Native Hawaiians. If necessary, the United States should engage in continuing negotiations to seek resolution of any outstanding issues with the sovereign Hawaiian entity."

Chapter 5

Historical Grievances (and falsehoods)

Two kinds of grievances, and how they are exploited for wealth and power

The Hawaiian grievance industry is flourishing today as never before. Ethnic Hawaiian institutions have become wealthy by getting large grants from the federal and state governments and from private philanthropies. The money is given because the institutions tell stories about bad things that happened historically, and provide evidence that their clients need help today. It's unclear whether current troubles are actually caused by events from 1778, 1820, or 1893; and it's unclear whether a causal connection would make any difference.

Large institutions with plenty of money hire lots of employees who then become emotionally loyal to coworkers and to the institutions. Employees are also financially dependent on their jobs. Large institutions with plenty of money hire businesses to do projects for them, and those businesses become dependent on that relationship. The institutions and their business partners need cooperation from politicians on topics like taxes, zoning, licensing, government contracts, labor laws, health and property insurance, etc. Cooperative politicians receive campaign contributions and votes from the institutions and their business partners, and from thousands of employees.

The Hawaiian grievance industry also generates political power for its institutions based on public perception of the "plight" of ethnic Hawaiians. "Aw, they're hurting so bad. What can we do for them?" There are two main types of grievances calling forth public sympathy: historical victimhood and current demographic victimhood. Some bad things happened long ago by accident or may have been inevitable; but the consequences reverberate until today. Some bad things were done deliberately.

Harm inflicted intentionally is a basis for anger and for demanding reparations. The fact that some damage was accidental or inevitable might mitigate blame or feelings of guilt; but in any case there's compassion for poor downtrodden people in need of help.

We've all heard about scammers who fraudulently file lawsuits or insurance claims for accidents or illnesses that never happened, or who file claims that grossly exaggerate the damages. The Hawaiian grievance industry is fueled by many false or overblown claims. There is strong competition for the privilege of being history's greatest victim because (wordplay on a familiar saying): to the victim go the spoils (of political patronage for government handouts). Civil rights activists are called "racist" when they resist being assaulted with political propaganda touting grossly overblown racial grievances. Refusal to "feel the pain" of those who are allegedly aggrieved is taken as evidence of continuing oppression.

Claims of current suffering might evoke compassion and generate political support for government and philanthropic handouts, regardless of whatever might have caused the suffering. Current victimhood claims will be dealt with in Chapter 6. But even if hard-hearted or evil people refuse to show compassion voluntarily, historical claims can be asserted as a basis for fixing blame and demanding reparations. The criminal must pay restitution whether he likes it or not. If necessary his assets will be seized and wages garnished.

Let's begin with historical claims that are false or twisted. There are a large number of them, and each one could be the topic for an entire chapter. The purpose here is neither to assemble a complete collection nor to provide detailed refutations. The purpose is to show the absurd falsehood of some of the claims, the dramatic exaggeration of others, and the zealotry of their assertion as instruments for promoting racial separatism and ethnic nationalism.

Genocide

The claim is that the number of native Hawaiians dropped by 95% during the first century following the arrival of Caucasians in 1778. Hawaiian zealots use the word "genocide." They want to evoke the sympathy we all feel for what happened to European Jews, and more recently to ethnic groups in Bosnia, Rwanda and Darfur.

Some zealots imply the decimation of native Hawaiians was done with deliberate malice. Most describe it as willful negligence, because

Captain Cook knew the effect European diseases had on native populations elsewhere. Cook issued orders that his men should not have relations with the eager native women who swam out to the boat; but he failed to enforce those orders.

Captain Cook's two ships arrived at Kauai in January 1778. His men had extensive contact with natives for several weeks at both Kauai and Niihau. Cook's ships then sailed north for several months. In November of 1778 the ships returned, first to Maui and then to Hawaii Island, where the famous events at Kealakekua Bay took place in January and February of 1779. Journals kept by Cook and his men report that on this second arrival in the islands they observed natives showing symptoms of venereal diseases. Captain Cook again tried to restrain his men; but again he was ineffective in doing so.

Are Americans responsible for the introduction of the diseases which ravaged the native population? No, Captain Cook and his men were British (and the United States was not yet a nation, being engaged in the Revolutionary war against Britain). Could the native Hawaiians forever escape the ravages of Western diseases? Clearly not; sooner or later Hawaii would be "discovered" and nature would take its course.

Did the population really drop by 95%? Nobody knows. Estimates of pre-contact population range from 200,000 to as high as 1,000,000 (all "pure Hawaiian", of course). The first U.S. Census of Hawaii in 1900 counted 29,799 full-blooded Hawaiians and 9,857 part-Hawaiians. David Stannard, a University of Hawaii Professor of "American Studies," wrote a book whose primary purpose was to inflate the pre-contact population estimate as high as possible in order to maximize the victimhood damages. The title of Stannard's book shows his intent: "Before the Horror."[67] Stannard, a Caucasian, also happens to be the long-time live-in boyfriend of one of the most zealous far-left ethnic Hawaiian activists, Professor Haunani-Kay Trask. For years they co-hosted a radical Hawaiian sovereignty TV program, until Stannard withdrew because it was too politically incorrect to have a Caucasian co-hosting the program.

How much of the native population decline was attributable to imported Caucasian (or later Asian) diseases? It's hard to know. Untold thousands (including women and children) were killed by Kamehameha and other warrior chiefs using new weapons of mass destruction (metal knives, guns, cannons, large ships). Greedy chiefs ordered thousands of commoners to leave their taro patches to gather sandalwood for the chiefs to use in trade for warehouses full of European luxury goods. Many people starved due to lack of food production until the sandalwood forests were exhausted and farmers were allowed to return to their taro patches. Human sacrifice for religious and cultural purposes took a toll, although with declining frequency, until perhaps as late as 1819.

A tiny book published in 2003 for the Christmas stocking-stuffer market is one of the biggest tear-jerkers in the Hawaiian grievance pity party. "Then There Were None" by Martha H. Noyes (based on Elizabeth Kapu'uwailani Lindsey Buyers' TV docudrama)[68] is an exploration of collective white guilt, focusing on the steady decline of the number of "pure Hawaiians." A "documentary film" on which the book was based was on tour throughout the U.S. and Canada for at least 7 years before the book was published. The film was televised nationwide on PBS. There was also a performance of the Honolulu Symphony Orchestra featuring narration from the book/film. Gregory Shepherd, the Advertiser's classical music critic, wrote a scathing review calling it "a tottering soapbox" and "a tendentious harangue about the evil haoles [Caucasians] (disingenuously called "the newcomers" in the film)."[69]

"Then There Were None" traces the history of Hawaii since 1778 with short descriptions of the terrible loss of population caused by disease and poverty, and the withering of native culture caused by the natives' warm embrace of Euro-American culture. The book is punctuated by several population milemarker pages where the entire page is a single sentence such as Page 35: "By 1836 there were only 108,000 pure Hawaiians left alive."

Of course it's true that the number of "pure Hawaiians" has steadily declined. That's because Hawaiian natives mated with Caucasians, and later Asians, as rapidly as possible. When Captain Cook first arrived native women swam out to the boats in large numbers, eager to trade sex for small bits of metal, and eager to acquire the imagined spiritual power of the sailors by sharing their bodies and hopefully making babies with them. Even late in the Kingdom period high chiefesses married Caucasian men for wealth and social prestige – including Princess Bernice Pauahi Bishop, Miriam Likelike Cleghorn (mother of the half-Hawaiian Princess Kaiulani), and Lydia Dominis (Queen Liliuokalani). The book "Then There Were None" apparently deplores interracial marriage, and denigrates children of mixed marriages by labeling them as less than "pure Hawaiian." Perhaps the author would recommend banning interracial marriage? Apparently rejecting 400,000 mixed ethnic Hawaiians as less than pure (including herself), she dedicates the book "To the five thousand piha kanaka maoli [pure-blood Hawaiians] who remain"

Interestingly, Census 2000 (Summary File 1) counted 80,137 pure Hawaiians!! How did that number come about? The year 2000 was the first time the U.S. Census Bureau allowed people to check more than one box for "race." Tycoons of the Hawaiian grievance industry waged a campaign encouraging ethnic Hawaiians to check only the one box for "Native Hawaiian" regardless how many other ancestries they might have and even though their percentage of native blood might be very low. According to "Then There Were None" perhaps 5,000 actually were "pure Hawaiian." But 75,000 chose to disrespect and reject the remainder of their genealogies – in most cases the largest portion of their ancestries. They did that because of zealotry for Hawaiian racial pride and because their leaders had told them there might be larger government handouts if there were a larger number of "pure Hawaiians."

Here's an optimistic way to look at ethnic Hawaiian population statistics. Throughout the Kingdom period the number of ethnic Hawaiians (the total of both "pure" and mixed) always declined. But then, after annexation, things improved. During the first century of American sovereignty in Hawaii, the number of ethnic Hawaiians multiplied tenfold – from fewer than 40,000 in Census 1900 to more than 400,000 in Census 2000. Ethnic Hawaiians are not a dying race. On the contrary, they are flourishing. According to a study released by the Kamehameha Schools' research/propaganda division (PASE) in September 2005, the population of "Native Hawaiians" is projected to more than double by year 2050, when there will be nearly a million.[70]

Professor Lilikala Kameeleihiwa actually had the nerve to respond to the PASE report by saying she wants "Native Hawaiians" to double their numbers in only 20 years rather than 50 years, so they will become a majority racial group as soon as possible! She wants to maximize the political bang of the ethnic Hawaiian population bomb![71] Recently released Census data show that ethnic Hawaiian girls are obeying her wishes, producing illegitimate babies at triple the rate of other ethnic groups[72] (while also presumably collecting welfare benefits the "oppressors" pay for). This deliberate explosion of an ethnic Hawaiian population bomb resembles the Lebensborn plan devised by Heinrich Himmler in 1936, whereby (according to Wikipedia) German men, especially SS soldiers, were encouraged to produce children with "racially pure" Aryan-looking women. The unmarried mothers could live in special homes and receive financial support, while the children would be adopted.

U.S. "armed invasion" in 1893, and U.S. apology resolution in 1993

The claim is that the U.S. staged an armed invasion of Hawaii in 1893, and the U.S. overthrew the monarchy. U.S. Senators Dorgan and Inouye repeated that claim on the floor of the Senate in June 2006 when debating the Akaka bill (see below). Here are additional, related claims: The Republic of Hawaii created after the monarchy was overthrown was merely a U.S. puppet regime. Annexation was illegal, both because the Republic had no legitimacy or standing to offer a treaty, and because the U.S. failed to ratify the treaty properly. The U.S. apology resolution of 1993 is a confession of a crime under international law – a freely given "statement against interest" constitutes a confession and is admissible as evidence in court.

These historical claims are significant for several reasons. They are used as a basis for claiming that the continuity of the Hawaiian nation under international law has never been interrupted. Therefore Hawaii is under a prolonged illegal belligerent military occupation by the U.S. The U.S. should withdraw and restore sovereignty to the still-living independent Hawaiian nation. The claim of illegal overthrow is used to justify demands for enormous reparations – both compensatory and punitive damages. Part of the claim is that the overthrow of the monarchy dealt a crippling blow to the self-esteem of ethnic Hawaiians in 1893 and continuing to today. Abandonment of culture and debilitating despair occurring in 1893 have reverberated down through the decades, allegedly causing today's ethnic Hawaiians to have poor health, poor education, low income, high rates of drug abuse and incarceration, and family dysfunction. "Pain and suffering" (both physical and emotional) of the victims of a crime is an important factor in setting the amount of restitution owed; thus, the victims have a vested interest in magnifying how much they suffer. Historical falsehoods are also used to inflame "righteous anger" and racial hostility in an effort to increase the level of zealotry, possibly leading to violence.

These historical claims are not asserted in a haphazard or frivolous manner – they are intended to be taken very seriously. These claims are put forward not only in Hawaii but also in Washington D.C. and in foreign lands. The claim that the Hawaiian Kingdom has an unbroken continuity of existence under international law, right up to now, was asserted at a hearing of an international arbitral tribunal at the Hague (see Chapter 9).

Portions of a "legal brief" filed at that hearing were assembled into what appears to be a scholarly paper by the author of the brief, Dr. Matthew Craven, Reader in International Law, University of London.[73] Kyle Kajihiro, the program director of the American Friends Service Committee in Honolulu, is very active in promoting Hawaiian independence and demilitarization. Kajihiro travels to the U.S. mainland, Puerto Rico, Asia and various Pacific islands coordinating anti-military protests and also pushing the message of Hawaiian independence. For example, on November 6, 2006 he attended an international meeting and presented a very well written four page summary about the illegal overthrow of Hawaii and the ongoing belligerent military occupation: "Hawai'i Report for the Asia-Pacific Consultation of Movements Against U.S. Military Bases"[74] On January 30, 2007 a Ph.D. candidate in Political Science presented an academic paper at a colloquium at the University of Hawaii allegedly on the topic whether ethnic Hawaiians should assert claims to being "indigenous" but in reality the paper was focused mainly on events surrounding annexation in 1898.[75] Articles and presentations like these are frequent events, and are often funded by wealthy, powerful institutions.

On June 7, 2006 the U.S. Senate was debating a cloture motion on the Akaka bill. Complete transcripts of four and a half hours of floor debate are available, including the two speeches excerpted below.[76]

Senator Dorgan (D, ND) made the following statements (Congressional Record page S5557): *"I will give a little bit of the history as vice chairman of the Committee on Indian Affairs. ... January 16, 1893 – that is a long, long time ago – the United States Minister John Stevens, who served, then, as Ambassador to the court of Queen Liliuokalani, directed a marine company onboard the USS Boston to arrest and detain the queen. This is the queen that served the indigenous people in Hawaii. She was arrested. She was placed under arrest for 9 months at the palace."*

Senator Inouye (D, HI) made the following statements (Congressional Record, page S5570): *"I think it is about time that we reach out and correct the wrong that was committed in 1893. Yes, at that time the representative of the people of the United States directed a marine company on an American ship to land and take over the government. They imprisoned our queen. No crime had been committed. When the new government took over and turned itself over to the government of the United States and said, Please take us in, the President of the United States was President Cleveland at that time. He sent his envoy to Hawaii to look over the case. When he learned that the takeover had been illegal, he said this was an un-American act and we will not take over. The queen is free."*

Hawaiian Apartheid

These Senators are probably honorable gentlemen. They wouldn't knowingly tell lies on the Senate floor (would they?). The same falsehoods are being taught to thousands of children in Hawaii's schools, and to college students. They are "urban legends" repeated so often that the general public comes to believe them. These falsehoods are so widely accepted as fact that two Senators felt comfortable asserting them on the floor of the U.S. Senate as justification for a controversial bill.

It's important to explain what really happened in 1893, in order to refute the falsehoods asserted by Senators Dorgan and Inouye.

The USS Boston had just returned to Honolulu from a training cruise to a different island. When the ship left on the cruise things had seemed politically stable; but when the ship arrived back in port the situation was frightening. The Queen had used bribery and intimidation to ram through some very controversial bills (distillery, lottery, and opium licensing bills) in the closing days of the legislature and then dismissed it. Immediately thereafter she announced that she would unilaterally proclaim a new Constitution giving herself near-dictatorial powers. According to some sources her new Constitution would also take away voting rights from everyone except ethnic Hawaiians (After the revolution she destroyed all copies of her proposed Constitution, so we'll never know).[77]

The Queen's cabinet (Caucasian men) refused to endorse her new Constitution. Some of them ran out of the Palace in fear for their lives when she threatened them. Ethnic Hawaiians assembled on the Palace grounds expecting to hear a new Constitution being proclaimed; and instead the Queen told them to go home because some obstacles had arisen. There were rumors that there would soon be riots and arson – several times in recent years there had been riots due to political instability, which had necessitated the landing of British and American sailors to restore order on those occasions. A group of 1500 local men, including several hundred who belonged to an armed militia, was known to be planning a revolution. Mass meetings had already been going on for several days after the Queen tried to proclaim her new Constitution, so there was no secret that a revolution was underway.

The American diplomat, Minister Stevens, had gone on the USS Boston's training cruise, taking his family along. When the ship headed back to Honolulu Stevens' daughter stayed behind on another island to do some sightseeing. She was killed in an accident there, which Minister Stevens learned about just before the revolution, possibly affecting his judgment and concentration. Now American residents pleaded with him to send sailors ashore as peacekeepers to protect American lives and property and to prevent rioting and arson. There were also citizens of other nations who were residents and business owners in Honolulu. Some of them begged Minister Stevens for help, pointing out that the USS Boston was the only foreign ship in port with men who had rifles and military training. The revolutionaries were mostly Caucasian, so Europeans and Americans living in Honolulu were fearful that violence might be directed against Caucasians in general.

At Minister Stevens' request the ship's captain sent ashore 162 armed sailors on January 16, 1893, two days after the mass meetings and one day before the local militia took over buildings and issued their proclamation. The sailors were under orders to remain strictly neutral in the political conflict. Some royalists imagined the sailors were landed to support the monarchy; some revolutionists imagined the sailors had come ashore to assist them. The sailors marched past the Palace and the Government Building (Aliiolani Hale) on the way toward a suburban area where they hoped to spend the night. As they passed the Palace they respectfully dipped their flags in salute to the Queen. When it turned out they had no place to spend the night, they made arrangements to sleep in a building (Arion Hall) located down a side street a block away from the Palace, with no direct view of the Palace or the Government Building. They went there that evening and remained in the building, or inside that building's fence.

The following day, January 17, the local militia finally completed its revolution by taking over the Government Building, where many armaments had been stored by the Queen's forces. The militia issued a proclamation abrogating the monarchy and announcing a Provisional Government. Shortly thereafter the militia took over other buildings and disarmed the Royal Guard. The militia had zero assistance or supplies from the U.S. peacekeepers. The local militia arrested the Queen and escorted her to her private residence a block from the Palace. The Provisional Government then assigned members of the ex-queen's own (former) Royal Guard to protect her from harm, and paid the Guards' salaries. Nobody touched the Queen or her property at her private home. There was some vandalism at Iolani Palace, and eventually the new government sold its furnishings. But vandalism is normal when revolutions overthrow a monarchy. Also, the Palace and its contents were the property of the nation, not the personal property of the head of state; so whatever government was in power had the right to dispose of Palace contents. One reason for the revolution was to put an end to the lavish lifestyle of a corrupt monarchy. The Queen was treated with extreme politeness and gentleness, especially when compared against what happened to the French and Russian royals when those countries had revolutions.

Throughout the revolution the U.S. peacekeepers remained strictly neutral. They never took over any buildings. They never surrounded the Palace or the Government Building. They never arrested the Queen. They never patrolled the streets. The armed revolutionary local militia easily maintained order, partly because they were strong and well trained, and partly because the Queen's forces were weak and had surrendered without a fight. She wrote a letter saying she was surrendering temporarily to the superior forces of the U.S. until such time as the U.S. government would hear her case and restore her power. But she had that letter delivered to the revolutionary Provisional Government, not to the U.S. diplomat; indicating she knew the local Provisional Government was in charge and not the U.S. She probably intended her letter of surrender, being addressed only to the U.S. and claiming it was only a temporary surrender, as a ruse. Being a clever politician she probably hoped a friendly but distant nation would undo her loss to the local militia who had actually defeated her.

The U.S. Senate Committee on Foreign Affairs, whose chairman was Senator John T. Morgan (D, AL), spent January and February of 1894 investigating the U.S. role in the Hawaiian revolution. They took testimony under oath, in open session, with cross examination. The committee's official 808-page report, known as the Morgan Report, provides documentation for the facts above.[78]

Senators Dorgan and Inouye stated outrageous falsehoods in the Senate debate on June 7, 2006.

Senator Dorgan was entirely wrong when he said "United States Minister John Stevens ... directed a marine company onboard the USS Boston to arrest and detain the queen." If that claim were true it would be a basis for blaming the U.S. for overthrowing the Hawaiian monarchy and demanding reparations. But it was false. The local militia of Hawaiian residents did all the heavy lifting of the revolution.

Senator Dorgan then continued with another sentence that contains a bit of truth but placed in the wrong time frame and falsely blaming the U.S. and Minister Stevens for what happened. Senator Dorgan says: "She was arrested. She was placed under arrest for 9 months at the palace." The ex-queen was indeed arrested and held at the Palace – but not in 1893, not in connection with the overthrow of the monarchy, and certainly not by the U.S. peacekeepers. In January 1895 – two years after the revolution! – Robert Wilcox, a half-Hawaiian racial demagogue, attempted an armed counter-revolution which failed. Guns and bombs were found buried in the flower bed of the ex-queen's private home. She was convicted of conspiracy in that treason. She did not spend 9 months under arrest in the Palace, as Senator Dorgan said; she spent only January 16 to September 6, 1895 – seven and oneself months. She had been sentenced to 5 years at hard labor and a $10,000 fine; but served only a few months in a huge Palace room with full-time maidservant. Her "hard labor" consisted of composing songs and sewing a quilt with monarchist political slogans and symbols. Later her friend, Republic of Hawaii President Sanford B. Dole, gave her a full pardon and allowed her to travel to Washington D.C. where she showed her gratitude by lobbying the Senate against Dole's most cherished dream of annexation.

Senator Dorgan also made a very misleading statement which ironically contained the truth about why Liliuokalani was overthrown. Dorgan said "This is the queen that served the indigenous people in Hawaii." Yes indeed! But her job as Queen was to serve all the people in her multiracial nation. Saying that she was Queen only of "the indigenous people" (i.e., ethnic Hawaiians) is what must be said to justify passing a racially exclusionary "Native Hawaiian Government Reorganization" bill. But the fact that she saw herself as serving "the indigenous people" exclusively or primarily is what caused her to be overthrown by those whom she was dis-serving.

Senator Inouye told similar falsehoods and also wrongly consolidated the events of 1893 with the events of 1895. Inouye was totally wrong when he said "... the representative of the people of the United States directed a marine company on an American ship to land and take over the government." Inouye was totally wrong when he said "They imprisoned our queen."

If Inouye is referring to 1895 when Liliuokalani was imprisoned at the Palace, he was totally wrong when he said "No crime had been committed." – Liliuokalani had indeed committed the crime of conspiracy in a violent counter-revolution in which men were killed. She allowed guns and bombs to be hidden in the flower bed of her private home, for which she was placed on trial, convicted, and sentenced to prison.

Inouye was also totally wrong to say the ex-queen's imprisonment was at the hands of the United States. The U.S. did not imprison her in the Palace in the 1893 revolution – it was the local militia which arrested her and escorted her to her private home where her former Royal Guard was paid by the Provisional Government to protect her against possible assassination. By 1895, when the ex-queen was indeed imprisoned, the U.S. peacekeepers were long gone from Hawaii – Grover Cleveland's hatchet man (Blount) had removed the few remaining peacekeepers on April 1, 1893. Those who arrested and jailed her in 1895 were officers of the Republic of Hawaii.

Following his incorrect statements about the imprisonment of 1895, Inouye then returns to 1893 to the period of several months after the revolution, showing that Inouye thinks 1895 and 1893 were all intermingled and all to be blamed on the U.S. Talking about the Provisional Government's offer of a treaty of annexation immediately after the revolution, Inouye says *"When the new government took over and turned itself over to the government of the United States and said, Please take us in, the President of the United States was President Cleveland at that time. He sent his envoy to Hawaii to look over the case. When he learned that the takeover had been illegal, he said this was an un-American act and we will not take over. The queen is free."* But of course by the time President Cleveland issued his message to Congress it was December 18, 1893, 11 months after the revolution. Grover Cleveland never proclaimed "The queen is free" because the Queen had never been under his authority for him to set her free!

It is inexcusable for U.S. Senators to assert such falsehoods in a high-stakes debate, especially when they have many researchers and staff members who had been preparing these speeches for a long time. It's equally inexcusable for schools and colleges to be teaching such falsehoods in their textbooks and lesson plans when reputable scholars could easily be contacted for fact-checking.

In 1993 the U.S. Congress passed, and President Clinton signed, the apology resolution. This was a resolution of sentiment to commemorate the 100th anniversary of the overthrow of the Hawaiian monarchy. The resolution is filled with historical falsehoods and distortions similar to the ones uttered by Senators Dorgan and Inouye. It would require a book to describe and document the errors. The beginnings of such a discrediting of the apology resolution can be found in Chapter 10 of Thurston Twigg-Smith's book "Hawaiian Sovereignty: Do the Facts Matter?".[79] Another useful analysis is found in a monograph by constitutional law expert Bruce Fein, "Hawaii Divided Against Itself Cannot Stand" which was reprinted in three installments in the Congressional Record of June 14, 15, and 16, 2005.[80]

A very interesting repudiation of the apology resolution is found in an article in the Wall Street Journal of August 16, 2005. Slade Gorton and Hank Brown, two former Senators who had fought against the apology resolution in 1993, published "E Pluribus Unum? Not in Hawaii."[81] They reminded a nationwide audience about some of the historical falsehoods and alerted readers to the fact that the apology resolution is being abused to support the Akaka bill. In 1993 Gorton and Brown had warned their Senate colleagues that the apology resolution would be used to demand race-based government handouts and to support a secessionist movement. Senator Inouye had promised his colleagues, on the floor of the Senate, that the resolution would never be used in any such way. Now 12 years later Senators Gorton and Brown were saying "See, we told you so."

In his short story "The Man Upstairs" P.G. Wodehouse wrote: *"It is a good rule in life never to apologize. The right sort of people do not want apologies, and the wrong sort take a mean advantage of them."* The way the apology resolution is being used today makes it abundantly clear that Wodehouse was right. The resolution should be repealed.

Fake Presidential Proclamation alleged to be by Grover Cleveland

This section of this chapter describes an example of extreme zealousness. Sovereignty activists have manufactured a totally false story about a (fake) Presidential proclamation by Grover Cleveland. They then staged a publicity circus traveling to New Jersey in April 2006 to honor Cleveland at his birthplace and gravesite. They issued a call for a national day of prayer and repentance on the same date which Cleveland's fake proclamation had called for 112 years previously. They somehow persuaded Associated Press to publish a news story nationwide reporting Cleveland's proclamation as being real. Back in Honolulu, even after being given clear and convincing proof that the proclamation was fake and had actually been political sarcasm directed against President Cleveland in 1894, the sovereignty zealots nevertheless went forward calling for the national day of prayer and holding a rally at a historically important church.

This is the sort of twisted history and propaganda which Hawaii's people are constantly bombarded with; and which they have come to believe because it is repeated so often. It is very easy for sovereignty zealots to twist history or to invent total falsehoods; it is very difficult for their opponents to discover the truth; and it is even more difficult to inform the public and set the record straight.

First some background about Grover Cleveland. Then the fake proclamation will be discussed.

Hawaiian Apartheid

Hawaiian sovereignty zealots regard U.S. President Grover Cleveland as a hero. Cleveland was a personal friend of Liliuokalani. He did everything in his power in 1893 (short of sending troops) to block annexation, to destabilize the revolutionary Provisional Government, and to restore Liliuokalani to the throne. He failed to destabilize the Provisional Government, and he failed to restore the Queen. But he succeeded in blocking annexation until after his term as President ended. He has the eternal gratitude of the Hawaiian sovereignty zealots.

In his first week in office, in March 1893, Cleveland withdrew the treaty of annexation offered by the Hawaii Provisional Government that had been sent to the Senate by his predecessor President Benjamin Harrison. Also during his first week in office President Cleveland appointed James Blount to be "Minister Plenipotentiary with Paramount Powers" and sent him to Hawaii with secret instructions. Cleveland never notified the Senate about Blount's appointment and never sought Senate confirmation – Blount was a "hatchet man" sent secretly on an emergency mission.

Immediately upon arriving in Honolulu (and thus presumably carrying out his secret instructions) Blount ordered the few remaining U.S. sailors to leave town and return to their ship. He immediately ordered the removal of the U.S. flag flying next to the Hawaiian flag on the Government Building where the Provisional Government had hoisted it as a show of stability and desire for annexation. He set up headquarters at the royalist hotel and conducted interviews, almost all of which were with royalists. Rumors were flying around town that Blount would soon restore the Queen. There was speculation that he had ordered the sailors back to their ship, and the removal of the U.S. flag, in hopes there might be a counter-revolution. He refused to receive some important revolutionists who wanted to tell their side of the story; and he twisted or falsely reported what a few revolutionists told him.[82] He then wrote a one-sided report blaming the U.S. for overthrowing the Queen, and hand-carried it back to Washington; still keeping its contents secret from the Provisional Government.

In the Fall of 1893 President Cleveland sent a new representative to Honolulu, who began negotiating with Liliuokalani, without knowledge of the provisional Government, for conditions under which she could be restored to the throne. In December Cleveland's representative sent a letter to Hawaii President Sanford Dole demanding that Dole resign and restore the Queen.

Meanwhile in Washington President Cleveland sent Blount's report to Congress along with a strongly-worded message that the U.S. had committed a grave wrong in overthrowing the Hawaiian monarchy. Cleveland referred the matter to Congress to decide what should be done.

In response the Senate Committee on Foreign Affairs held two months of hearings taking sworn testimony under oath and with cross examination. The resulting Morgan Report repudiated Blount's report and concluded the U.S. had neither instigated nor supported the Hawaiian revolution. The Senate then passed two resolutions saying that neither the U.S. nor any other nation should interfere in the internal affairs of Hawaii. In effect the Senate rebuked President Cleveland for his efforts to overturn the Provisional Government and told Cleveland to leave Hawaii alone. This rebuke to Cleveland, a Democrat, is all the more significant because the Democrats were the majority party in the Senate; and John T. Morgan, chairman of the committee which wrote the report, was also a Democrat.

For the remainder of his term in office President Cleveland continued to block annexation; but he did comply with the Senate resolutions. Cleveland extended full diplomatic recognition to the newly formed Republic of Hawaii, and conducted negotiations with President Dole regarding further implementation of Kingdom treaties. Thus even the ex-queen's strongest ally and supporter finally acknowledged that the overthrow would not be undone and that the Republic of Hawaii was the legitimate successor government of the continuing independent nation of Hawaii.

Because of his strong support of the Queen, President Cleveland is treated as a hero by today's sovereignty activists. A grandson of Grover Cleveland visited Hawaii in 2006, made public appearances at sovereignty events, and was featured guest on a cable TV program. A small park located on a sidestreet near Aliiolani Hale (the Government Building of the Kingdom) has a plaque dedicating the park to Grover Cleveland and honoring him for his resistance to annexation.

The Hawaiian sovereignty zealots are not satisfied with the great service President Cleveland rendered to their cause. They feel a need to embellish the story by creating a totally fake piece of history. Here's a "Presidential Proclamation" posted on many websites, apparently beginning around 1999-2000 and continuing through today.

FOOLS' DAY A FAST DAY

To My People: Whereas, my good and great sister and fellow sovereign, her gracious majesty, Liliuokalani, queen of Hawaii, has been wickedly and unlawfully dethroned by the machinations of Americans and persons of American descent in those islands, being instigated thereto by the devil, one John L. Stevens; and whereas, my well-concieved plans for the restoration of her sacred majesty have not had the result they deserved but her majesty is still defrauded of her legal rights by her refractory and rebellious subjects, and her position is a just cause of sympathy and alarm; now, therefore, I, Grover Cleveland, President of the United States, do hereby ordain and appoint the last day of April next as a day of solemn fasting, humiliation and prayer. Let my people humble themselves and repent for their injustice to me and my great and good sister, and pray, without distinction of color, for her speedy return to the throne and the discomfiture of the miserable herd of missionaries and their sons, her enemies and traducers.

Long Live Liliuokalani, the de jure queen of Hawaii

Done at our mansion in Washington this 25th day of February, 1894.

Grover Cleveland

A true copy. Attest,
Walter Q. Gresham,
Secretary of State

  Anyone reading the proclamation should certainly be suspicious. Would a President of the United States actually use such language in an official government document? And why does the heading refer to "Fools' Day" when the date specified for fasting and repentance is April 30 and not April 1 (April Fools Day)?
  It turns out that the proclamation was actually a newspaper advertisement or editorial on page 6 of "The New York Sun" of February 27,

1894. It was intended as sarcasm against President Cleveland because of his strong support for a corrupt ex-queen who was his personal friend. It was published at the same time the Morgan Report was being published, which repudiated the work of Cleveland's hatchet-man Blount.

It turns out that the same page of the newspaper also has another fake "special message" from President Cleveland calling for the Senate to be abolished. This is clearly sarcasm against President Cleveland, reflecting the fact that the Morgan Report repudiated the Blount Report that had been specially commissioned by Cleveland.

A SPECIAL MESSAGE

To the Senate and House of Representatives,

The experience of my first term as President has been corroborated and fortified by my experience thus far in my second term, leading me to believe that the powers and duties now vested by the Constitution in the Senate would be more safely and usefully vested in the Executive. Especially is this the case in reference to the confirming power, which, as now employed by the Senate is a serious obstacle to the Executive and to good government. The Senate, composed of men elected from the several States and at various times, has no unit and principle of responsibility. It is not elected, as the President is, by the people and its possession of the power to thwart the will of the people, expressed through the President, is an unconsecrated anomaly in our institutions.

I know from my own experience that the Senate commits a grave injury and wrong on every occasion when it opposes the wishes of the President. I cannot admit that the Senate should have the right to revise and undo or even to consider what I in my wisdom have determined. Furthermore, the habit of the Senate to criticise and review the foreign or domestic policy of the President is, in my judgement, a monumental evil. A careful consideration of the whole matter has convinced me and I doubt not will convince you, that the abolition of the Senate is necessary to the independence of the Executive, and the equilibrium of the Government. Even the power of impeachment should belong to the Executive.

Hawaiian Apartheid

I therefore suggest to you that a joint resolution for an omnibus constitutional amendment, striking out all references to the Senate, and conferring upon the President all the powers now possessed by that body, should be passed by you and submitted to the several States for ratification. I cannot entertain a doubt that such amendment of the Constitution is eagerly desired by the people.

I append further with full memoranda of my wishes in this matter.

Grover Cleveland
Executive Mansion, Feb. 26, 1894

The same newspaper page also contains the following two items:

Liliuokalani's Double Game

Who was responsible for the overthrow of Liliuokalani? Was it Minister Stevens, representing a passing Administration of the United States? Was it the foreign population or the business interests of the islands?

Neither! It was the premeditated and deliberate purpose of the Queen herself.

As is now universally admitted, Liliuokalani is a characterless woman, caring alone for her own material pleasure, restless and fearful under responsibility, craving for the pomp and ceremony of position and the luxuries of wealth, but shirking the duties and restraints accompanying them.

Tempted by the offer of half a million of dollars a year from the lottery and opium syndicate, she placed herself in a position to accept, thinking she would either win this enormous sum or precipitate annexation to the United States, which would retire her on a pension from this Government, under which she could live in luxury with the honors of an ex-Queen wherever she might choose, and free from all care and danger, indulge to their full her demoralized tastes.

Heads or tails, she would win!

But the whirling coin unexpectedly landed upon the edge, remained upright, and she lost.

F. A. R.

Seven to Two for Annexation

The Senate Committee on Foreign Relations, which has been investigating the Hawaiian question, consists of nine members, five Democrats and four Republicans.

With what was already known concerning their views on the subject of the ultimate annexation of Hawaii, the various reports submitted to the Senate yesterday from this committee show how the nine members stand on the main question.

Senator Morgan, the Chairman, has declared himself squarely for annexation.

The four Republicans, Mr. Sherman, Mr. Frye, Mr. Dolph, and Mr. Davis, are all annexationists, differing only as to the method by which Hawaii should come into the Union; Senator Sherman, for example, suggesting that the islands ought to become a part of the State of California.

Of the four Democrats besides Senator Morgan, whose views were already known, Mr. Butler and Mr. Turpie file a supplemental report, in which they say that they are "heartily in favor of the acquisition of these islands by the United States in a proper manner."

The fact that the two remaining Democrats, Senator Gray of Delaware and Senator Daniel of Virginia, did not join with Senator Turpie and Senator Butler in this supplemental report, indicates that they are opposed to annexation at any time or in any shape. That may be the case with them, or it may not: nevertheless, there is good reason to put them down as opponents of annexation.

The Senate Committee on Foreign Relations stands seven to two in favor of annexation by proper methods.

This should encourage our friends in the islands. It only remains to find the proper method, and the American flag will fly again and forever over these beautiful islands of the sea.

How did the fake proclamation come to be regarded as real? It all goes back to a book by Helena G. Allen entitled "The Betrayal of Liliuokalani."[83] She made a lot of errors in regard to this alleged proclamation. It's unclear whether the errors were accidental, or whether they were deliberate acts of fraud committed by a Hawaiian sovereignty zealot. The title of her book should give pause to anyone who thinks she might be providing a fair and balanced view of history.

On pp. 314-315 Helena Allen provides the text of the fake proclamation exactly as copied above. Her footnote reads as follows: "New York Sun, February 26, 1894." An examination of microfilm of the February 26, 1894 edition of the New York Sun showed no trace of any such proclamation. Further investigation revealed the proclamation to be in the New York Sun of February 27, 1894, page 6, immediately following the fictitious "Special Message" attributed to Cleveland demanding the Senate be abolished. Clearly Helena Allen would have seen those other items, and she would have known the proclamation was phony. The proclamation was also incorrectly quoted by Helena G. Allen, as it referred not to the LAST day of April next (April 30), but the FIRST day of April next (April Fool's Day).

Was Allen's changing of the date for the national day of prayer and repentance from April 1 to April 30 merely an honest error, or was it an effort to cover up the fact that this "proclamation" was intended as an April Fools joke? Was her changing of the date of publication in the newspaper from February 27 to February 26 merely an honest error, or was it an effort to prevent scholars from finding the other clearly anti-Cleveland articles published on the same page? Allen provides the text of that proclamation in the context of discussing the Constitution of the Republic of Hawai'i, which was not issued until 4 months later; and then she says about that Constitution "President Cleveland jokingly expressed contempt in a proclamation: FOOLS' DAY A FAST DAY." In that quote

Allen is claiming that Cleveland's proclamation was real, and that it was sarcasm against a Constitution which was not issued until 4 months after the date on the proclamation!

In any case, Rev. Kaleo Patterson, a Hawaiian independence zealot, issued a press release including an announcement of a Honolulu church service. Featured speakers included Patterson, and also independence zealot Hayden Burgess alias Poka Laenui. Here are excerpts from the press release:

In a February 1894 letter to the New York Sun, President Grover Cleveland selected April 30, 1894 as a national day of prayer to recognize the United State's role in the illegal overthrow of Hawaii's monarch Queen Liliuokalani. "Let my people humble themselves and repent for their injustice to my great and good sister Queen Liliuokalani, and pray without distinction for color, for her speedy return to the throne," wrote Cleveland. President Cleveland's call for prayer has become the inspiration for April 30th, 2006 - A National Day of Prayer for Hawaiian Restoration.

Rev. Dr. John Thomas, President of the United Churches of Christ states: "I am honored and pleased to be included in the list of persons sharing in the April 30th - Hawaiian Restoration Day of Prayer."

On April 21, 2006, a delegation of Na Kanaka Maoli traveled to New Jersey in preparation for the upcoming day of prayer.

They honored President Grover Cleveland by visiting his birthplace and gravesite in Caldwell, NJ. The delegation attended worship services at the First Presbyterian Church of Caldwell where he was baptized. Another delegation of Native Hawaiians including Leon Siu, artist and Executive Director of Aloha Ke Akua Ministries, will also attend services in Caldwell this Sunday, April 30 to commemorate the national Day of Prayer for Hawaiian Restoration at Cleveland's birthplace.

WHAT: Event to raise awareness of the National Day of Prayer for Hawaiian Restoration. Native Hawaiians and church and community leaders will gather to commemorate President Cleveland's call for prayer recognizing the United State's illegal overthrow of Queen Lili'uokalani.

WHEN: Saturday, April 29, 2006, 6:00 p.m.

WHERE: Church of the Crossroads 1212 University Avenue

CONTACT: Rev. Dr. Kaleo Patterson, President, Pacific Justice and Reconciliation Center: (808) 330-3769, pjrc@pacificpeace.org

----

So the national president of the United Churches of Christ was hoodwinked into making a public statement to the effect that Cleveland's proclamation was real. But he wasn't the only one to be fooled.

Associated Press wrote an article which it distributed to all its affiliated newspapers. Many of those newspapers published part or all of the article. The article does not merely report that Patterson is calling for a national day of prayer – the news report states as fact that Cleveland's proclamation was real. Here are excerpts from the version of the AP "news report" published in a newspaper serving the Philadelphia suburbs:[84]

"President Grover Cleveland ... is getting some respect from an unusual source: Native Hawaiians who credit Cleveland with sticking up for their rights and national sovereignty in the 1890s ... three Native Hawaiians landed at New York's LaGuardia Airport, toting about 20 leis ... searched for Cleveland's birthplace in Caldwell ... about 25 miles west of Manhattan and 5,000 miles northeast of Honolulu - and at his grave site in Princeton. "We just wanted to come and visit and get a firsthand knowledge of the person and history of Cleveland," the Rev. Kaleo Patterson said after arriving in New Jersey. The journey is part of the events leading to an April 30 national day of prayer for Hawaiian natives that groups on the islands have been organizing. ... is meant to raise support for efforts to reduce poverty and crime among Hawaiian natives, as well as the granting of some form of self-government and self-determination. ... The day of prayer has a direct connection to New Jersey's only native-son-turned-president, because it was Cleveland as president who set aside April 30, 1894 as a day of prayer and repentance over the U.S. role in the Hawaiian monarchy's overthrow. On Sunday, they plan to attend a morning service at the Caldwell church, placing leis on the church's alter. They

then plan to take the leis to Princeton and lay them on Cleveland's grave and pray. Patterson said they have a special flower lei just for the former president, a lei that is usually reserved for royalty."

In case anyone missed it in the excerpts above, here's the falsehood reported throughout the world as fact by Associated Press (not merely attributed to Reverend Patterson), and which Reverend Patterson uses as a basis for his April 30 2006 "national day of prayer for Hawaiian natives":

"...it was Cleveland as president who set aside April 30, 1894 as a day of prayer and repentance over the U.S. role in the Hawaiian monarchy's overthrow."

Civil rights activists Ken Conklin (Kaneohe HI) and Jere Krischel (California) collaborated closely and intensively to discover what was true.

Krischel contacted Rev. Patterson with the information that the alleged Grover Cleveland proclamation cannot be found in the newspaper where it was reported to have been published, and that in any case a review of all of Grover Cleveland's compiled Presidential proclamations and statements showed that the President never published any such proclamation. Krischel asked Patterson to stop perpetuating this falsehood. Patterson replied to Krischel that whether or not Cleveland ever published such a proclamation, the April 30, 2006 National Day of Prayer for Native Hawaiian Restoration will go forward because it's good to pray for reconciliation and peace. (in other words, we've got this big propaganda circus planned, and we will not allow concerns for historical accuracy to stand in our way).

Krischel produced a webpage documenting all the information he discovered.[85]

Conklin also produced a webpage which includes some of the e-mails exchanged between Krischel and Rev. Patterson.[86]

Perhaps readers of this book might think it was silly to waste so much time to discover the truth about such a small detail. This overly lengthy section of this book is evidence of how easy it is for Hawaiian sovereignty zealots to manufacture totally false historical claims; how easy it is for them to get tremendous publicity for their falsehoods; how difficult it is to disprove even one small falsehood; and how energetically the zealots push their lies even after they have been decisively proved false.

Hawaii puppet regime had no legitimacy to offer a treaty of annexation

The claim is that the revolutionary Provisional Government from January 17, 1893 to July 4, 1894 was a U.S. puppet regime installed and kept in power under U.S. military occupation; and that the Republic of Hawaii, July 1894 through August 1898 continued to be a puppet regime. Therefore, the claim is that neither the Provisional Government nor the Republic of Hawaii had any legitimacy to speak on behalf of the Hawaiian nation; and certainly no authority to submit a treaty of annexation to its puppet master U.S.

In the previous section we saw that the 162 U.S. sailors present during the final stages of the revolution were sent ashore as peacekeepers to be ready if needed to protect American lives and property and to prevent rioting and arson. They were under strict orders to remain neutral. They never fired a shot, did not take over any buildings, did not surround the Palace or Government Building, stayed in a building down a side street out of sight of those buildings, and did not patrol the streets.

Was Hawaii ruled by a U.S. puppet regime for five and a half years, from January 1893 to August 1898? Indeed, was Hawaii ruled by a U.S. puppet regime for any period of time at all?

Immediately after the revolution the Provisional Government wrote a treaty of annexation and sent it to Washington. President Benjamin Harrison (Republican) submitted it to the Senate; but it was not acted upon because his term in office was at an end.

The new President Grover Cleveland (Democrat) was a personal friend of Liliuokalani. Less than a week after taking the oath of office President Cleveland withdrew the annexation treaty from the Senate. Cleveland sent a political hatchet man, James Blount, to Honolulu. Cleveland appointed Blount "Minister Plenipotentiary with paramount powers" even though he kept the appointment secret from Congress and never sought Senate confirmation. Cleveland gave Blount secret orders to destabilize the Provisional Government and to write a one-sided report for Cleveland to use for the purpose of turning public opinion against both the Provisional Government and annexation. Blount stayed at a Honolulu hotel owned and run by royalists. He did his "fact-finding" by doing nearly all his interviewing with royalists. He twisted the statements made to him by those few revolutionists he spoke with – some of them later gave sworn statements to the Morgan committee telling what they had told Blount and how Blount had twisted or falsely reported their words.[87]

During the weeks following the revolution the commander of the USS Boston had gradually been sending the peacekeepers back to the ship since they were not really needed in town. On April 1, 1893, within days after his arrival, Blount ordered the remaining sailors to return to their ship. For a few weeks the Provisional Government had been flying the U.S. flag alongside the Hawaiian flag on the Government Building, as a sign of stability to reassure Americans and Europeans still fearful of racial hostility and as a symbol of their hope for annexation. On April 1, when he ordered the remaining sailors back to their ship, Blount also ordered the removal of that U.S. flag. Perhaps he was hoping that the sudden removal of the U.S. flag and sailors would trigger mob action leading to counter-revolution; but that did not happen. The Provisional Government was firmly in control, as it had been right from the beginning on January 17 without any U.S. assistance. People were going about their business quite normally, and there was no agitation to restore the monarchy.

President Cleveland later used Blount's report as a basis for his message to Congress on December 18, 1893 in which Cleveland blamed the U.S. for illegally overthrowing the sovereign Queen of a friendly and confiding nation. Cleveland thereupon referred the matter to Congress to decide what should be done next (implying that U.S. forces should undo the Hawaiian revolution). The Senate Committee on Foreign Affairs promptly held two months of hearings and produced the Morgan Report which repudiated the Blount Report. The Senate then passed two resolutions that there should be no further interference (by President Cleveland or any other nation) in the affairs of Hawaii. These actions by the Senate are especially remarkable because committee chairman Morgan, and the Senate leaders, were all members of the the President's own Democrat party.[88]

Throughout the Summer and Fall of 1893 U.S. government agents in Honolulu had been trying to find a way to put Liliuokalani back on the throne. Her stubborn refusal to make any concessions made that impossible. The Blount report still remained secret, and the discussions between the U.S. and Liliuokalani also remained secret. In mid to late December there was a sudden flurry of correspondence. Hawaii President Dole wrote the U.S. diplomat in Honolulu to inquire what was going on. Dole received a response stating that the U.S. demands the Dole government to step down and restore Liliuokalani.[89] Dole sent a lengthy, blistering reply on Christmas Eve. Dole said that although Hawaii desires annexation, that has not happened; and so long as Hawaii remains an independent nation the U.S. has no business ordering it to change governments.[90]

There never was a U.S. puppet regime in Hawaii. The 162 peacekeepers sent ashore on January 16 were never used. The revolutionary militia was strong and got the job done without any help. The Queen's forces were weak and surrendered without a fight. The number of peacekeepers was gradually reduced because they were not needed, and the last remaining ones left town about ten weeks after the revolution. The U.S. flag that had flown for a few weeks alongside the Hawaiian flag on the Government Building, as a show of stability and desire for annexation, was removed. The U.S. President was demanding that his friend, the ex-queen, be put back on the throne. Throughout his four years in office President Grover Cleveland continued to oppose annexation and never tried to use military force to control Hawaii. The only puppet strings he pulled were those of his appointed diplomatic representatives whom he ordered to oppose the Hawaiian government and support the ex-queen for an entire year, from March 1893 through February 1894, until the Morgan Report was issued.

Was the Provisional Government legitimate? It clearly was not democratically elected. It probably did not have the support of most of those who had voting rights in the Kingdom. But the same can be said about most revolutionary provisional governments throughout the world, then and now.

From the standpoint of "international law" the Provisional Government was clearly legitimate. Within two days after the revolution the Provisional Government received letters of de facto recognition from the local consuls representing every government that had previously had diplomatic relations with the Queen's government. The nation had not been overthrown; only the government had changed hands. The Queen and her four cabinet ministers lost their jobs, but all the department heads, bureaucrats, and judges remained in office. De facto recognition is all that was possible at first. There were only low-level consuls present in Hawaii, who would need to get instructions from their governments (much like today's honorary consuls who usually have other full-time jobs in the local economy). There was no internet, telephone, or telegraph; so communication was possible only through letters sent by ship. Also, the Provisional Government hoped soon to be annexed. Governments which call themselves provisional are seen as only temporary and therefore do not seek or receive full permanent recognition.

As time went by no foreign government filed any diplomatic protest about the revolution either with the Hawaiian Provisional Government or with the United States. In particular, those nations who had treaty relations with the Kingdom continued doing business with the Provisional Government without protest, just as happens today when the U.S. government changes hands from one political party to another. From March 1893 to February 1894 it slowly became clear that President Cleveland would not succeed in restoring Liliuokalani to the throne. The U.S. Congress investigated, determined that the U.S. had not done anything wrong in the revolution, refused to support Cleveland's efforts to undo the revolution, and passed resolutions that the U.S. and foreign nations should leave Hawaii alone. Hawaii officials began planning for the years ahead as an independent nation.

On July 4, 1894 the Provisional Government gave way to the Republic of Hawaii with a Constitution and an elected legislature. The Speaker of the House, John Kaulukou, was ethnic Hawaiian and had formerly been a royalist. The Republic was now ready to receive full diplomatic recognition as the permanent government of Hawaii. In August of 1894 the minutes of the Executive Council of the Republic of Hawaii recorded that President Grover Cleveland had sent a letter of full diplomatic recognition – the same Grover Cleveland who had previously tried to destabilize the Provisional Government and restore the monarchy. The Hawaiian Star newspaper reported on November 15, 1895 that Queen Victoria's government had sent a letter of full diplomatic recognition – the same Queen Victoria who had previously entertained Liliuokalani at Victoria's coronation in London, and who had been godmother to baby Prince Albert born to Alexander Liholiho Kamehameha IV and his wife Queen Emma.

There can be no doubt that the Republic of Hawaii was standing on its own and was not a U.S. puppet regime. There can be no doubt that the Republic had diplomatic recognition from all the nations that had formerly recognized the Kingdom; and none of them had ever protested the revolution to the governments of either Hawaii or the U.S. The Republic of Hawaii had the right to speak as the government of the nation, and to offer a treaty of annexation to the U.S. And that's exactly what Hawaii President Sanford Dole did as soon as U.S. Democrat President Grover Cleveland was replaced by Republican President William McKinley.

Illegal annexation

The claim is that the annexation of Hawaii to the United States was illegal. Another way of putting it is: the annexation "never happened." Therefore Hawaii remains the independent nation it always was (but its rightful government is ineffective because of a prolonged belligerent military occupation).

Those who make this claim often do not mention that the Republic of Hawaii in 1897 offered a treaty of annexation. When confronted with this fact the zealots respond that the Republic was illegitimate; but that claim has already been disposed of.

Allegedly the U.S. unilaterally reached out and grabbed Hawaii. It did that by passing a joint resolution of annexation in 1898. Joint resolutions are merely internal laws of the U.S.; they have no force or effect outside. The zealots say the only way to do an annexation legitimately is through a treaty, and the U.S. Constitution requires a treaty to be ratified by a 2/3 vote in the Senate. The treaty submitted by the Republic in 1887 was defeated when it failed to get the 2/3 vote needed in the Senate. End of story. The joint resolution of annexation, passed by majority vote of both House and Senate in 1898, is illegal because treaties need a 2/3 vote of the Senate.

Here's the true story. The Republic of Hawaii had full international recognition. It offered a treaty of annexation in 1897. The U.S. Senate was unable to get the 2/3 vote required by U.S. law for ratifying a treaty. However, the Spanish-American War then suddenly got started. The U.S. urgently needed to use Hawaii as a coaling station and rest stop for troop ships on the way to and from the Philippines. That would not be possible without violating the neutrality of an independent Hawaii. The solution was for Congress to accept the treaty so that Hawaii would be a part of the U.S.

Southern sugar planters did not want competition from Hawaii. Southern politicians were still recuperating from the post Civil War reconstruction, and were busily implementing Jim Crow racial laws – they did not want to make U.S. citizens out of Hawaii's predominantly dark-skinned population of Hawaiians and Asians. It seemed the treaty once again might not get the necessary 2/3 vote in the Senate. But 50 years previously Texas had been annexed by joint resolution, requiring only a majority vote of both the House and Senate. The leaders of Congress decided to follow that precedent. When the matter was put to a vote, the Senate approved the annexation resolution by 42-21, the House approved it by 209-91, and President McKinley promptly signed it.

Hawaiian sovereignty zealots say it's contrary to international law for the U.S. to use a joint resolution as its method for approving a treaty. But that's absurd. International law cannot dictate to any nation the method whereby that nation chooses to ratify a treaty. Some nations don't even have a Senate!

Anyone familiar with the fundamentals of contract law can understand what happened. Two parties, both of which were competent and acting freely, negotiated the terms of a contract. One party offered the contract and the other accepted it. There was an exchange of value – Hawaii gave control of the ceded lands to the U.S. to hold in trust for the people of Hawaii, and the U.S. paid off the Hawaiian national debt (which was larger than the market value of the ceded lands). The party that makes an offer has no standing (no right) to complain later about the method whereby the other party makes its own decision to accept the offer. It was entirely up to the U.S. to decide by what method the U.S. can ratify a treaty. The U.S. did not pass an internal law that unilaterally reached out and grabbed Hawaii. Hawaii first made an offer, and the U.S. then accepted the offer by a process it had every right to choose for itself. The question, whether it was proper for the U.S. to use joint resolution as its method of accepting the Republic's offer, was debated heatedly in the media and in Congress in 1898. But those favoring annexation won the debate. Even the Southern Senators who opposed annexation never tried to file a lawsuit in the Supreme Court to challenge the ratification of Hawaii's annexation treaty by means of a joint resolution, and no other nation (including the Kingdom's numerous treaty partners) made any complaint.

Anti-annexation petition signed by 95% of ethnic Hawaiians

The claim is that in 1897 a petition opposing annexation was signed by 38,000 people in Hawaii, representing nearly all ethnic Hawaiians then living. The petition was presented to the Senate and caused the annexation treaty to fall short of the 2/3 vote needed for ratification.

Here's the truth. There was indeed a petition opposing annexation in 1897. It might have played a role in persuading some Senators to vote against annexation, although opposition from Southern sugar planters, and racial concerns, were probably more important factors than the petition.

But there were only 21,269 signatures on the petition opposing annexation, not 38,000. The petition and all signature pages are available on the internet.[91]

That petition was formally presented to the Senate, so it was then placed in the U.S. National Archives. The petition was found there a century later by a Hawaiian independence zealot who made photocopies of it. Photos of all the signature pages were posted on public view at the Hawaii state Capitol and at sovereignty rallies at Iolani Palace, and made available for sale; as part of the August 1998 commemoration of the 100th anniversary of Hawaii's annexation. They are now available on the internet through the University of Hawaii library website. Thousands of ethnic Hawaiians took great pride in finding the signatures of their ancestors. Many were thereby inspired to sovereignty activism as a way to follow in the footsteps of their ancestors' resistance to the U.S. and patriotism toward the nation of Hawaii.

Where did the figure alleging 38,000 signatures come from? In 1897 there were two different ethnic Hawaiian political organizations sponsoring two different petitions. The petition with 21,269 signatures was specifically in opposition to annexation. The other petition allegedly had about 17,000 signatures but it was on a very different topic – demanding the restoration of Liliuokalani as Queen. Today's sovereignty zealots add up the signatures from both petitions, even though they were on very different topics and even though it seems likely that most of the people who signed the petition to restore the Queen would also have signed the petition opposing annexation. We'll never know whether that monarchy restoration petition actually existed (it probably did), nor how many signatures it contained, nor how many of the signatures were on both petitions (probably most). In any case it is clearly irresponsible to add up the totals for the two different petitions. That tactic is typical of the way sovereignty zealots twist history.

Indeed, the gap of 4,000 signatures between the two petitions could be interpreted to mean that there were 4,000 natives who opposed annexation but also opposed restoring the monarchy and wanted the Republic of Hawai'i to continue as an independent nation under the coalition of white and Hawaiian oligarchs!

The monarchy restoration petition was never presented to the Senate, and therefore is not in the National Archives. That petition has never been found. It's hard to imagine how such a politically important petition with so many signatures could be lost. An even greater mystery is why nobody wrote about either of the petitions for many decades after their signatures were gathered. The sovereignty zealot who "discovered" the anti-annexation petition in the National Archives made many inflammatory public statements that the petition had been "hidden" and "suppressed" by evil Caucasian annexationists and by historians ever since then. But there were royalist newspapers publishing openly anti-annexation articles in Hawaiian language, as well as English, throughout the 1890s (and right up to 1948). Liliuokalani wrote personal diaries continuously until her death in 1917. Yet we know that neither the newspapers nor the diaries ever mentioned either one of the petitions. The sovereignty zealot who "discovered" the petitions in the National Archives is fluent in Hawaiian language and has made a career of poring through the old newspapers. She continues to maintain, even ten years after rediscovering the petitions, that the existence of the petitions was suppressed and hidden. Thus it is clear that during ten years of reading and translating the old newspapers, and studying native resistance to American "imperialism," she still has not discovered any mention of the petitions.

The anti-annexation petition did not go unchallenged in 1897. Lorrin A. Thurston, who was a leader of the revolution and a leading annexationist, wrote a report discrediting the anti-annexation petitions, which is now available on the internet.[92] He pointed out that some individuals signed the petition multiple times in their own names on different pages, and also forged the signatures of numerous others (their handwriting was remarkably the same as the forger's!). Hawaiians in the 1800s frequently gathered petitions on many subjects. Thurston, who had been an elected member of the Kingdom legislature, reports that some of his ethnic Hawaiian colleagues routinely gathered entire pages of signatures on otherwise blank documents, and later filled in the top of the petition with whatever cause they desired. The ages of some small children were also changed to make it appear they were adults.

How significant were the 21,269 signatures on the anti-annexation petition, even assuming they were all legitimate? In 1890 the Kingdom Census counted 40,622 pure or part Hawaiians representing 45% of the population; in 1896 the Republic Census counted 39,504 for 36% of the population; and in 1900 the U.S. Census counted 39,656 representing 26% of the population (there was substantial immigration from Japan, China, and the U.S., causing the percentage of Hawaiians to drop dramatically) Straight-line interpolation yields 39,542 as the number of full or part Hawaiians in 1897, the year of the anti-annexation petition.

Assuming all 21,269 signatures were from ethnic Hawaiians, that figure would represent about 54% of the ethnic Hawaiian population of

39,542. So on average, today's ethnic Hawaiian looking for the signatures of his Hawaiian ancestors would find that half of them did not sign the petition. There was a massive effort to gather signatures from all corners of the nation, and strong pressure from family and community leaders (just like today!). The absence of nearly half of ethnic Hawaiians on the signature pages probably reflects that there were many brave individuals who resisted signing either because they supported annexation or because they just didn't care.

But there's more to the story. The signatures have no relationship to voter registration. Only adult men were allowed to vote; but most of the signatures are by women and children. Furthermore, everyone acknowledges that some of the signers were not ethnic Hawaiians, since there were many Caucasians and Asians who were royalists.

The signers did not have to be ethnically Hawaiian, and did not have to be registered voters. So the correct way to judge the significance of the number is by comparison against the entire population. The whole population in 1896 was 109,020; in 1900 it was 154,001; so interpolation yields 120,265 as the population in 1897. That means the 21,269 signatures represent less than 18% of the population.

Hawaiian language was made illegal[93]

Hawaiian sovereignty zealots like to say that "Hawaiian language was made illegal." They like to say that "After our Queen was overthrown we were forbidden from speaking Hawaiian here in our own homeland, and our grandmothers have told us they were beaten for speaking it."

The activists like to assert this historical grievance because it magnifies their claim to victimhood status. "It's one more way those evil Caucasians turned us natives into strangers in our own homeland – a poor, downtrodden people who have the worst statistics for education, health, incarceration drug abuse, etc. So of course we feel deep pain, we're angry, and we're entitled to huge reparations for the damage done to us."

But here's the truth. Hawaiian language was never banned in the society and culture of Hawaii. There were Hawaiian language newspapers publishing continuously from the 1830s right up through 1948 when they finally died out. Today those newspapers are available on the internet. Hawaiian language was spoken along with English in the Territorial Legislature, where bills were printed in both Hawaiian and English.

The remnant of the "illegal language" claim is that Hawaiian language was banned in the schools. That is also absolutely false. Here's what's true.

Just as today, every child in the Kingdom, Republic, and Territory of Hawaii was required to attend school (and not merely labor in the taro patch or fishpond). But what standards must a "school" meet in order to be accepted by the government as fulfilling the attendance law? The Republic of Hawaii was concerned that there was tremendous immigration from Portugal, China and Japan. Ethnic Portuguese, Japanese and Chinese children born and raised in Hawaii should all be able to speak the language that was actually dominant in everyday life. A law was passed in 1896 requiring that English must be the language of instruction in all schools (public or private) seeking certification as satisfying the compulsory attendance law. Hawaiian language was not singled out; the law applied to all Asian, European, and other languages. Courses where Hawaiian language (or any other language) was the subject matter were specifically allowed by the carefully written law.

The 1896 law did not prohibit private schools for after-school instruction in language and culture. The law only said that such "language immersion" schools (as we would call them today) could not be the main school that the government would recognize as meeting the compulsory school attendance law. Impoverished Japanese plantation workers somehow found enough money to create such Japanese schools for their children; ethnic Hawaiians (whose wage scale was higher) chose not to do that.

English had already become the dominant language for everyday use. By 1892 (the year before the monarchy was overthrown) 95% of all the government schools were already using English as the language of instruction, because that's what the ethnic Hawaiian parents and the sovereign monarchs wanted for their people.

And yes, if granny spoke Hawaiian in school as a little girl she might have been punished by the teacher, just as the little Japanese girl was punished for speaking Japanese. But children were not "beaten" – instead of using a baseball bat or fist, the teacher might use a ruler to rap a child's hand much as Catholic school nuns reportedly still do today. Even at home, granny as a little girl might have been punished by her own parents for speaking Hawaiian in the home. Hawaiian parents recognized that the path to social and economic success would be through English. The parents would speak to each other in Hawaiian, but would speak only English with their children. The parents did that not because the language was illegal, but rather because they wanted what was best for their beloved children.

On August 2, 2005 the 9th Circuit Court of Appeals handed down a ruling that the racially exclusionary admissions policy of Kamehameha Schools is illegal (since then reversed by a 7-6 vote of an en-banc panel). The 3-judge panel made the following observation on page 6 of the pdf copy of the ruling: "As the Schools' 1885 Prospectus observed: 'The noble minded Hawaiian chiefess who endowed the Kamehameha Schools, put no limitations of race or condition on her general bequest. Instruction will be given only in English language, but The Schools will be opened to all nationalities.'" So here we have the most wealthy and powerful native Hawaiian chiefess, able to set up her school to use whatever language she preferred. And here we have the trustees she appointed, opening a school 8 years before the overthrow of the monarchy, and two years before the "Bayonet Constitution," when the Hawaiian "merrie monarch" King Kalakaua ruled and was reviving hula and Hawaiian language. And that school is conducting its courses solely in English language. That was clearly a free choice, and clearly illustrates that Hawaiian language went into a coma due to natural causes and not because of suppression.

This language ban/suppression falsehood is one of the most tenacious historical errors, repeated innumerable times in newspapers, magazines, and TV broadcasts both in Hawaii and throughout the U.S. It is often asserted quickly, as a matter of common knowledge, in the middle of a sentence that goes on to recite other victimhood claims. When an attempt is made to correct the record, angry replies are published saying "How dare you question what my Hawaiian teachers and my grandmother have told me with tears in their eyes." Perpetuating the falsehood that Hawaiian language was banned in society, or in school, serves the agenda of the sovereignty zealots to portray ethnic Hawaiians as victims. It deliberately stirs up resentment and anger where none is appropriate.

"Treaties are the supreme law of the land."

The claim is that the Kingdom of Hawaii had treaties with the United States, especially including a treaty of perpetual friendship and commerce (true). But then the U.S. violated that treaty by staging an armed invasion in 1893 (false, as discussed previously). The U.S. further violated that treaty by passing an internal law (joint resolution of annexation) that unilaterally reached out and grabbed Hawaii (false, as discussed previously).

But treaties are the supreme law of the United States, according to its own Constitution (we'll examine that claim next). Thus the treaty of friendship would take priority over the annexation resolution which was merely an internal law. The U.S. is required by its own Constitution to uphold its treaty of friendship, which as a treaty takes priority over and thereby nullifies the resolution of annexation. And under terms of the treaty of friendship the U.S. must withdraw its prolonged belligerent occupation of Hawaii.

The claim that treaties are the supreme law of the United States is interesting because it provides a typical example of how Hawaiian sovereignty zealots knowingly take statements out of context, using partial truths or half-truths to twist history and score points with public opinion. Part of what makes this example typical is that it is very easy and quick to say "Treaties are the supreme law of the land and therefore the U.S. must live up to its treaty of friendship with the Hawaiian Kingdom"; but it is very complicated and time-consuming to set the record straight. People with short attention spans are impressed with the easy rhetoric and then lack patience or intelligence to sift through facts and logic (Dear reader, are you still paying attention?).

Hawaiian independence zealots love to quote the following snippet from Article VI, Section 2 of the U.S. Constitution: "... treaties ... shall be the supreme law of the land." But the activists don't include the ellipses that would indicate there are things they left out, and they take the quote out of context.

Could any intelligent person seriously believe the Constitution would make treaties the supreme law of the land – period! – standing higher than the Constitution itself? Indeed, the Constitution is the authority for the Senate to ratify treaties. The Constitution is the document which is allegedly conferring upon treaties the authority to stand above the Constitution itself.

Here's Article VI, Section 2 in its entirety. This entire section is one single sentence, and must be taken as a whole. Shame on the sovereignty zealots for always cutting and gluing together two separate parts of the single sentence while leaving out the rest of it, as though quoting a single fundamental principle.

"This constitution, and the laws of the United States which shall be made in pursuance thereof; and all treaties made, or which shall be made, under the authority of the United States, shall be the supreme law of the

land; and all the judges in every state shall be bound thereby, anything in the constitution or laws of any state to the contrary notwithstanding."

The entire sentence makes clear that its purpose is to establish the principle that federal law is superior to any state law that might contradict it. If a federal law and a state law are in conflict, the federal law wins. A good example is Rice vs. Cayetano, where the U.S. Supreme Court cited the 15th Amendment of the U.S. Constitution to rule that a portion of Article 12 of the State of Hawaii Constitution is illegal. The racial restriction that only ethnic Hawaiians can vote for OHA trustee (state constitution) was nullified because it was in conflict with the U.S. Constitution 15th Amendment sentence that says the right to vote shall not be denied or abridged on account of race. The whole purpose of Article VI, Section 2 of the U.S. Constitution is to make sure that the U.S. Constitution, U.S. statute laws, and U.S. treaties will trump any state Constitution or state statute which might conflict with any of them.

Now let's take the entire first part of Article VI, Section 2, not leaving anything out, to see that there are three things that are the supreme law of the land, not only treaties. "This constitution, and the laws of the United States which shall be made in pursuance thereof; and all treaties made, or which shall be made, under the authority of the United States, shall be the supreme law of the land ..."

Note that the first thing mentioned is the Constitution, because it is more important than the other two (indeed, it's the Constitution which grants power to the other two!). Then the next thing mentioned is the laws passed by Congress, because that is more important than the third item. Then, finally, the third item is treaties. Treaties are the least important among the three items which, taken all together, are the supreme law of the land, taking precedence over any state Constitution or law.

The U.S. has on occasion unilaterally abrogated some of its treaties. It does that by Congress passing a law, or resolution, which the Secretary of State implements by giving notice to the treaty partners that the treaty is abrogated. Even without action from Congress the President alone, or cabinet officers acting under his authority, occasionally has used general authority given to them under acts of Congress (such as regulations governing interstate commerce) to abrogate portions of treaties in regard to import/export, regulations governing the size and weight of trucks crossing the border from Mexico under the NAFTA treaty, etc. One major treaty abrogated in its entirety in recent years was the treaty with the Soviet Union prohibiting missiles that could defend against missiles – testing now under way for the "Star Wars" missile defense system would have been contrary to that treaty, so the U.S. abrogated it.

Perhaps the Hawaiian independence zealots, clutching at straws, would reply that the U.S. never notified Hawaii that it was abrogating the treaty of friendship. But even that lame claim would be false. The annexation documents exchanged between the U.S. and the Republic of Hawaii agree on what will happen to treaties Hawaii had with foreign nations and treaties Hawaii had with the U.S. No nation ever protested annexation, and all nations thereafter dealt with the U.S. as the sovereign power for Hawaii; thereby showing that everyone agreed the treaties were abrogated.

Article III of the Republic's offer of annexation, dealing with treaties with foreign nations, is completely identical with the language in the U.S. acceptance except that where the Republic refers to its offer of a "treaty" of annexation, the U.S. refers to a "joint resolution" of acceptance. The identical wording establishes the common-sense disposition of treaties as described above. Here is the wording:

"The existing treaties of the Hawaiian Islands with foreign nations shall forthwith cease and determine, being replaced by such treaties as may exist, or as may be hereafter concluded, between the United States and such foreign nations. The municipal legislation of the Hawaiian Islands, not enacted for the fulfillment of the treaties so extinguished, and not inconsistent with this joint resolution nor contrary to the Constitution of the United States nor to any existing treaty of the United States, shall remain in force until the Congress of the United States shall otherwise determine."

The language is also identical between the two annexation documents dealing with the commercial relations between (the former Kingdom of) Hawaii and the U.S. and foreign nations:

"Until legislation shall be enacted extending the United States customs laws and regulations to the Hawaiian Islands the existing customs relations of the Hawaiian Islands with the United States and other countries shall remain unchanged."

Thus all treaties between the Kingdom of Hawaii and other nations, including the United States, were forever extinguished in 1898 for two reasons: (1) As a result of the overthrow of the monarchy, the new Hawaiian governments in 1893 (Provisional) and 1894 (Republic) took control of and continued to enforce the treaties of the Kingdom, unless such treaties were changed by the Republic of Hawaii through negotiation with the treaty partners (for example, President Grover Cleveland and President Sanford Dole negotiated onshore and submerged land rights for an international telecommunications cable linking Japan, Hawaii, and California). (2) As a result of the annexation, all treaties of the Republic of Hawaii (and therefore of the Kingdom whose treaties were assumed by the Republic) were either abrogated or became the responsibility of the United States to administer, in accord with the provisions of the agreement of annexation.

Hawaiian flag publicly torn into souvenir pieces given to the Caucasians, as a way of humiliating ethnic Hawaiians at the time of overthrow or annexation[94]

This totally false claim is normally asserted as pertaining to the ceremony of annexation at Iolani Palace in August of 1898. However, the claim is sometimes asserted as pertaining to the overthrow of the monarchy in January of 1893. Sovereignty zealots who don't know much about history often blur the two events, as well as others in between such as the Wilcox attempted counterrevolution of 1895 and the ensuing imprisonment of the ex-queen for conspiracy in it. It's not unusual to hear someone run together falsehoods covering the entire period from 1893 to 1898 by shouting something like this: "The U.S. staged an armed invasion, overthrew the monarchy, imprisoned the Queen, made Hawaiian language illegal, and tore up the Hawaiian flag for souvenirs for the guys who did it. Thurston Twigg-Smith still has his grandfather's piece." Wow! Everything in that sentence is false, but it makes emotionally rousing propaganda.

Senator Dan Akaka told the falsehood on the floor of the U.S. Senate on July 31, 1990 in a short speech commemorating "Hawaiian Flag Day." Besides asserting the flag desecration lie, the speech was notable for its double-entendre timing. July 31 was a national holiday of the Kingdom of Hawaii, "Ka La Hoihoi Ea" (sovereignty restoration day), commemorating the return of sovereignty from Britain to Kauikeaouli Kamehameha III after a rogue British naval captain had seized control for several months. The fact that Senator Akaka made a point of commemorating this date indicates his clear leanings in favor of the Hawaiian independence movement, which stages a sparsely attended celebration of this revived Kingdom holiday on July 31 each year in downtown Honolulu.

From the Congressional Record for the Senate, July 31, 1990, page S11232:

Kenneth R. Conklin, Ph.D.

"Mr. AKAKA. Mr. President, it gives me great pleasure today to join the people of my home State of Hawaii in saluting the Hawaiian flag. Today, July 31, marks Hawaiian Flag Day, or 'La Hae Hawai'i'. The Hawaiian flag, also known as the Kamehameha flag, flies proudly as a living symbol of a people and their beloved land. ... The Hawaiian flag also symbolizes a once sovereign nation which was overthrown by business leaders in 1893. It was at this time that the Hawaiian flag was lowered, cut into pieces, and given to the crowd as souvenirs. The American flag was then raised in its place and it was not until Hawaii become a U.S. territory that the Hawaiian flag officially flew again, now as a companion to the American flag."

Besides the lie about the shredded flag being used for souvenirs, Akaka was also wrong in saying that the Hawaiian flag did not fly from the time of the 1893 overthrow until the 1898 annexation. The Hawaiian flag flew throughout that time. The U.S. flag flew briefly alongside the Hawaiian flag on the Government Building, by order of the Provisional Government (as a symbol of stability and hope for annexation) until the U.S. flag was removed by order of President Cleveland's hatchet man James Blount on April 1, 1893. The Hawaiian flag remained the flag of the Provisional Government and the Republic. It was still flying atop Iolani Palace in August 1898 when it was replaced with the U.S. flag during annexation ceremonies.

Three years after Senator Akaka's speech, Senator Dan Inouye showed his own ignorance of history, and his demagoguery, on the floor of the U.S. Senate. There was a short debate before passing the apology resolution. Here's the relevant portion of Senator Inouye's speech from the Congressional Record for the Senate for Wednesday, October 27, 1993, (103rd Congress, 1st session), regarding 139 Cong Rec S 14477:

"Mr. INOUYE: We are here to recognize the results of the unfortunate events of that day. ... it is significant as a first step in that process, as my colleague has so eloquently stated, to bring about some understanding and reconciliation ... just a few footnotes in history, and this might give one a better picture of what happened. This so-called revolution that overthrew of our Queen was engineered by 12 men, leaders of the business community, owners of great sugar plantations and shipping companies. They called themselves the Committee of Safety [correction: the Committee of Safety had 13 members]. On that fateful day when the flag of the Kingdom of Hawaii was lowered over Iolani Palace and the American flag went up, it is reported that one of the Committee of Safety remarked to the others: "This is a glorious day. We need something to

Hawaiian Apartheid

remind us of this auspicious moment." So someone is reported to have suggested, "Why don't we cut that flag in 12 parts; each of us take a piece, a piece of the action?" And that is what happened. It is said that one piece remains today, the last remaining piece of the flag of the Kingdom of Hawaii."

Did anyone tell Senator Inouye that what he said was false? Apparently not, because seven years later he was still saying it. He corrected it slightly by placing the flag desecration at the time of annexation rather than overthrow. In July 2000 Inouye was busy in the Senate just getting started on the Native Hawaiian Recognition bill (which also contains numerous falsehoods). He repeated the shredded-flag lie as fact while talking with a local reporter in Honolulu. On July 18, 2000 columnist Bud Smyser wrote the following in the Honolulu Star-Bulletin:

"No one has the potential for more effective arm-twisting and persuasion than Hawaii's powerful, fourth-most-senior member of the Senate, Daniel K. Inouye. He told me in a recent extended interview that he will work harder for this than for any other legislation in his 37-plus years in the Senate.

The Democratic political sweep in Hawaii in 1954 put Inouye into the territorial House of Representatives. The former throne room in Iolani Palace was its meeting place. He refused to join presiding officers in operating from the raised replicas of the thrones. It was a desecration, he says, as was the Aug.12, 1898, act of cutting into memento pieces the Hawaiian flag that was lowered from the palace at the U.S. annexation ceremonies. It should have been preserved for a museum, he says. The 1893 revolutionaries also tried to suppress the Hawaiian language and hula."

The Honolulu Star-Bulletin of August 14, 2000 briefly mentioned it again, saying: *"The local urban legend about the mutilation of the Hawaiian flag has a life of its own. It was repeated as gospel recently by none other than Sen. Dan Inouye, who should know better."*

Nobody knows for sure how the shredded flag story got started. By the late 1950s the flag-shredding story had become sufficiently widespread that James Michener included it in his FICTION novel "Hawaii." Here's a quote from James Michener, "Hawaii" 1959 edition, Chapter IV, "From the Starving Village", page 704, describing the ceremony of annexation at Iolani Palace on August 12, 1898:

"But when the ceremonies were ended, a most shameful thing occurred, and to Malama it would always epitomize the indecency by which her nation had been destroyed. As the Hawaiian flag fell, an American caught it and, before he could be stopped, whisked it away to the palace

cellar where, with a pair of long shears, he cut the emblem into strips and began passing them out as souvenirs of the day. One was jammed into Micah's hand and he looked down to see what it was, but his eyes were so strained from writing letters on behalf of Hawaii that he could not easily discern what he held, and imprudently he raised it aloft. Then he saw that it contained fragments of the eight stripes symbolizing the islands of Hawaii and a corner of the field, and he realized what a disgraceful thing had been done to this proud flag. Hastily he crumpled it lest his wife see and be further offended, but as he pushed the torn cloth into his pocket he heard from behind a cry of pain, and he turned to see that his wife had at last been forced to cover her face in shame."

In 1997, just in time for the 1998 centennial of annexation, WGBH (PBS in Boston) produced a nationally broadcast "documentary" entitled "Hawaii's Last Queen" hosted by the golden-voiced David McCullough. This hour-long "documentary" was the centerpiece of a PBS webpage that included a transcript of the TV show plus numerous lesson plans for school teachers, based on the show. At 51 and a half minutes into the program, the transcript has Malcolm Chun reporting as follows: *"On the actual day of annexation, the queen shuttered herself at Washington Place, surrounded by her court, by the princes, by her ladies in waiting, and they had a solemn picture taken. On the other side at 'Iolani Palace, there were sharpshooters pointed out. There was still tension in the air that something might happen. But when the Hawaiian flag was lowered, it was said that it was cut into small little, two to three inch ribbons and given out a tokens of remembrance to the sons and daughters of the missionary families, so that they could keep those as little tokens of their great victory over the Hawaiian kingdom and the end of the tyranny of the Hawaiian monarchy."* The PBS lesson plan offered to teachers says: *"With the Spanish American War in 1898, the need for Hawaii is evident. President McKinley decides to annex it. On August 12, 1898 President Dole yields to the U.S. The American flag is raised over the Palace. The Hawaiian flag is cut into pieces and given away to the children of the missionaries as tokens of their victory. The disposed [sic] Queen Lili'uokalani would live for another 20 years. Her death at age 79 was marked by strange events in nature."*

Thurston Twigg-Smith, grandson of a leader of the 1893 revolution, wrote a book "Hawaiian Sovereignty: Do the Facts Matter?" published in 1998. On page 319 Mr. Twigg-Smith explains it this way, describing what the story said and also providing some information on how widespread it is.

Hawaiian Apartheid

"Fiction: The 1997 Public Television video, Hawai'i's Last Queen, included an emotional episode that said the Hawaiian Flag taken down at Annexation was "cut up into little ribbons by the missionaries and given to their children as souvenirs of what they had done to the Hawaiians."

"Fact: There is no historical record of any such incident. The producers of the video knew no Hawaiian historian had ever mentioned such an act and knew this fable first appeared in the 1950s as an item written by a newspaper columnist known for her often fictitious tales of old Hawai'i. They used it anyway, telling this writer that it captured the spirit of the Annexation period. H.J. Bartels, curator of 'Iolani Palace and sympathetic in a rational way to sovereignty issues, believes this flag incident is fictional. He suggests it may have sprung from an item in the August 5, 1898, Pacific Commercial Advertiser, page 1, column 3. The item related that a commercial firm had approached President Dole with the idea of raising and lowering the flags on a colorful ribbon-like lanyard that then could be cut into pieces and sold as souvenirs. There is no report this was ever done but the Dole family in the 1970s sold to antique dealer Robert Van Dyke a piece of cloth resembling this description, which may have been the lanyard sample shown to President Dole. At any rate, there were no missionaries alive at the time of Annexation and the four missionary descendants who were involved in leadership of the Revolution and the Provisional Government — Castle, Dole, Smith and Thurston, all attorneys — certainly didn't spend their time cutting up Hawaiian flags."

Later, on page 321, while disposing of another scurrilous falsehood (regarding an alleged assassination attempt against the ex-Queen by Thurston), Twigg-Smith again quotes Bartels: *"It was just a rumor,"* notes Bartels. *"We left it in because it caught the state of mind of the times."* Interestingly, that's about what the producer of Hawai'i's Last Queen said to me in a letter about the flag-cutting incident: *"It may not be true, but we think it catches the flavor of the period."* In other words, what's wrong with a little baloney if it makes the stew taste better?"

Another version of the story was told a few years ago by one of Hawaii's most famous racial demagogues, "Uncle" Charlie Maxwell, in his response to a student asking a question on his internet discussion bulletin board. The youngster asked: *"I have recently been searching for help on a research paper. Any help that anyone could provide would be fantastic. I am doing it on the roles that Liliuokalani played in order to prevent the annexation of Hawaii. Thanks for all your help. Jessica"*

Maxwell replied [verbatim, not corrected for grammar or spelling]: *"Aloha Jessica. The role that Queen Liliuokalani played was very dra-*

matic and hurtful to her and her people. Just think that a small group of business men who were mostly descendants of the first missionaries (Thurstons, Twiggs, Smith, Baldwins, Castles, Cooks etc., formed an alience and planned her overthrow. They were friendly to the commissioner of the United States J. L Stevens, who used the powers of the United States to force the surrender of the Kingdom with armed troops at Iolani Palace. The Queen yielded to the United States and after President Cleveland sent down M. S. Blount to investigate what happened. He took down the American Flag and replaced the Hawaiian Flag. The Provisional Government consisting of the haole business men told the United States that they did not have jurisdiction on Hawaiian soil and with the help of "crooked" Congrassmen and Senators Annexated Hawaii to the United States. 16 White people signed the Treaty of Annexation in 1898 and when they took down the Hawaiian Flag for the last time, they cut it in 16 pieces and gave it to the people that signed the "illigal" treated. Please check my webpage about the law which President Clinton signed called the "Appoligy Law for the illegal Annexation of Hawaii" Hope I have helped. Uncle Charlie"

Proving that something never happened is nearly impossible. But in the case of the shredded flag falsehood there is rock solid evidence.

John "Butch" Kekahu was well known in the community for leading two "Aloha March on Washington" events in 1998 and 2000. Butch was an advocate for Hawaiian independence. The August 2, 1998 Sunday Honolulu Advertiser had a front-page photo whose caption states, "Allen Hoof, left, and John 'Butch' Kekahu examine the Hawaiian flag that was replaced at Iolani Palace 100 years ago by the U.S. flag." The accompanying article, on page A-3, says,

"John 'Butch' Kekahu, a Hawaiian rights activist from Kauai who happened to be in the archives, instead [instead of looking at the preserved U.S. flag which had been hoisted on annexation day] focused on the Hawaiian flag that came down from the palace at 11:46 a.m. in 1898. It was so tattered Hoof didn't want to unfold it any more from the acid-free roll it hangs on [in the archives] ..."

And so, although he may not have intended to do so, Butch Kekahu put to rest that scurrilous historical lie about the Hawaiian flag being ripped to shreds at the 1898 annexation and pieces being passed out as souvenirs to the 1893 revolutionaries.

The Honolulu Star-Bulletin of August 14, 2000 had a feature story that begins with a photograph whose caption reads: *"The Hawaiian flag that was flown above Iolani Palace during the 1893 coup is locked in a*

Hawaiian Apartheid

vault at Hawaii State Archives, contrary to stories of its destruction." The story, by columnist Burl Burlingame, has the headline "Mutilation of Hawaiian flag a myth"

Burlingame says: *"The local urban legend about the mutilation of the Hawaiian flag has a life of its own. It was repeated as gospel recently by none other than Sen. Dan Inouye, who should know better. Since this weekend was the anniversary of annexation by the United States, let's shake this particular eyewash. ... When the U.S. annexed Hawaii on Aug. 12, 1898 ... there was a formal ceremony at Iolani Palace where the Hawaiian flag was lowered and the stars 'n' bars run up. Here's a picture of a Yankee sailor atop the Palace getting ready to lower the Hawaiian flag. It is not known if this is the same flag that flew over the Palace during the 1893 coup, but it likely is. According to Inouye and certain sovereigntists, the palace's Hawaiian flag was enthusiastically cut up for souvenirs by the Americans and ceased to exist. It should have been preserved for a museum, Inouye complained to the Star-Bulletin's Bud Smyser last month. It was, sort of. At least it was never cut up. It rests today in the vault of the Hawaii State Archives. It's complete and in one piece. Archivist Luella Kurkjian says it's too fragile to be taken out but the flag was certainly preserved for history."* In a later article on September 11, Burlingame adds: *"This week, we're back to Hawaiian flags that made history – and what happened to them. To update an earlier urban legend, there was a particularly vicious rumor that the Hawaiian flag that was lowered from Iolani Palace on Admission Day in 1898 was cut up for souvenirs, a whopper repeated recently by Sen. Dan Inouye. The flag is actually safely stored in the State Archives. The basis for that myth, as it turns out, is likely James Michener's novel "Hawaii," which noted that the flag was cut into strips. A fiction!"*

Mauna Ala (The Royal Mausoleum in Honolulu) today remains sovereign territory of the Kingdom of Hawaii, and U.S. law does not apply there[95]

The Royal Mausoleum contains the tombs of Kamehameha II, III, IV, V, King Kalakaua, Queen Liliuokalani, and other notables of the Hawaiian Kingdom including Englishman John Young and Princess Bernice Pauahi Bishop. The U.S. flag has never flown there, out of respect for the sensitivities of those who bitterly resent the overthrow of the monarchy and annexation to the U.S. even now, more than a century later.

The claim is that the Royal Mausoleum today remains the sovereign territory of the still-living Kingdom of Hawaii; and the laws of the U.S. and the State of Hawaii do not apply within its boundaries. The claim is that at the time of annexation, the 3.5 acres of the Royal Mausoleum were held back and not included in the ceded lands.

This claim has been repeatedly asserted in recent years in published newspaper articles intended to be taken as factual reports. There are so many historical falsehoods in today's Hawaiian sovereignty movement that it would be impossible to cover most of them here. This one is included because it illustrates an extreme level of zealotry grasping at a very thin reed of hope. The Kingdom still lives, firmly entrenched on 3.5 acres of land in the middle of urban Honolulu. Today the mausoleum, tomorrow the entire archipelago! It illustrates how political correctness and compassionate generosity are abused, so that a custom of refraining from flying the U.S. flag gets twisted into a grotesque assertion of national continuity. It also illustrates how Hawaiian zealotry makes use of mystery-mongering, the spiritual power of ancestral bones, and the living presence of historical figures to whom prayers are addressed in hopes they will intervene to restore the nation.

"Midweek" newspaper contains supermarket circulars and a substantial number of serious news reports and political commentaries. It is distributed free of charge every week to all households on the island of Oahu (including Honolulu). It is owned by the Honolulu Star-Bulletin. Don Chapman, editor of Midweek, authored a very lengthy article in two installments appearing as the cover stories of Volume 20, No. 4 of May 19, 2004 and No. 5 of May 26, 2004. An additional, related article was published in the Honolulu Star-Bulletin on Sunday October 30, 2005. The Midweek article was accompanied by photos of Mausoleum grounds, the Hawaiian flag flying alone, the beautifully decorated Kalakaua key to an underground crypt, etc. The article featured a lengthy interview with the man described in a front-page photo caption: *"William Kaihe'ekai Mai'oho, descended from two brothers chosen by Kamehameha the Great to hide his bones, continues a family tradition as curator of the Royal Mausoleum at Mauna Ala"*

On May 19 the following statements were made, some as comments by Chapman and some as quotes of Maioho:

"Our story is also about the only place in Hawaii where neither state nor federal land laws apply. These peaceful 3.5 acres are the last surviving remnant of the Kingdom of Hawaii." ... *"And who made it safe in that respect was Queen Lili'uokalani and George Wilcox [correction: should be Robert Wilcox]. Although they were political rivals and really didn't like each other, they worked together — he had the in as Hawaii's first delegate to Congress. "In May 1900 (seven years after the overthrow of the native monarchy) when the Organic Act was passed by the Congress of the United States, creating the Territory of Hawaii, Lili'uokalani and Wilcox worked to have Mauna Ala removed from the public domain. Which means that federal land laws do not apply to the grounds of Mauna Ala, nor now state laws. Mauna Ala is the only place that flies the Hawaiian flag by itself, honoring our ancestral chiefs. By American law, whenever a public facility opens, the American flag is highest, the state flag second. Here at Mauna Ala is proudly displayed only the flag of the nation of Hawaii, created by Kamehameha. So it's even more intense, even more of a symbol of Mauna Ala's separateness and sovereign status. I tell people, when you come to Mauna Ala, you enter a different world. ... It's magnificent and overwhelming, this thing, for lack of a better word, they created to care for us, the Hawaiian people. So Mauna Ala in this sense, this separateness again, it is a place of refuge. It is where our iwi, the most important part of our being, links us through the generations, to remember them and their aloha to us. ... Mauna Ala is immovable, and Queen Lili'uokalani did that for her ancestors, and for the Kamehamehas, to keep them secure and sacred, to have this inserted into the Organic Act. So only the flag of Kamehameha and the nation of Hawaii flies here. ... Queen Lili'uokalani, perhaps, is winking somewhere. Her kingdom was stolen, but she preserved a bit of it for all time at Mauna Ala by using the laws of the nation that helped steal her throne."*

A lengthy article in the Honolulu Star-Bulletin of October 30, 2005 describes an effort by mausoleum caretaker Maioho to get two sacred sticks returned by Kunani Nihipali of Hui Malama, who had "borrowed" them several years before. In the article are the following quotes:

Kenneth R. Conklin, Ph.D.

"Mai'oho said that when someone crosses the threshold of the gold-tipped gates of Mauna 'Ala, they come onto 3.5 acres of royal land under the Hawaiian flag. He said the Western world and its laws and customs are left behind on Nuuanu Avenue and that Hawaiians can relate to one another completely on Hawaiian terms. "If you are Hawaiian, your word is life and death, especially here," said Mai'oho. "Here, on Mauna 'Ala, we can be completely Hawaiian with one another." He noted that everything that is of Mauna 'Ala belongs there, including the pulo'ulo'u. "Even the dirt is consecrated here," he said. "It is blessed and it isn't taken from here."

So, what is the truth about ownership of this place, and about the claim that it was exempted from the transfer of the ceded lands?

A computer search of the complete text of the Organic Act shows that the words "Mauna Ala" or "Royal Mausoleum" were never mentioned. But as always with Hawaiian sovereignty claims, there is a mole hill factual element that got elevated into a mountain of sovereignty nonsense.

A joint resolution passed by Congress on May 31, 1900 as Public Resolution No. 28, says the following (nearly two years after annexation and one month after the Organic Act, as an afterthought):

"Resolved by the Senate and House of Representatives of the United States of America in Congress Assembled, That the following described lands lying and being situate in the city of Honolulu, Hawaiian Islands, heretofore used as a mausoleum for the royal family of Hawaii, to wit: the mausoleum premises, beginning at ... [detailed description of meets and bounds] ... be withdrawn from sale, lease, or other disposition under the public-land laws of the United States."

The following points from that resolution provide further evidence that Mauna Ala was never exempted from the Organic Act or in any way preserved as sovereign territory of the Kingdom of Hawaii following annexation: (1) That Mauna Ala resolution was a joint resolution of Congress, exercising control over Mauna Ala – the U.S. Congress clearly had control of Mauna Ala at the time the resolution passed on May 31, 1900. (2) Presumably Congress had that jurisdiction because Mauna Ala was part of the ceded lands. Note that the lands were ceded at the time of Annexation in August 1898, and that full implementation of annexation including all land issues were resolved in the Organic Act passed by the U.S. Congress on April 30, 1900; whereas the Mauna Ala resolution was passed on May 31, 1900. (3) The closing sentence of the resolution regulates disposition of Mauna Ala "... under the public land laws of the United States", not under the public land laws of the Kingdom of Hawaii. (4) The clear purpose of the resolution is to ensure that no U.S. bureaucrat in the Department of Interior will be able to sell, lease, or otherwise dispose of those 3.5 acres without an act of Congress – the resolution does not in any way exempt those lands from U.S. or Territorial law except for preventing their lease or sale. If a murder or theft were committed at the mausoleum today, the crime would be investigated and prosecuted by the State of Hawaii, not the Kingdom of Hawaii.

The City and County of Honolulu maintains careful records of all the real property on the island of Oahu, including assessed valuation and building permits. That information is now available at a government website. The address of Mauna Ala is 2261 Nuuanu Ave., as printed at the end of the newspaper article. Also, the correctness of that address is confirmed by the records contained on the property tax website for that address containing the name Royal Mausoleum in one of the building permits.

The "property information" for this address in 2004 (regarding the caretaker's home) said: Building Value: 75,700 ; Building Exempt: 75,700; Land Value: 2,615,800; Land Exempt: 2,615,800; Land Classification: Unimproved Residential. "Owner information" clearly says: STATE OF HAWAII Fee Owner. We can also find that a building permit was issued for a new curators' house in 1977, and the permit was issued not to the Kingdom of Hawaii but to "State of Hawaii/DLNR Div of State Parks - new curators residence at the Royal Mausoleum State Monument"

Is Hawaii legitimately the 50th state?

This issue was already discussed in Chapter 4. The claim is that the statehood vote of 1959 was contrary to international law because the ballot question failed to offer independence as a choice (and also because the United Nations requires an occupying power to remove its military forces before a status plebiscite takes place). But in Chapter 4 it was shown that the United Nations never required a three-way choice in a status plebiscite until at least a year and a half after the Hawaii statehood vote; and even years later the choices to be offered and the conditions for holding a status vote were very vague. There is nothing that binds the U.S. to follow whatever the zealots claim to be "international law." Those few people who might have wanted independence in 1959 could have voted "No" on the statehood question to show their displeasure; but in fact 94% voted "Yes." After the statehood vote the United Nations did in fact remove Hawaii from the list of non-self-governing territories eligible for decolonization. No other nation objected to doing that at the time; and no other nation has ever since then asked that Hawaii be reinscribed on the decolonization list.

Chapter 6

Current Victimhood Claims (Junk Science Fueling the Hawaiian Grievance Industry)

What claims are being made, and for what purpose?

How many times have we heard it said? Native Hawaiians are at the bottom among all Hawaii's ethnic groups on most important measures of well-being.

Hundreds of ethnic Hawaiian victimhood claims are asserted as generalities describing the entire racial group as being the worst, most disadvantaged, most poor and downtrodden. Sometimes the claims are limited to a single broad category such as income, education, disease, homelessness. Sometimes there are also specific claims about particular diseases or social dysfunctions like cancer, diabetes, drug abuse, incarceration for felonies, etc. Occasionally the claims are accompanied by specific percentage figures. Source citations are rarely given and are usually too general for a reader to be able to follow up or verify independently; for example: "The American Cancer Society reports that ..."

Ethnic Hawaiian victimhood "studies" are usually not subjected to peer review. By contrast, scientific journals require an article to be reviewed by a panel of outside experts before it can be published. Ethnic Hawaiian victimhood studies are often written in a way that makes them impossible to evaluate for validity or reliability. By contrast, scientific studies clearly explain how the data are relevant to a hypothesis, how the data were gathered, and what method was used to perform statistical analyses; thus scientific studies can be replicated by other researchers who might doubt the results. The purpose of the Hawaiian "studies" is not scientific but political.

The sheer number of victimhood claims, and the amount of data necessary to prove or disprove them, makes it impossible for any individual or small group to deal with them effectively. Huge amounts of government and philanthropic money are spent to create these "studies"; comparable megabucks and large staffs would be needed to evaluate them objectively. Hawaiian victimhood studies are often released at a time chosen for political purposes. Short summaries can be used for immediate propaganda value, while opponents have no time to make a rebuttal before the political process reaches its conclusion. Money and political backing are readily available to create victimhood "studies" but there is neither money nor glory for debunking them.

The purpose of putting forward victimhood claims is not merely to solicit sympathy and hand-holding. We've all complained to a friend about how bad life is, just to "get it all out" and get some TLC (tender loving care). The friend's job is to listen sympathetically, not to give hardheaded advice or charity. We share our feelings and bond emotionally.

But Hawaiian victimhood claims are not merely pleas for sympathy – they are demands for handouts. They are the kinds of statements made by an aggressive beggar who goes far beyond holding out a tin cup – he chases you down the street, grabs you by the collar, shakes you and yells in your face the reasons why he is begging and why you owe him money.

The Hawaiian grievance industry is big business. Powerful institutions with large highly-paid staffs comb through data collected by others such as the U.S. Census Bureau or the National Institutes of Health. The "researchers" look for data that can be used to portray ethnic Hawaiians as desperately in need of help, while ignoring conflicting or mitigating data. The results are then published as a "study." These studies are given to the media as press releases, or attached to applications for government or philanthropic grants. Much of the grant money is then spent to gather more data and generate more studies.

Sometimes grant money is actually used to deliver services to needy people; but usually such services are racially exclusionary, for ethnic Hawaiians only. The result is a severe racial skewing of social services. People lacking a drop of Hawaiian native blood are ignored or pushed to the side because hospitals, community health clinics, universities, and law schools turn toward the sources of money in the same way as the leaves of a plant turn toward the sun. There's plenty of money for breast cancer or diabetes screening and drug trials for ethnic Hawaiians; but far less money is available for Filipinos or Caucasians or for the general population. The most talented doctors, nurses, and administrators are sidetracked into racially exclusionary programs. They and their institutions feel compelled to pursue more racially exclusionary grants to keep their programs going; and they feel intimidated into supporting the political agenda of the Evil Empire.

Liberal politicians love to give the impression they are reaching out to help needy people. Liberal voters love to vote for such politicians and send them political contributions. Thus the Hawaiian grievance industry grows wealthy and powerful by using poor, needy people as poster-boys.

"Help Hawaii's indigenous people. Do it for the keiki (children). Native Hawaiians have the worst statistics among all Hawaii's ethnic groups. Save the next generation from this terrible fate. Mean-spirited haoles (Caucasians) are attacking programs that provide help to poor downtrodden Native Hawaiians – they are abusing civil rights laws passed after the Civil War that were intended to ensure equal treatment for former slaves. We need to protect the Hawaiian programs by passing the Akaka bill so that Native Hawaiians are provided the same political recognition as Native Americans and Native Alaskans. Fairness and justice demand it. America owes it to Native Hawaiians, to fulfill the reconciliation and restitution promised in the 1993 apology resolution."

Let there be no doubt why Alu Like, Papa Ola Lokahi, PASE(KSBE) and other race-based institutions are so eager to do research and gather data. They are not doing scientific studies just for the pleasure of increasing human knowledge, or appreciating the beautiful patterns in the data. They are looking for data to support their predetermined conclusions that ethnic Hawaiians have the worst statistics for whatever terrible thing is being studied. There's no money to be gotten for showing that Hawaiians are well off. The government gives money to institutions who produce the "right" evidence demonstrating a need for it. Drug companies give money to universities and research institutes to do studies that will provide evidence that a new drug produced by that company is safe and effective. There may or may not be unethical drug research like tossing out disagreeable data, selecting a sample likely to produce "good" results, etc. Drug companies have a long-term incentive not to use manipulated data to get FDA approval for a drug that is actually dangerous, because the company knows it will be sued if people die. Professors and scientists know their reputations are at stake because their work will be peer-reviewed and tested for replicability. But there are no such incentives for honesty in the Hawaiian grievance industry – all the incentives go toward proving Hawaiians are suffering.

There's also a vicious kind of racial profiling, stereotyping, and social injustice going on. Statistics is all about patterns and averages. Even if ethnic Hawaiians as a group have average results worse than other groups, that does not mean that all ethnic Hawaiian individuals are in bad shape. There are wide variations; with many ethnic Hawaiians doing extremely well. Nevertheless, if a study shows the average is bad, then government grants may be given to the group as a whole to provide benefits to every individual, including those who are already well off. Truly needy individuals of other groups get no help, because all the help is going to the "disadvantaged" group including individuals who are not disadvantaged at all. Thus an impoverished ethnic Filipina woman who already knows she has breast cancer and cannot afford treatment, might actually be paying taxes to provide breast cancer screening for a healthy, wealthy ethnic Hawaiian woman simply because "Native Hawaiians have the worst rate of breast cancer."

A few examples of some specific victimhood claims and their debunking

Later in this chapter there's an important general analysis of what's wrong with ethnic Hawaiian current victimhood claims. But first let's take a look at a few specific claims asserted in a typical newspaper article and why they are false or misleading. Readers should keep in mind that such claims are asserted frequently and in large numbers. It would require many books to list all the claims and debunk them. There's room here only to give a few examples.

A typical Hawaiian grievance industry "news report" was published in the Honolulu Advertiser on June 20, 2005. Ethnic affairs reporter Gordon Pang's article was entitled "Forced assimilation may hurt Hawaiians."[96]

"News reporter" Pang writes "'Cultural trauma' caused by forced assimilation into Western culture continues to wreak havoc on the health and well-being of Native Hawaiians even today, according to a Hilo, Hawai'i, researcher." The article then cites one brief assertion about the lifespan of ethnic Hawaiian men; and several paragraphs of data regarding the percentages of various ethnic groups and genders who smoke tobacco.

Was there really "forced assimilation" in Hawaii? If so, who was to blame? And what connection would there be between events from more than two centuries ago and current health statistics?

Hawaiian Apartheid

"Forced assimilation" in Hawaii was done first by Kamehameha the Great, who ruthlessly killed all his opponents and decimated entire villages in order to unify Hawai'i under his dictatorship. Kamehameha succeeded where others had failed because he was clever enough to trade local commodities produced by slave labor (sandalwood, taro, sweet potatoes, fresh water) in order to get spectacular new technology never seen in Hawaii before, to use as weapons of mass destruction (guns, canons, metal knives, and large ships). The military force that made all the natives assimilate to the control of one ruthless dictator was wielded by a native, not an outsider. The destruction of Hawaii's sandalwood forests, and starvation of countless families forced out of their taro fields to gather sandalwood to enrich their chiefs, was done by natives to other natives.

The next candidate for "forced assimilation" was the abandonment of the ancient native religion and its replacement with Christianity. But the ancient religion was abandoned by order of Liholiho Kamehameha II and regent Ka'ahumanu in 1819. They publicly broke an important taboo at a large luau in order to impress everyone that they were overthrowing the old religion (The taboo was that men and women were not allowed to eat together; and the penalty was instant death. So when the King and his regent stepmother sat down together in public and began to eat, that shocking and terrifying event utterly destroyed the old religion; and they did it intentionally with full knowledge of the consequences). These native chiefs then publicly ordered the heiau (temples) to be destroyed and the wooden god-idols to be burned. Then they won a short civil war against a minority of chiefs who wanted to keep the old religion. These things happened several months before the first Christian missionaries arrived in 1820.

Those Christian missionaries came to Hawaii because natives invited them. Several natives (including the crown prince of Kauai) had found their way to Yale divinity school and became Christians. Opukahaia (Christianized to Henry Obookiah) pleaded with his new friends at Yale to send missionaries to save his people from their heathen ways.[97] At Yale, and then during the long voyage to Hawaii, the natives taught the missionaries how to speak Hawaiian, and helped them create an alphabet and a written version of the language. Once the missionaries arrived, Hawaii's natives were so glad to learn reading and writing, and so delighted to have a new religion to replace the old one, that they converted to Christianity in droves.

Thus, assimilation to Christianity and to the replacement of oral tradition with written language was entirely voluntary, not forced. Those men who would have been killed as human sacrifices to the old gods, and those women who would have been executed for the capital sin of eating a banana, were undoubtedly glad their nation assimilated to Christianity.

The next candidate for "forced assimilation" was the adoption of a written Constitution in 1840, replacing autocratic power; and the adoption of private property deeds in 1848, replacing feudal land ownership. These things were done by the request and under the authority of King Kauikeaouli Kamehameha III. A few natives (e.g., David Malo) protested the changes and the role of the King's white advisors; but the King (with the consent of nearly all the chiefs) exercised self-determination on behalf of his people to embrace this "assimilation" voluntarily, not because of outside force.

The second part of Gordon Pang's article reports a few health statistics. "... a study done by the state Department of Health in 2002 concluded that a Hawaiian male, on average will die six years earlier than the average male in all other populations ..." That citation was far too sketchy to trace. Using the internet it was possible to find a webpage healthtrends.org which said it was relying on the State of Hawaii statistical abstract databook for 2003.

According to those tables,[98] in 1990 the average life expectancy in Hawaii for men and women combined was was 78.9, while ethnic Hawaiian life expectancy was 74.27. That's a difference of 4.63 years. We know that women live longer than men, so perhaps a comparison of men with men would indeed yield a discrepancy of 6 years (rounded up), as the article says.

However, what was left out of the newspaper report is also very interesting. The same results cited above also show that in 1990 the average life expectancy in Hawaii for Caucasians was 75.53, Chinese 82.93, Filipino 78.94, ethnic Hawaiian 74.27, Japanese 82.06. Caucasians were "hurting" almost as badly as ethnic Hawaiians, living only one year longer than them; while all three Asian categories (Chinese, Japanese, Filipino) have substantially longer lifespans. So, why are there no studies about the short life expectancy of Caucasians in comparison with the overall Hawaii average, and especially in comparison with Chinese who live to 82.9 while Caucasians live to only 75.5? Why are there no studies about Caucasians? Because there is no Office of Caucasian Affairs. There are plenty of Congressional acts appropriating money for Papa Ola Lokahi, but not one penny for (non-existent) Papa Ola Haole.

Some very important topics were never mentioned on the issue of life expectancy. The life expectancy of ethnic Hawaiians has increased dramatically and steadily throughout the ten decades of U.S. sovereignty in Hawaii. Data seem to be unavailable for the life expectancy of native Hawaiians prior to the arrival of Captain Cook in 1778, and for the period of the Hawaiian kingdom. But the same webpage cited earlier reports the following: "Life expectancy in Hawaii has improved dramatically since 1910 when it was less than 44 years. It was not until 1950 that life expectancy in Hawaii surpassed that of the U.S. and has continued to exceed the U.S. since then." The life expectancy for all Hawaii's population (all ethnicities and men and women combined) was as follows: 1910: 44; 1920: 45.7; 1930: 54.0; 1940: 62.0; 1950 69.5; 1960: 72.4; 1970: 74.2; 1980: 77.8; 1990: 78.9; 2000: 79.9. The life expectancy of ethnic Hawaiians has increased in proportion to that of Hawaii's overall population. Assimilation, U.S. sovereignty, and statehood have been good for everyone, including ethnic Hawaiians. But Gordon Pang chose not to report that fact.

The National Cancer Institute sums it up nicely in its report "Cancer in Native Hawaiian Women."[99] On page 6 the report says *"life expectancy for Native Hawaiian women has increased considerably since the beginning of the century; life expectancy went from 32 years in 1910 to 64 years in 1950 and to 77 years in 1990 (Park et al., 1979; Braun et al., 1997; Yang et al., 1996). The gap among ethnic groups has been diminishing. Whereas in 1970 there was a 6-year difference in the life expectancy of Native Hawaiian women compared to White women, in 1990 the difference had decreased to 1.5 years (Anderson, 1998)."* It's interesting that the data reported by NCI differ significantly from the earlier "health-trends" webpage.

Here's another important point not mentioned by "news" reporter Gordon Pang. The life expectancy of ethnic Hawaiians in Hawaii compares very favorably with the life expectancy of ethnic Tongans in Tonga. This comparison is important in discussing the effects of "forced assimilation" or political sovereignty. Tonga remains an independent nation under a monarchy, just as the Hawaiian Kingdom was and just as some Hawaiian sovereignty activists would like Hawaii once again to become. The people of Tonga are Polynesians, just like Native Hawaiians. But the life expectancy of ethnic Hawaiians in Hawaii is significantly better than for Tongans in Tonga. Indeed, many Tongans come to Hawaii for both jobs and healthcare, while few if any Hawaiians go to Tonga for jobs or healthcare – that says a lot about which place is more desirable to live in and which place has a better economy and healthcare system.

Tonga's population in 2002 was estimated at 110,237. Life expectancy in Tonga (98% are ethnic Tongan) in 2002 was 68.56 (male and female combined), whereas life expectancy in Hawaii for ethnic Hawaiians in 1990 (12 years earlier) was 74.27 (male and female combined) and higher by 2000 and 2002. It's also worth mentioning that in Tonga, according to the U.S. State Department fact sheet, the Gross Domestic Product per person in 2004 was estimated to be $1,287 in U.S. dollars.[100] According to Census 2000 the median family income for ethnic Hawaiians in 1999 was $49,282 and 13.1% of them had incomes above $100,000 even though their median age was only 25.3 (compared to a statewide median age of 36.2).[101]

In his "news report" Gordon Pang says *"... The findings reaffirmed earlier studies that showed Native Hawaiians with a greater prevalence of smoking than other ethnicities, and a greater percentage of Native Hawaiian women who smoke than Native Hawaiian men. The research by Kaholokua's group showed 20.8 percent of Native Hawaiians smoke, a larger percentage than the other groups studied. Among other groups, 17.6 percent of Filipinos, 11.6 percent of Caucasians and 7.7 percent of Japanese surveyed smoke. What's more, Kaholokua's group found that 22.1 percent of Native Hawaiian women smoke, more than Filipinos (13.8 percent), Caucasians (11.1 percent) and Japanese (3.7 percent). Among men, 23 percent of Filipinos reported smoking, followed by Native Hawaiians (19.2 percent), Caucasians (12.1 percent) and Japanese (11.8 percent)."*

But something is badly wrong about those data. For example, the U.S. government Centers for Disease Control reported Current Cigarette Smoking Among Adults Aged 18 and Older, 1997 – All States 23.2%, Hawaii 18.6%; By Gender Men 21.4% Women 15.8%. Also Current Cigarette Smoking Among Adults by Race/Ethnicity, 1996-1997, White 20.3, Black 20.9, Hispanic 23.8, Asian/Pacific Islander 19.2.[102]

Periodically the U.S. Census Bureau adds a supplemental interview on tobacco use onto its regular monthly Current Population Survey. Based on data collected during 2000 and 2001, the results were reported by the Substance Abuse and Mental Health Services Administration of the U.S. Department of Health. The report includes data tables showing what percentage of people in each of various ethnic groups are tobacco smokers. However, in that report, the row for "Native Hawaiian" has a * rather than a percentage number; and this is true for every table in the report. The * refers to a footnote which says "Low precision, no estimate reported." So, we must wonder how Keawe'aimoku Kaholokua was able to get reliable data when the U.S. Census Bureau and the prestigious SAMHSA felt compelled to report "Low precision, no estimate reported."[103]

That's enough fooling around with statistics. There are thousands of studies of Native Hawaiian income, longevity, health, etc. mostly paid for with taxpayer dollars. Somebody is getting rich, and it's not those poor, downtrodden, disease-ridden ethnic Hawaiians! For example, the National Cancer Institute compiled a list of several dozen studies focusing mostly on the topic of cancer in ethnic Hawaiian women.[104] Reading the titles of those studies, we must wonder how many women actually received treatment because of them, vs. how many dollars were funneled into the bloated bureaucracies that cited the studies in their grant applications for funds to do more studies.

Gordon Pang's article "Forced assimilation may hurt Hawaiians" is typical of the sort of nonsense the media publish in Hawaii, combining both junk history (distortions, half-truths, and outright falsehoods) and junk science (statistics not backed up with sources, data carefully selected to bolster a predetermined outcome when other data might support an opposite conclusion). These junks are shouted through the media megaphone so often that everyone comes to believe them. The junks are stated very matter-of-factly and with great brevity, while evidence and arguments to the contrary would require extensive research, lots of time to assemble, and highly specialized expertise available only to those who have plenty of time or money. What we've seen in this section of this book is an example of the difficulty of correcting a very short junk-history slogan ("forced assimilation") by providing historical evidence and reasoning to counteract it, and correcting some junk science (hurting Hawaiians) by providing preliminary results of a few hours of inexpert research that suggest the facts might be inaccurate or incomplete.

Kamehameha Schools PASE – the Daddy Warbucks among tycoons of the Hawaiian grievance industry

According to the will of Princess Bernice Pauahi Bishop, the sole purpose of Bishop Estate (whose name is now changed to Kamehameha Schools) is to establish and sustain two schools, one for boys and one for girls. There was nothing in the will that required admissions to be limited to ethnic Hawaiians only. There was nothing that required even a racial preference, except for the one category of children who were orphans or indigents. Yet Kamehameha Schools has practiced near-total racial exclusion for 120 years. And it has expanded its mission beyond the wildest imaginings of Princess Pauahi. Its land holdings and investment portfolio are now valued at an estimated $8-15 billion depending how the land assets are valued – more than the endowment of Harvard or Yale University. Kamehameha owns enormously valuable property including the Royal Hawaiian shopping center in Waikiki, and Windward Mall in Kaneohe. It provides millions of dollars to public charter schools focused on Hawaiian culture, and to ordinary public schools where significant numbers of ethnic Hawaiians are attending. But Kamehameha also uses its massive wealth to help other racially exclusionary institutions gather data, apply for government grants, and launch propaganda campaigns.

PASE is the Policy Analysis and System Evaluation branch of Kamehameha Schools, which does research and report writing on many topics. Its website[105] describes its mission as follows: "As the research and data gathering arm of Kamehameha Schools, PASE is committed to advancing Kamehameha Schools' mission: 'To fulfill Pauahi's desire to create educational opportunities in perpetuity to improve the capability and well-being of people of Hawaiian ancestry.' PASE supports this mission through objective, nonpartisan research on social and educational issues that affect the lives of Hawaiians." PASE produces numerous "studies" to highlight ethnic Hawaiian victimhood statistics, and also to falsely portray ethnic Hawaiian charter schools as being incredibly successful at improving the education of children previously left behind by the ordinary heterogeneous public schools.

In September 2005 Kamehameha's publishing arm "Pauahi Publications" produced a monster grievance book by PASE. "Ka Huaka'i": a "Native Hawaiian Educational Assessment" gathered together 450 pages of the most impressive victimhood "studies." But even before the book was actually printed they rushed to give reporters and the general public an "executive summary" that was truly astonishing. That summary, at 11,462 kilobytes, required 45 minutes to download using dialup internet; and the pdf file was only 20 pages long! The lengthy download was necessary because the 20 pages were filled with beautiful pictures of children and flowers. The sparse amount of text was written in a slick style, arranged to fit in the petals of tropical flowers. It was a real propaganda masterpiece – form with hardly any substance.[106]

The timing of "Ka Huaka'i" was crucial. The Akaka bill was poised for action in the Senate, partly justified by claims that ethnic Hawaiians are poor, downtrodden victims of history. A lawsuit against the Office of Hawaiian Affairs was underway, in which part of the defense was the claim that ethnic Hawaiians are an indigenous people desperately in need of help. It was also the very moment when Kamehameha Schools was seeking en banc review of an unfavorable 9th Circuit Court decision regarding Kamehameha's racially exclusionary admissions policy – a decision where the District Judge had ruled in favor of Kamehameha primarily on the theory that Kamehameha is providing affirmative action for sorely-needed remediation of educational deficits. The slick 20-page executive summary was publicized in the newspapers (and in Congress) even though the 450-page book was not yet printed. Thus the forthcoming book got its big propaganda bang before the contents were available for scrutiny and possible debunking. Even if the data had been released immediately, they would be so massive that a group of experts would need years to determine whether the data are both valid and reliable; i.e., whether the data actually address the claims being made and whether the method of analysis was scientifically and mathematically correct. The group of experts would need to include statisticians, medical doctors, educators, sociologists, etc. If such a study were being published in a scientific journal it would be sent out for peer review before being published; and the review might well take a year.

In 2004 PASE published a 15-page report by Iwalani R.N. Else entitled "The Breakdown of the Kapu System and Its Effect on Native Hawaiian Health and Diet."[107] The report claims that abolishing the old religion (nearly 200 years ago!) is responsible for bad health statistics among today's ethnic Hawaiians, and the solution might be Dr. Shintani's "Waianae" diet based on poi and other traditional foods. Else says: "Since 'discovery' in 1778 by Captain James Cook, Native Hawaiian culture and practices have changed substantially. In a land they once called their own, Native Hawaiians found themselves alienated not only from the land, but also from themselves and others. This article focuses on historical changes in Hawai'i and how the breakdown of the precontact system in Hawai'i led to the adoption of Western culture and practices. In particular, the article examines how diet changes affected general health of Native Hawaiians."

However, no cause-and-effect relationship is argued, and no comparison between ethnic Hawaiians and other ethnic groups is offered to see whether switching from high-fat fast-food diets to the Waianae diet is especially good for Hawaiians, or whether it is equally helpful to all ethnic groups. The report merely provides a review of the ancient Hawaiian taboo system and some of the changes that took place, interspersed with modern statistics focusing on high rates of metabolic diseases among ethnic Hawaiians. The report is mostly propaganda, using the device of mentioning two different things at the same time as a way of implying (but never proving) that one is the cause of the other.

Another short essay entitled "Legacy of a Broken Heart"[108] literally claims a connection between a metaphorical broken heart and a physical broken heart. The abstract reads: *"This article reviews the Native Hawaiians' health-status and socio-economic survival in general, and the co-morbidity of depression and cardiovascular disease in particular. The etiology of chronic depression among Native Hawaiians is examined in theoretical paradigms that take into account the historical context of colonization and cultural disintegration. An argument is made to assert that the severe psychological effects of cultural conflict and acculturation of Native Hawaiians are reflected by their poor physical health status, notably the high mortality rate for heart disease. Special attention is given to the discussion of sovereignty as a solution to the survival of the Native Hawaiian people."*

Why ethnic Hawaiian victimhood statistics are unreliable or misleading, and what terrible prescriptions we must write if they are correct

(1) Age

It's shocking but true: the average age of ethnic Hawaiians is 14 years younger than the average age of Hawaii's non-ethnic-Hawaiians. The average age of ethnic Hawaiians in Hawaii is only 25. The general population of Hawaii (including ethnic Hawaiians) has an average age of 36. But ethnic Hawaiians are about 20% of Hawaii's population. Simple arithmetic shows that removing ethnic Hawaiians from the population would result in an average age of 39 for everyone else.

At age 25 people have only recently finished school. They're just getting started on a career, and their incomes are low. But by age 39 people have gotten well established in their careers and are earning much higher salaries. Of course people with average age of 25 have high unemployment, incarceration, drug abuse etc. compared to people with average age of 39. The sins of youth! Thus many "Native Hawaiian" victimhood claims are not really about "Native Hawaiians" at all – they are about age.

Although the average income of "Native Hawaiians" is somewhat lower than the state average, the difference is only about 9%. That seems entirely reasonable in view of the fact that "Native Hawaiians" have an average age of only 25, compared with 36 for the state as a whole.

In Census 2000, the median household income for "Native Hawaiians" was $45,381, and their median age was 25.3. In Census 2000, the median household income for the population of Hawaii as a whole was $49,820, and the median age was 36.2. Also in Census 2000, 12% of all "Native Hawaiians" had household income ABOVE $100,000. Surely those wealthy people should not be eligible for government handouts based on the racial profiling of "Native Hawaiians" as poor and downtrodden.[109]

A related issue was addressed by another Kamehameha PASE report publicized in another Gordon Pang Advertiser article on September 27, 2005. "Native Hawaiian" population is projected to more than double by year 2050, with the average age becoming even younger.[110] Thus we might reasonably conclude that the poor statistics for income, drug abuse, criminality, etc. can be expected to worsen. A frequent spokesperson for ethnic Hawaiians, Lilikala Kameeleihiwa, actually urges "her people" to try to double their population in only 20 years rather than 50, as Gordon Pang reported in his article. She wants them to become a majority of the state's total population as soon as possible and thereby gain political power.[111] There's evidence that ethnic Hawaiian girls are eagerly working to make Kameeleihiwa's dream come true, since ethnic Hawaiian girls are having illegitimate babies at triple the rate of other ethnic groups – the State of Hawaii data book for 2002 shows that 55% of ethnic Hawaiian babies in Hawaii are born to unmarried women, as opposed to 17% for Caucasian babies.[112] Thus we can expect the bad ethnic Hawaiian statistics to become even worse in the years ahead, partly caused by a deliberate political strategy to make babies as fast as possible.

(2) The "one drop" rule

All that's required to be called "Native Hawaiian" is to have one drop of Hawaiian native blood. Most "Native Hawaiians" are mostly not of Hawaiian native ancestry. Perhaps 75% of all "Native Hawaiians" have more than 75% of their ancestry from Asia, Europe, and America. The actual percentages are probably not known, and might not be knowable. There seems to be no systematic collection of blood quantum data. Furthermore, people might not report their genealogy accurately, especially when government and philanthropic handouts are at stake.

Kenneth R. Conklin, Ph.D.

The number of Hawaiians with 50% or more native blood quantum SHOULD be knowable, because every such person is eligible to be placed on the waiting list for a Hawaiian Homestead lease under terms of the Hawaiian Homes Commission Act of 1921. The State of Hawaii Department of Hawaiian Homelands maintains the list of those who have signed up, but has no way of knowing how many additional people who qualify simply do not know about the program or chose not to sign up.

When someone with 1/64 Hawaiian native blood quantum is diagnosed with breast cancer, the Hawaiian grievance industry chalks up one full tally mark. That's clearly wrong.

Any honest statistical analysis that claims to assign specific outcomes to specific racial groups should either assign those outcomes to the racial group with the highest percentage of blood quantum in that individual's ancestry, or else (much better!) allocate a fractional tally mark to each race equal to that person's fraction of blood quantum.

Such fractional allocation would also make it possible to show whether women with higher native blood quantum also have higher rates of breast cancer than women with lower native blood quantum, thus providing evidence that being "Native Hawaiian" is highly correlated with (and might be a genetic cause of) this disease. Just imagine how many millions of dollars Papa Ola Lokahi could get from the National Institutes of Health to gather the data and perform the statistical analysis! What a wonderful guarantee of job security in the institutional bureaucracy! Why don't they do it? Perhaps they know that the resulting data analysis would blow a huge hole in the Hawaiian grievance industry.

Allocating tally marks in the way the Hawaiian grievance industry currently does it, by counting any smidgen of native blood quantum as a full tally mark for ethnic Hawaiians, and following that same policy for every racial group, we might discover some remarkable data. For example, here's a totally fictitious illustration of what might be discovered: 40% of incarcerated criminals are ethnic Hawaiian, 60% are ethnic Chinese (many Hawaiians are also Chinese; or is it the other way around?), 70% are ethnic Filipino (they are more recent immigrants and therefore less assimilated and more rowdy), 50% are ethnic Japanese, and 40% are ethnic Caucasian. That total of 260% doesn't yet include the Koreans, Vietnamese, Tongans, Samoans, Africans, Hispanics, etc. The percentages total far more than 100% because so many people have so many races mixed in their ancestries.

Allocating one tally mark per person according to the single race that is the highest percentage in an individual's makeup would produce much tamer results, adding up to 100%. Allocating fractional tally marks according to fractional blood quantum percentages would also add up to 100%, and would clearly be the most accurate way to attribute outcomes to racial groups.

Fractional allocation of outcomes is not only appropriate for race – it should also be applied to culture. The underlying concept of giving fractional tally marks for a single case of breast cancer to different racial groups based on fraction of blood quantum is not limited to physical outcomes nor to racial causes. It could also be applied to cultural outcomes and cultural causes. It would be extremely difficult and politically controversial to develop a taxonomy of cultural behaviors. But such a taxonomy is necessary to find correlations between race and culture. For example: having the Hawaiian gene might be correlated with (or might actually cause) a desire to eat poi or a tendency to engage in thievery. Such a taxonomy of cultural behaviors might also facilitate "studies" showing correlations between cultural upbringing and physical victimhood. For example: working in the taro patch or eating poi causes breast cancer.

There are many victimhood claims asserting that ethnic Hawaiians have bad statistics for disease and social dysfunction. The grievance industry is unclear whether the bad results are being attributed to genetics or lifestyle. The grievance industry really doesn't want to know – all they care about is to make demands for race-based (or is it culture-based?) government handouts and political power. It's politically incorrect to say that ethnic Hawaiians are doomed to failure because of either their genes or their Hawaiian culture. But the only way to find out whether ethnic victimhood truly exists, and whether it is caused by genetics or by culture, is to gather blood quantum data and allocate victimhood tally marks fractionally among various races and cultures. That's also the only way to generate plausible hypotheses for a cure.

(3) Mortality rates

Everyone eventually dies. Shocking, but true! And nobody dies more than once. So when the Hawaiian grievance industry says that "Native Hawaiians" have the highest mortality rate for breast cancer, isn't it obvious that they must also have the lowest mortality rate for some other disease? There are only so many Hawaiians, and each one can only die once. Furthermore, whatever diseases "Native Hawaiians" have comparatively low mortality rates for, it must be true that some other ethnic group has comparatively high mortality rates for those diseases. So, in order to protect the interests of Caucasians (for example), there should be a Papa Ola Lokahi Haole funded by millions of federal dollars to gather and analyze the data for all those diseases for which white people have comparatively high mortality rates. Likewise a Papa Ola Lokahi Kepani to do the corresponding job for people of Japanese ancestry. Of course it's silly to propose the haole and Japanese institutions. Why then do we not see that it is equally silly to have the Hawaiian institution? But there's nothing silly about the obvious fact that if a racial group is to be singled out as having a high mortality rate for some diseases, then that same group must have low mortality rates for other diseases while other racial groups have higher mortality rates. Because everybody dies, and only dies once. It is statistically impossible for "Native Hawaiians" to have the worst mortality rates for the majority of deadly diseases, just as it is statistically impossible for the majority of children to have above-average intelligence.

(4) Evolution and species differentiation in an isolated environment

Darwinian "natural selection", or evolution, might explain why "Native Hawaiians" have bad statistics (both physically and socially). This is not as silly as it might sound.

We know there are many species of animals and plants endemic to Hawaii (i.e., totally unique and found nowhere else in the world). Those endemic species (or varieties) are the result of ancestors of a parent genus or species who somehow came to Hawaii, found themselves isolated with no further outside contact, and engaged in many generations of inbreeding and adaptation to the local environment.

When humans first arrived in Hawaii 2,000 years ago, they made changes to the physical and cultural environment. They brought new animals and plants that resulted in the extinction or crippling of some endemic species. New diseases caused problems for endemic species, along with changes to the physical environment such as fishing, making fires, channelizing water, plucking particular colors of bird feathers, etc.

Today's Hawaiian activists like to say they have been here from time immemorial. Archeological evidence (and the Polynesian voyaging propaganda) suggests about 2,000 years. "Native Hawaiians" have had perhaps 100 generations of inbreeding, with perhaps no outside additions to the gene pool or culture between the Tahitian invasion (circa 1200 AD?) and the European arrival in 1778.

It seems perfectly reasonable to suggest that native Hawaiians adapted to the local physical and cultural environment in ways that became genetically encoded through inbreeding and the survival of the fittest (that's the core principle of the theory of evolution). Inbreeding was magnified because of cultural customs favoring the mating of brothers and sisters with each other and with close relatives. Inbreeding was also magnified because Hawaii's geography of valley ridges running from mountains to sea, and a feudal system of land tenure, made it difficult for most people to mate outside their small geographic area.

When Western civilization arrived, new diseases were introduced. There were also huge changes in the physical environment caused by whaling, the sugar industry, the creation of private property, introduction of metal and gunpowder, the mechanization of food production and preservation, etc.

It takes many generations before an organism can adapt to a changing physical environment. Thus "Native Hawaiians" may simply be physiologically (genetically) unable to cope with today's physical environment. The same argument might be made regarding the cultural environment.

Some activists say that race (genealogy) somehow is related to culture, or that cultural skills (such as Polynesian voyaging) are genetically encoded through "racial memory" of "deep culture." A theory of "Hawaiian epistemology" says that anyone with a drop of Hawaiian native blood has genetically encoded unique ways of thinking and of perceiving the world. Theories of racial memory, deep culture, and Hawaiian epistemology will be discussed in Chapter 8. The logical conclusion is that ethnic Hawaiians need a separate education system where they control what subject matter gets taught and what methods are used for teaching it.

Assertion of genetic determination of social needs and cultural behavior is very dangerous, and has been the cause of great misery in places like Germany, Bosnia, Rwanda, Zimbabwe.

Is the claim being made that there is some kind of genetic factor whereby the Hawaiian gene causes cancer, or alcoholism, or criminal behavior? A lot of scientists got in a whole lot of trouble for suggesting that such a question might perhaps be studied scientifically with regard to "Negroes." Harvard University expelled Professor Arthur Jensen for daring to raise such questions. We today condemn the Nazis for suggesting that Jews had genetic predispositions to immorality or criminality and the best solution would be "the final solution."

Nevertheless, it seems that the "Native Hawaiian" victimhood "studies" are intended to lead to precisely that kind of conclusion – the studies seem designed to prove that the mere fact of BEING Hawaiian is sufficient to warrant at least reasonable suspicion, or perhaps probable cause, that an individual is doomed to cancer, drug abuse, and incarceration; and must be given massive amounts of government assistance administered by highly paid bureaucrats in institutions belonging to the Council for Native Hawaiian Advancement.

If "Native Hawaiians" are either biologically or culturally incapable of living in modern "Western" society, what are the alternatives? It seems there are only two possibilities, neither of which is morally acceptable or politically feasible.

Science fiction novels describe the choice facing human settlers on planets where the environment is inhospitable to human biology. Either biomorph or terraform. Biomorph: engineer changes to the genome of the human settlers to make future generations whose bodies are more compatible with the planet's environment (would they still be human with one eye, eight tentacles instead of two arms, and an exoskeleton like a lobster?). Terraform: engineer changes to the planet's environment to make it more like Earth (destroying all environmental features and life forms hostile to humans as humans are presently constituted).

The biomorph solution to ethnic Hawaiian victimhood is genetic therapy to change the "Hawaiian" gene, to make "Native Hawaiians" more like the Caucasians and Asians whose genetic composition has clearly proved to be superior to the Hawaiian genome in terms of survival and flourishing in the existing physical and social environment of Hawaii. But we have already seen that "Native Hawaiians" are strongly opposed to doing anything remotely close to genetic engineering. There are strong objections to digging up the bones of long-dead distantly-related ancestors. Even artifacts buried with the dead are sometimes regarded as untouchable (the Forbes Cave controversy).[113] Recently there was heated objection to a proposal that the University of Hawaii might do genetic engineering of taro to make it more able to resist modern diseases and snails – because taro is mankind's elder brother and a part of the Hawaiian genome according to the creation legend in Kumulipo.

The terraform solution to ethnic Hawaiian victimhood is to hand over the entire physical and cultural environment of Hawaii to racially (or culturally) defined "Native Hawaiians" so they can put everything back the way they need it to be ("Pono" – everything in balance). At the extreme, that restoraton of "pono" might include knocking down all the high-rise buildings, demolishing the expressways, requiring everyone to give several days of labor per month to communal projects like digging ditches to send water to taro patches, and sending all non-ethnic Hawaiians to live in restricted areas or to leave the islands.

The Akaka bill is being pushed today partly by saying it is needed to "empower" "Native Hawaiians" to begin exercising that second option – "Native Hawaiians" are entitled to "self-determination" so they can control their own (and everyone else's) physical (land) and cultural (intellectual property) environment. The claim is that "indigenous rights" grant racial supremacy to anyone with a drop of Hawaiian native blood, because they are the hosts in their ancestral homeland and everyone else is merely a guest. Scary. Can't we all just get along?

(5) A needs-based social welfare system

Suppose help is given to people in a race-neutral way based on need alone. Then "Native Hawaiians" will automatically get the lion's share of the help, if "Native Hawaiians" truly have the worst statistics among all ethnic groups. The 450-page Kamehameha monster victimhood book is actually a 450-page proof that "Native Hawaiians" will get more help than other ethnic groups if help is given based on need alone. For "Native Hawaiians" to demand more government and philanthropic assistance than would be warranted by their needs is both selfish and racially divisive.

(6) Hawaii's race-based programs have failed miserably

Lyndon Johnson's "War on Poverty" has been stunningly unsuccessful despite 40 years and trillions of dollars. We saw that most dramatically when Hurricane Katrina ripped through New Orleans, exposing a vast underbelly of poverty.

Likewise, in Hawaii we see that Kamehameha Schools, with $8-$15 billion in assets, has been unable to give ethnic Hawaiians the same educational level as other ethnic groups, despite 120 years of racially exclusionary programs. Alu Like has been getting racially exclusionary federal grants for 30 years; yet ethnic Hawaiians still (allegedly) have the worst statistics for income, unemployment, and social dysfunction. OHA, with about $400 million in assets, has been unable to make a dent in the (allegedly) bad economic and social statistics of ethnic Hawaiians despite 25 years of racially exclusionary benefit programs. The Hawaiian Homes Commission Act of 1921, administered since 1959 by the State of Hawaii, has created racial ghettos where poor Hawaiians are prohibited by law from participating in the most wealth-creating activity available to most Americans – ownership of homes which grow in capital value.

(7) Good news: ethnic Hawaiians in other states have above-average well-being statistics (despite lack of Hawaii's race-based handouts)

Recent Census data from other states show that "Native Hawaiians" in those states are actually doing better than average for the populations of those states. This is stunning news. Why do ethnic Hawaiians outside Hawaii do spectacularly better than ethnic Hawaiians inside Hawaii? It seems clear that no good has resulted from the large number of race-based handouts given over a period of many years by the State of Hawaii, where ethnic Hawaiians suffer bad statistics. Ethnic Hawaiians in other states are thriving despite not having access to Hawaii handouts.

A reasonable conclusion is that ethnic Hawaiians in Hawaii have actually been harmed by the race-based welfare programs. Perhaps the harm is caused because many ethnic Hawaiians get handouts which make it unnecessary for them to struggle for success like everyone else. They are robbed of motivation, knowing their basic needs will be met by government handouts even if they do nothing to earn a living.

Of course there are many ethnic Hawaiians in Hawaii who work hard. There are many who earn or inherit great wealth, and can easily pay for the best quality of housing, healthcare, and education. But at the lower end of the scale ethnic Hawaiians can do in Hawaii what they cannot do in other states, and what other ethnic groups cannot do in Hawaii – kick back; enjoy a heavily subsidized lifestyle with low but acceptable income, healthcare, and housing. Ethnic Hawaiians in Hawaii who choose to accept the plethora of government and philanthropic race-based handouts can spend their time not working, but complaining about historical grievances while agitating for even more handouts.

Following is the complete text of an article published by Jere Krischel in Hawaii Reporter newspaper (online) on January 11, 2007. The article cites U.S. Census data gathered in 2005 for ethnic Hawaiians living in California, the state with the largest population of ethnic Hawaiians (65,000) outside Hawaii (about 250,000).[114]

Hawaiian Apartheid

Census: Native Hawaiians Do Better When Treated Equally
By Jere Krischel

The 2005 American Community Survey for California, recently released by the U.S. Census Bureau, confirms Native Hawaiians' ability to prosper without special government programs. The estimated 65,000 Native Hawaiian residents of California, with no Office of Hawaiian Affairs or Hawaiian Homes or other such race-based entitlements, enjoyed higher median household ($55,610) and family ($62,019) incomes, relative to the total California population ($53,629 and $61,476 respectively) despite having smaller median household and family sizes.

California is particularly appropriate for comparing earning power, because California has the greatest Native Hawaiian population outside of Hawaii; and it happens that the median age of Native Hawaiians residing in California (33.7 years) is almost identical to that of the general population of California (33.4 years).

The fact that Native Hawaiians are quite capable of making it on their own was suggested by Census 2000 which showed the then-60,000 Native Hawaiian residents of California enjoyed comparable relative median household and family incomes despite their 5 year younger median age.

California a fluke?

Some may argue that the Native Hawaiian statistics in other states represent an out-migration of well-to-do Native Hawaiians. The idea of large swaths of rich Native Hawaiians leaving paradise for the mainland seems counter intuitive, but for argument's sake, let's consider it.

If in fact all the rich Native Hawaiians are leaving the state of Hawaii, let's say because of onerous taxes or the lack of fine avocados, the lower statistics of those Native Hawaiians who have stayed in Hawai'i are simply an artifact of the well-off moving away, and not due to any systemic bias against Native Hawaiians. Removing the rich from our calculations hasn't made anyone poorer, but will obviously lower the group average.

It is much more likely that those Native Hawaiians who have chosen to leave the state did so for economic reasons, and their significant success outside of the state reflects poorly on the race-based programs only implemented in the Islands.

Media Misrepresentation

Oblivious to the respectable earnings of Native Hawaiians, some media in Hawaii have cited the 2005 ACS as showing "Poverty still grips Hawaiians" and "Census survey shows need for assistance to Hawaiians." But the 2005 ACS sample survey for Hawaii shows Native Hawaiians in Hawaii, who average only 24.6 years of age, enjoy median family income of $56,449; and 55% of them occupy homes they own. Hispanics in Hawaii, in comparison, average 24.2 years of age, have a median family income of $54,803 and only 46.2% of them occupy homes they own. If anything, if one were looking for an ethnic group in Hawaii that was needy, the census data might suggest Hispanics. But nobody is anywhere near suggesting race-based programs for Hispanics in Hawaii - that "honor" is reserved for Native Hawaiians alone, and the census data has been carefully selected and misrepresented to fit that political point of view.

Could it Be Age?

The sample chosen in Hawaii for the ACS 2005 survey showed a 14 years difference in the median age for Native Hawaiians living there. Age makes a huge difference in earning power. For example, the Census 2000 data shows Hawaiians 35 to 44 years had over $9 thousand greater household income than Hawaiians ten years younger. This more than erases the difference reported of less than $6-8 thousand between Native Hawaiians and the total population of Hawaii.

The Ulterior Motive Becomes Apparent

Now with this backdrop of improved Native Hawaiian prosperity when treated equally, and a clearer understanding of the effects median age can have on income statistics, imagine how surprised we all are to learn of the shocking information discovered by the Honolulu Advertiser and Jim Dooley, "OHA push for Akaka bill topped $2M". (Adv. 11/27/06.) Well over $2 million of taxpayer money spent to lobby for a bill to break apart the State of Hawaii and give away much, perhaps all, of the state and its governing power & jurisdiction to a brand new sovereign nation of, by and for Native Hawaiians.

The Akaka Bill got started when once well-intentioned race-based programs were challenged in Hawaii - programs that have existed for decades, and have apparently done a great disservice to the overall health, wealth and well-being of Native Hawaiians when compared to their counterparts in other states without such race-based entitlements. In addition to the millions for lobbying to break up the State with the Akaka Bill, the bloated (and very powerful) bureaucracies of OHA and HHCA have cost the State of Hawaii over $1 billion just since 1990. Federal entitlements for Native Hawaiians have added over $1 billion more.

By continuing to paint Native Hawaiians as a special victim class, through willful misrepresentation of the data, supporters of race-based entitlements preserve their rationale at the expense of truth.

The Future

There is no doubt that there are people in need in Hawaii - but these people are of all races and backgrounds. We neglect too many of those in need when we target our help only to a certain ethnicity, and do more damage than good to the ethnicity we target. Race is an illusion, compelling yet meaningless - and a closer look at the statistics used to promote that illusion shows us clearly that no Hawaiians, of any race or ethnicity, have a need for the Akaka Bill.

Jere Krischel was born and raised in Hawai'i and now resides in California with his wife and two young children. He also is a member of the Grassroot Institute of Hawaii.

Reductio ad absurdum: left-handed breast cancer

For many years the media and public have been bombarded with Hawaiian victimhood statistics which sometimes seem strange, exaggerated, and useless. How are we to understand a claim that Native Hawaiian women have the highest rate of breast cancer of all the ethnic groups in Hawaii? What should we do about that if it is true? Where exactly did that statistic come from? Should we also note more detail, that white women have a higher rate of breast cancer being diagnosed (but a lower mortality rate) than Native Hawaiians? Will there be a struggle as large institutions seeking government and philanthropic grants try to protect their "turf" by citing statistics to prove that Native Hawaiians are really the worst victims, while suppressing statistics that prove otherwise? Does the racial stereotyping of ethnic Hawaiians by KSBE/PASE victimhood statistics have a bad effect on their self-esteem and social status?

Recent medical studies have made the startling discovery that young women who are left-handed are more than twice as likely to get breast cancer as young women who are right-handed. However, ethnic Hawaiian women of any age are far less than twice as likely to get breast cancer as women of other ethnicities.

Thus, being left-handed is a far greater predictor of breast cancer than being Native Hawaiian. So according to the logic used by KSBE/PASE, money spent to study and treat breast cancer in Native Hawaiians should instead be spent to study and treat left-handed women regardless of race. And of course, if we help all left-handed women we will also be helping ethnic Hawaiian left-handed women.

Here's the "study." On September 25, 2005, Patricia Reaney of Reuters News reported:[115] *"Left-handed women are more than twice as likely as right-handers to suffer from breast cancer before reaching menopause, Dutch scientists said on Monday. More than a million women are diagnosed with breast cancer worldwide each year... Researchers at the University Medical Center in Utrecht in the Netherlands speculate that there is a shared origin early in life for both left handedness and developing breast cancer, possibly exposure to hormones in the womb. ... Cuno Uiterwaal, an assistant professor of clinical epidemiology at the university ... and his colleagues studied 12,000 healthy, middle-aged women born between 1932-1941 who were part of a breast screening program. The scientists determined their hand preference and followed up their medical history to see which women developed breast cancer. ... 'We found that left-handed women are more than twice as likely to develop pre-menopausal breast cancer as non-left handed women,' the researchers said in the report published online by the British Medical Journal."*

Post-menopausal left-handed women also have a significantly higher risk of breast cancer than post-menopausal right-handers; and even in the post-menopausal group the increased risk from left-handedness is higher than the increased risk from being ethnic Hawaiian. Reuters Health, on March 9, 2000, reported[116] that "Left-handedness was modestly associated with breast cancer risk, with an odds ratio of 1.42."

If we're going to allocate scarce resources based on group membership, then the resources should go to the groups that are most at risk rather than to the group (ethnic Hawaiians) that has the wealthiest patron (Kamehameha Schools) or the most aggressive propaganda (PASE victimhood studies).

The solution: a welfare system based solely on need regardless of race

The ethnic Hawaiian victimhood statistics really serve only two purposes — to provide evidence in support of applications for race-based handouts from governments or philanthropies; and to acquire race-based political power by soliciting sympathy from the general public and the politicians they elect.

Social justice requires that needy people be given help based on need alone, regardless of race. If ethnic Hawaiians are truly the most needy ethnic group, then a needs-based welfare system would automatically give them the lion's share of handouts. Racial identity politics only serves to promote racial divisiveness.

There are only two good reasons to identify the race of someone with a medical problem or social dysfunction: curing the problem genetically or managing the problem culturally.

If a medical problem is genetically caused, then perhaps today's victim can be cured by gene therapy; and perhaps tomorrow's victim can be prevented by genetic engineering or genetic counseling for couples contemplating parenthood.

If a victim needs help to cure or manage a medical disease or social dysfunction, the help may very well need to be tailored to that individual's lifestyle and belief system. In some cultures people can only be interviewed or treated by people of the same gender. In some cultures people may be ashamed to acknowledge their problems; or elderly people might refuse to confide in someone younger or someone who is not a family or tribal member. But these are cultural issues, not racial ones. In Hawaii there is no necessary connection between race and culture. Some ethnic Hawaiians are cultural practitioners and some are not. Some people lacking Hawaiian native ancestry nevertheless hold values and participate in practices commonly called "Native Hawaiian." Community outreach programs and public health campaigns should be directed toward neighborhoods and cultures rather than toward racial groups.

Chapter 7

Anti-American, Anti-Military Activism

Most ethnic Hawaiians reject both racial separatism and ethnic nationalism, and are patriotic Americans

Chapters 3 and 4 described the two main approaches to Hawaiian sovereignty: racial separatism and ethnic nationalism.

Racial separatism is the concept found in the Akaka bill and also in Akaka Plan B. A racially exclusionary governing entity (comparable to an Indian tribe) would be set up for ethnic Hawaiians; and huge amounts of money, land, and law-making authority would then be transferred to it from the State of Hawaii and from the U.S. government.

Ethnic nationalism is the proposal that the entire State of Hawaii should once again become an independent nation. But unlike the actual Kingdom of Hawaii of the 19th Century, the new nation would guarantee racial supremacy for ethnic Hawaiians under a theory that "indigenous people" are entitled to special rights under international law. The great majority – those with no native ancestry – would be allowed to live and work in Hawaii, and perhaps could own property in restricted parts of Hawaii as resident aliens; and some of them might be able to have voting rights either as descendants of Hawaiian Kingdom subjects or as newly naturalized citizens. There would be special lands set aside exclusively for the "indigenous people" who also continue to share in all the lands. Voting rights would be restricted to ethnic Hawaiians on many topics, such as immigration, foreign affairs, land use, public education, and Constitutional amendments; while ethnic Hawaiians would also enjoy voting rights on all other topics. The superior land and voting rights guarantee racial supremacy for the ethnic Hawaiian minority in a multiracial society where everyone else would be second-class citizens, similar to blacks in South Africa under apartheid or similar to Asian Fijians in today's Fiji.

Most Hawaiians of native ancestry are not sovereignty activists, and probably not favorable to either version of Hawaiian sovereignty. They are proud to be Americans and totally uninterested in re-establishing Hawaii as an independent nation. They also do not want an apartheid partitioning of Hawaii that would occur through the creation of a race-based (tribal) government under the Akaka bill. There have been two automated telephone surveys by Grassroot Institute of Hawaii which called all households in Hawaii, in 2005 and 2006. Both surveys showed 67% of Hawaii residents oppose the Akaka bill, and about half of ethnic Hawaiians oppose it. The 2006 survey also asked whether people would vote for Hawaii to become a State if that question were on the ballot today. 78% of all people said yes, while 61% of ethnic Hawaiians said yes.[117] Those numbers are lower than in the actual statehood vote of 1959, when 94% of all voters said yes to Statehood, including 97% of voters on Molokai which has the largest percentage of ethnic Hawaiians among the major islands. The across-the-board lower support for statehood today may be due to voter discontent with the war in Iraq and with President Bush in this overwhelmingly Democrat state.

Perhaps surprisingly, it often seems the aggressiveness of sovereignty activism is inversely proportional to blood quantum. Some of the most zealous crusaders for sovereignty are those who have a very low percentage of native blood. A few leaders among both the racial separatists and ethnic nationalists have no native ancestry at all – they are wannabe Hawaiians who are very active in cultural affairs and perhaps married to an ethnic Hawaiian; or they are "save the whales" yuppie liberals feeling pangs of "white guilt."

Degrees of anti-Americanism

There are various degrees of anti-Americanism among both the independence activists and supporters of the Akaka bill. Mild forms of anti-Americanism include quiet resentment against the U.S. because of the overthrow and annexation; accompanied by frustration that time has moved on and it's fruitless to try to undo the past after more than a century. To ease the resentment for historical grievances and achieve some degree of reconciliation, reparations are owed in the form of billions of dollars of money and land. Such reparations might be funneled through a "Native Hawaiian" tribe under the Akaka bill, which would also provide some degree of self-governance.

More virulent hatred against the U.S. is seen in on-going political and anti-military activities intended to push the U.S. out of Hawaii and rip the 50th star off the flag. For many years activists have used international forums to challenge American sovereignty in Hawaii. It seems quite logical they will form partnerships with nations hostile to the United States to engage in anti-American political activity. Some Hawaiian sovereignty activists may even perform acts of espionage or sabotage, either to weaken the U.S. in hopes of forcing it to withdraw from far-away expendable Hawaii, or in return for foreign government recognition of Hawaiian independence. Such a possibility will be explored at the end of this chapter.

Some supporters of the Akaka bill might be patriotic Americans with distinguished military careers

Some ethnic Hawaiians who want to create an Akaka tribe are loyal Americans. They are mistaken in thinking that Hawaiians are similar to American Indians. But they are correct that it is entirely proper under U.S. law for loyal Americans who happen to be Indians to belong to Indian tribes. It is certainly possible for tribal members to be loyal Americans, despite their tribes' historical grievances against the U.S. For example, Navajo "code-talkers" risked their lives as soldiers in World War II, using their native language like a secret code which the enemy could never break.

There are several issues here which need to be distinguished, because Senators Inouye and Akaka, and OHA, are fond of intermingling and obfuscating them.

Have there been ethnic Hawaiians who served with bravery and heroism in the U.S. military? Absolutely yes! Are there ethnic Hawaiians who are loyal and patriotic toward America? Probably the vast majority are. Would those people support the Akaka bill? The dead ones can't speak. Most of the live ones will never speak or vote on this topic, but probably most either oppose the bill or don't care.

Can we rely on the fact that many, perhaps most, ethnic Hawaiians are loyal and patriotic toward America; to draw the conclusion that all ethnic Hawaiians are loyal and patriotic? Obviously not. Are most of those who support the Akaka bill loyal and patriotic toward America? We will never know. But it is clear that many supporters of the bill see it as a temporary way of getting money and land from the U.S. even while hating the U.S. and continuing to work toward independence.[118] So it is entirely possible that some supporters of the Akaka bill, who join the tribe and

Hawaiian Apartheid

receive federal government benefits, might nevertheless engage in espionage or sabotage against the U.S.

Many ethnic Hawaiians have served with distinction in the U.S. military, including some who suffered severe wounds or died for our country. Herbert K. Pililaau of Waianae got the Medal of Honor for his heroic death in the Korean War.[119] A huge transport ship was named after him, with the blessings of his justifiably proud family, and has been actively participating in the war in Iraq.[120] A review of Asian/Pacific Islanders who received Distinguished Service Crosses during WW2 led to upgrades to the Medal of Honor, reflecting the fact that racial discrimination in the 1940s might have prevented the men from receiving the highest award to which their heroism entitled them. In June, 2000 President Clinton awarded 22 Medals of Honor for such WW2 service. Twelve of those new Medals of Honor were awarded to ethnic Hawaiians.[121] Another upgrade to Medal of Honor was awarded to Hawaii Senator Dan Inouye for his distinguished service in Italy during WW2 (and he is the most powerful supporter of the Akaka bill).

On July 15, 2002 ethnic Hawaiian Brigadier General Irwin K. Cockett, Jr., United States Army, Retired gave a speech in the U.S. Senate Committee on Indian Affairs summarizing the contributions of ethnic Hawaiians in the U.S. military. It is filled with interesting historical tidbits.[122] He told how George Kaumualil of Kauai, and Thomas Hopu, enlisted in the U.S. Navy during the War of 1812 and served on the USS Enterprise that fought against the HMS Boxer. He noted that In 1818 two anti-Spanish privateers, the Santa Rosa and Argentina, recruited 80 Hawaiians in Honolulu for an attack on Spanish-held San Francisco; the Hawaiians, armed with long spears, led the assault on the Presidio of Monterey and were the first to haul down the Spanish Flag. He told about the contributions of ethnic Hawaiians in both world wars, the Korean War, etc. Senator Akaka told his own story about how he was in a high school ROTC unit at Kamehameha School and witnessed the bombing of Pearl Harbor from the school's campus; and later as a draftee serving on Tinian Island in the Pacific he watched the airplanes take off carrying the atomic bombs for Hiroshima and Nagasaki.[123]

But some of that "evidence" is simply irrelevant to either American patriotism or to the Akaka bill. For example, General Cockett noted that George Kaumualii and Thomas Hopu had served on an American warship in battle in 1812. But of course 1812 was 86 years before Hawaii became a part of America. In 1810 Kamehameha finally intimidated King Kaumualii of Kauai into knuckling under to Kamehameha's rule. George

Kaumualii, son of the King, had just been stripped of his future in Hawaii. With no more battles available for fighting in Hawaii, Kaumualii and Hopu, two young adventurers in search of action, ran off to the nearest war they could find. Likewise the 80 Hawaiians who fought for America in 1818 against the Spanish in San Francisco. Hawaii offered them absolutely no use for their spears and their desire to be warriors. So far as we know, none of these men abandoned their Hawaiian citizenship to become Americans. It was adventure, not patriotism. There is also no evidence that any of the 20th-21st Century ethnic Hawaiians who who did feel patriotic toward America (some of whom died heroically in America's wars) would have supported the Akaka bill.

Ethnic Hawaiian adventurers, like adventurers of other races, eagerly join up with other nations' armies just for fun. "Have spear, will travel." For example, consider Prince Jonah Kuhio Kalanianaole, heir to the throne if the monarchy had continued. After being released from prison for his role in the attempted Wilcox counter-revolution of 1895, Mr. Kuhio went off to South Africa on an adventure. He did not remain in Hawaii to fight against annexation alongside his deposed Queen, Liliuokalani. He went to South Africa to join the Boer War, as a soldier in the British army, on behalf of one colonial power (England) fighting the descendants of another colonial power (the Dutch) to see who would control the indigenous people of a nation halfway around the world. He spent about three of the most crucial years in Hawaiian history, 1899-1902, on his "excellent adventure." Why did he abandon his own homeland in its time of great need? Maybe as a rifle-toting bomb-throwing "freedom fighter" with Wilcox in 1895 he developed a taste for violence? In today's slang we might call him a "cowboy."

Historical grievances against the United States produce a simmering anti-Americanism even among wealthy Hawaiians and well-established institutions not (yet) seeking independence

There are common core attitudes held by all sovereignty activists, including supporters of the Akaka bill. White sailors from England who "discovered" Hawaii in 1778 brought diseases which soon wiped out 95% of native Hawaiians. White missionaries from America "forced" native Hawaiians to adopt religious views contrary to native culture, and smoothed

Hawaiian Apartheid

the way for colonialism. White businessmen from America colonized Hawaii and eventually conspired with the U.S. government to overthrow the native government. The United States staged an armed military invasion in 1893 which overthrew the monarchy, and established a puppet regime. After a few years the puppet regime was able to get Hawaii annexed to the United States despite a written protest signed by nearly all ethnic Hawaiians. The puppet regime both before and after annexation made Hawaiian language illegal and suppressed the native Hawaiian culture. Hawaii is now under military occupation by the United States. Native Hawaiians are oppressed and their culture is trivialized by a tourist industry using it to reap huge profits.

That is the version of history that all sovereignty activists believe to be true. Many elements of that story are false or exaggerated, including complaints that became part of the apology resolution passed by Congress in 1993 to commemorate the centennial of the overthrow of the monarchy. The historical grievances, plus current victimhood claims, are spelled out in greater detail in the "findings (preambles) of some of the legislation providing racially exclusionary benefits to ethnic Hawaiians in the areas of housing, education, and healthcare.

Independence activists cite the apology bill as a confession of a crime, and demand independence as the only rightful restitution. The Akaka bill incorporates the apology resolution as justification for providing "reconciliation" in the form of federal recognition of a "Native Hawaiian" tribe. University of Hawaii Professor Haunani-Kay Trask is famous for her vitriolic public statements expressing those historical grievances and also denouncing American culture and foreign policy; and she does not hesitate to make racist verbal attacks in public against white students.[124]

The University of Hawaii Center for Hawaiian Studies is a propaganda factory indoctrinating the next generation of ethnic Hawaiian leadership.[125]

Many other academic departments work closely with CHS to ensure that their own lecture halls are filled with Hawaiian students and their own students and professors will have field activities, research opportunities and grants available to them: Political Science, History, Anthropology, the biological sciences, teacher education, the law school and medical school, etc. In 2001 newly hired UH President Dobelle gave the keynote speech to the first annual convention of the Council for Native Hawaiian Advancement, pledging to politicize UH by harnessing it as a vehicle to help turn the dream of Hawaiian nationhood into reality; and he then gave a massive cash infusion to CHS.[126] UH is a hostile work environment for anyone seeking a balance of views on Hawaiian sovereignty. Academic freedom regarding Hawaiian sovereignty is nonexistent for both professors and students, some of whom have suffered blatant intimidation to enforce political correctness.[127]

The theory of history as grievance is also taught as fact to children from kindergarten through grade 12 in many of Hawaii's public schools. Some of these schools are extremely zealous in their support of Hawaiian sovereignty. They indoctrinate the children with religious beliefs supporting the view that ethnic Hawaiians have a genealogical, family relationship with the lands of Hawaii and with the gods, and therefore ethnic Hawaiians are entitled to racial supremacy in political power.

If someone truly believes his native land has been colonized, invaded, and forcibly annexed by a foreign country whose people are of a different race, he would naturally be angry against that country and race. If the land, culture, and language were stolen, the thieves should pay reparations, and be punished and deported. If the foreign occupier takes over huge portions of the homeland for use as military bases, and conducts military training activities that burn and pollute the sacred land, and stations nuclear weapons and tens of thousands of troops on those bases for many decades, the natives become bitter and feel justified in doing whatever it takes to expel the occupier from their homeland.

If the natives are brothers to the land, and both the natives and the land are descended from the gods; then the natives are entitled to racial supremacy in land "ownership" and management. The religious theory supporting Hawaiian racial supremacy (see Chapter 8) is believed by all sovereignty activists, and also by many ethnic Hawaiians who are patriotic to America and do not realize the fascist implications of those religious views.

Thus there is a common core of beliefs underlying both the independence viewpoint and the tribal viewpoint.[128] This common core became clear during two "red shirt" marches in the Fall of 2003,[129] and another one in 2004.[130] Depending who did the counting, somewhere between 7,000 - 20,000 ethnic Hawaiians and their supporters wore red shirts symbolizing the blood that unifies and defines who is Native Hawaiian. The red shirts also symbolize the ominous red cloud that is the name of the lead organization in the march, Ilioulaokalani (red dog [cloud] in the sky). The river of red shirts flowing through the streets also symbolically represents the schools of red fish, aweoweo, whose rare appearance portends a time of major change, such as the death of the Queen. More ominously the red shirts also harken back to the Wilcox rebellion of 1889 when Wilcox' army of 80 men all wore red Garibaldi shirts.[131] The fact that so many people can coordinate their coming together at the same time and place, wearing the same red shirt, intentionally serves as a reminder of the collective group consciousness that people who claim to be "indigenous" believe runs through their blood. Virulent anti-Americanism was shown in large signs and banners displayed on the grounds of Iolani Palace during the rallies following those marches, although the anti-Americanism was kept to the edges in order to broaden the base of support and to permit the participation of Governor Lingle and other "establishment" politicians.[132]

At rallies like these, dozens (perhaps hundreds) of Hawaiian (Kingdom) flags are always carried and displayed, often upside-down to indicate distress or emergency. But there is never a single U.S. flag. It would be inconceivable for anyone to carry a U.S. flag in any such event. The Office of Hawaiian Affairs, and Kamehameha Schools, (who aggressively promote these events and demand passage of the Akaka bill to save their programs) always like to say they are not anti-American. They say they are merely using the provisions of American law to ask the American Congress to pass a bill; and they are seeking their rights as "indigenous" people of the United States, comparable to the Indian tribes and Alaska natives. But OHA, Kamehameha Schools, and other organizations in control of these marches know that the mob would never tolerate the presence of an American flag, because the propaganda for many years has been that America colonized Hawaii, staged an armed invasion, overthrew the monarchy, suppressed the language and culture, illegally annexed Hawaii to the U.S., stole the land, and illegally conducted the statehood vote of 1959. Thus, any display of respect for America would be very unwelcome. These activists resent living under U.S. law where the 14th Amendment equal protection clause makes it unconstitutional to have racially exclusionary government programs like OHA and DHHL, and where even a private benevolent institution like Kamehameha Schools is given a hard time by the U.S. Office of Civil Rights, U.S. Internal Revenue Service, and the courts.

Some people with no native ancestry are active supporters of Hawaiian sovereignty. Some of these non-natives support total independence; some support the Akaka bill. The independence supporters tend to be political leftists who also support other leftist causes such as environmentalism, demilitarization, and gay rights. Some non-native supporters of the Akaka bill are professors, lawyers, bankers, and bureaucrats who earn high salaries as employees or contractors to institutions serving racially exclusionary beneficiaries – institutions which need the Akaka bill to defend their racial policies against legal challenges.

Well-meaning non-natives often feel sorry for ethnic Hawaiians because of the historical grievances, and therefore support either independence or the Akaka bill or "whatever the Hawaiians want." Ethnic Hawaiians have become Hawaii's favorite racial group, partly because of the grievances and partly because Hawaiian culture is the core that holds together Hawaii's rainbow of races and cultures. Ethnic Hawaiians as a group are a sort of state mascot to be petted and pampered.[133] Like all forms of racial profiling or stereotyping, there are many individuals in the group who do not want or deserve to be stereotyped, but they are included nevertheless.

The question whether there are loyal and patriotic Americans who support the Akaka bill is somewhat similar to the question whether there are loyal and patriotic Americans who criticize U.S. foreign policy in Iraq or Israel. The answer to both questions is "Yes, of course." But when the critics of American foreign policy get shrill, and they never have anything positive to say about America, one does begin to wonder about their love for America.

The corresponding question regarding the Akaka bill is more clear. Perhaps it might be true that most Americans who are critical of the Bush administration's foreign policy are loyal and patriotic Americans who fear we have lost our way and want to bring us back to our idealistic principles. But it is very clear that most supporters of the Akaka bill are not like that. In their hearts most supporters of the Akaka bill would like independence. They keenly feel those historical grievances against the U.S., but they realize as a practical matter that America will not let go of Hawaii, at least not anytime soon. Meanwhile lawsuits threaten to dismantle OHA, and other lawsuits against Kamehameha School threaten to desegregate it. The only way to keep government money flowing and to preserve racial exclusion is to pass the Akaka bill. Hawaiians feel entitled to huge reparations for historical grievances, so the Akaka bill is a small downpayment.

Perhaps it's appropriate to paraphrase Jesus' comment about whether a rich man can get to heaven: it is as difficult for a supporter of the Akaka bill to be a loyal and patriotic lover of America, as it is for a camel to fit through the eye of a needle.

Racism, threats of violence, and actual violence

The racism of the Hawaiian sovereignty movement is different from historic racism by whites against blacks; and far more dangerous. The Hawaiian sovereignty movement presents an outward appearance of multiracial partnership; but it is racist to the core. Hawaiian metaphysical racism is a fundamental religious belief that possession of even a small amount of Hawaiian native ancestry carries a genetically encoded racial supremacy based on a family relationship among the gods, the land, and ethnic Hawaiian people. That brand of religious fascism will be explored more fully in Chapter 8. Such a belief logically justifies the existing institutional racism, where racially exclusionary private and government agencies comprise the bricks in Hawaii's growing wall of apartheid.

To expand Hawaii's institutional racism and defend it against legal attacks, politicians have introduced legislation in Congress (the Akaka bill) to authorize a phony new Indian tribe to be created out of thin air, whose only rule for membership is possession of a drop of Hawaiian blood. Hawaii's politicians overwhelmingly favor this bill, to keep federal dollars flowing to Hawaii through the established racially exclusionary institutions.

Some people with no native ancestry support metaphysical and institutional racism, and support either total independence for Hawaii, or the Akaka bill. They support these things partly to ensure job security; but also because they admire Hawaiian culture, consider ethnic Hawaiians an endangered species, and feel compassion in the face of victimhood propaganda. The Hawaiian sovereignty movement is anti-American and anti-white for historic reasons. Ethnic Hawaiian activists also try to build solidarity with Asians to create a large majority of Hawaii's people who will see the Hawaiian sovereignty movement as a struggle of dark-skinned people against oppression by whites and by the U.S. government. A large webpage explores Hawaiian racism.[134]

Will Hawaiian sovereignty zealots use violence to achieve their goals? This topic is explored on a webpage, some of whose contents are summarized here. The webpage provides more detailed analysis and full documentation for what follows.[135] There have already been threats of violence made so aggressively as to cause actual disruption and cancellation of events. Threats of violence are a form of actual violence when people are caused to change their behavior because of the threats. There have also been threats of violence in the form of predictions by community leaders, elected politicians, and academics warning that unless the zealots get what they want there will be violence. On one hand it should be possible to have open and honest academic and friendly discussion of the possibility of violence, perhaps as a way of avoiding it. On the other hand, there's the mafia man in a business suit with a nasty-looking enforcer standing next to him who tells a restaurant owner in a very polite way that the owner would be well advised to hire the mafia man to protect him because it's a bad neighborhood and nobody can predict what might happen otherwise. There has also been actual violence in the form of physical attacks damaging the body or property of some individuals.

Hawaiian sovereignty zealots have already been using violence for many years in the form of verbal and physical threats and intimidation against individuals who dare to express views they don't like, or who dare to participate in activities where they "don't belong." Sometimes the threats have actually turned to physical violence. In 1976 major anti-white hostility erupted on the first voyage of the canoe Hokulea as ethnic Hawaiians insisted they should be exclusive owners of this important element of Hawaiian history and culture. One ethnic Hawaiian man who ran for Governor and received thousands of votes was arrested in 1998 for throwing rocks and stealing a white man's surfboard. The Hawaiian yelled at the "haole" saying "You took my land, so I'm taking your board."

In 1993 a man carrying an American flag tried to enter the grounds of Iolani Palace during an event commemorating the 100th anniversary of the overthrow of the monarchy. He was "escorted" roughly off the Palace grounds by a big tough-looking ethnic Hawaiian who told him the American flag is not welcome there. In 2002 Hawaiian sovereignty zealots forced the University of Hawaii to cancel a course by threatening the program director and the students who had signed up – university officials did nothing to protect academic freedom. The professor and his students nevertheless managed to hold the course in an undisclosed location on campus, buoyed by a news report followed by an editorial in the Honolulu Advertiser supporting academic freedom. In 2006 Hawaiian sovereignty zealots disrupted and prevented a celebration of the official Statehood Day holiday by verbally abusing and menacingly approaching children in a high school marching band and by rushing the adult participants who were brave enough to remain, standing nose-to-nose and yelling in their faces.

A "reverend" perceived as a community leader has repeatedly warned in published newspaper articles and speeches that "Hawaiians are a warrior people" and must be given what they demand. Senator Akaka in his January 2007 speech introducing the Akaka bill on the Senate floor warned that there will be racial trouble in Hawaii unless the Akaka bill is passed. A professor at the University of Hawaii had his students do a project interviewing ethnic Hawaiians on whether they approve of violence and whether they think violence will happen in the sovereignty movement. Interestingly, only a small minority of those interviewed said they favor the use of violence to achieve sovereignty, and a larger minority (1/3) said they support sovereignty; but a majority said they believe violence will actually happen because young people today are being raised to believe they are entitled to it and to believe they are being oppressed.

On one hand it's a good thing to study this issue in an academic setting and to have open and candid discussions about it. On the other hand, putting that information out for public attention in the newspaper can be interpreted as threatening the general public that they'd better give ethnic Hawaiians what is demanded "or else." How would one spouse feel if the other spouse says "Honey, I think we should find out all about the laws regarding divorce, and what happens to the money and the kids afterward." Would that be simply an interesting intellectual exercise, or a topic for lighthearted banter; or would it be perceived as a threat?

Hawaiian activists seeking independence by "working within the system" through U.S. domestic activity including the banking system, tax evasion, and "peace" churches

Earlier it was said that it is as difficult for a supporter of the Akaka bill to be a loyal and patriotic lover of America, as it is for a camel to fit through the eye of a needle. If that's hard for a supporter of the Akaka bill, then it is by definition impossible for a Hawaiian independence activist. The whole idea of ripping the 50th star off the flag is anti-American, in the same way as the secession of the Confederate States in 1860 was anti-American. To this day there are still Southerners who say "The South shall rise again!" There are still Southerners who feel insulted when someone calls the war of 1860-1865 the "Civil War." The more genteel lovers of the Confederacy call it "The War Between the States" because they consider that states' rights trumped the right of the United States to remain unified. They treat "United States" as a plural, not a singular; thus they say "The United States ARE prosperous" rather than "The United States IS prosperous." The more zealous partisans of the Confederacy still refer to that war as "The War of Northern Aggression" because the North invaded the South, pillaged and plundered, and refused to allow the Southern states to exercise self-determination (just as Hawaiian activists say the U.S. invaded Hawaii and continues to occupy it).

Hawaiian sovereignty activists are already using the university and the public schools as madrassas to indoctrinate children with attitudes of Hawaiian racial supremacy and attitudes of historical grievance against the United States. But some independence activists have tried to seek independence for Hawaii by following procedures within the U.S. financial, political, and legal systems.

For example, Bumpy Kanahele styles himself as head of government of the Nation of Hawaii. His "nation" consists of a large and interesting website whose webmaster is a white man living in Hana (Hawaii island); plus a small "village" on land leased from the State of Hawaii in Waimanalo (Oahu island). The lease was extorted as a settlement under Governor Waihee (also a Hawaiian sovereignty activist) as a "gentleman's agreement" (conspiracy to rip off the State) to end a politically uncomfortable long-term protest in which some of Kanahele's people illegally occupied a public beach, highway, and other highly visible areas in Waimanalo. Since completing a prison term for harboring a fugitive, Kanahele has changed his public image to "working within the system." For example, at a meeting of the Asian Development Bank in Honolulu, he provided "security" (i.e., he told his friends not to interfere with the meeting) in return for permission to distribute literature inside the convention hall about Hawaiian independence. A more recent caper by Kanahele was to file a protest with bank regulators, and a lawsuit, in an attempt to block the merger of Bank of America and FleetBoston in order to try to extort a payoff of money he claims was owed to his group by Bank of America to help found a bank for his Hawaiian nation.[136] In 2006 he was a candidate for trustee of the Office of Hawaiian Affairs, on a platform calling for OHA to establish his ethnic Hawaiian bank.

Another way independence activists operate within U.S. domestic systems is to quietly or publicly refuse to pay taxes to the federal and state governments. If Hawaii is not legitimately part of the U.S., then citizens of the nation of Hawaii do not owe taxes to the U.S. And if the State of Hawaii is merely a puppet regime under a belligerent U.S. occupation, then Hawaiians do not owe taxes to the State either. For example, in November 2003 it was announced that 30 Honolulu bus drivers had been arrested for tax evasion based on claims of Hawaiian sovereignty. From 2000-2004 numerous stories were published about a Honolulu tax preparation company that had prepared about 5000 tax returns, many of which asserted Hawaiian sovereignty claims.[137]

One sovereignty claim that even non-ethnic-Hawaiian newcomers can try to use, even while freely admitting they are U.S. citizens, goes like this: since Hawaii is not a part of the United States, therefore money earned from jobs in Hawaii can be exempt from tax under the foreign earned income tax credit. Another ethnic Hawaiian, attorney Hayden Burgess (alias Poka Laenui), often states publicly on radio and television programs that he has not paid federal or state income taxes since 1979, based on Hawaiian sovereignty arguments. Although he does not directly encourage others to evade taxes, that is the clear implication of his propaganda and his praise of the bus drivers and other tax resisters. Laenui is an independence activist who also supports the Akaka bill as a way of gaining money, land, and power to facilitate the drive for secession. Tax evasion is a way for a few individuals to feel good about their own "witnessing" for the movement; but if enough people begin not paying taxes, it could actually destabilize the government.

Another way some independence activists work domestically within the United States is to publish articles and give speeches to politically liberal organizations likely to support their view of history. These activists state historical, legal, and moral arguments for independence, laying a guilt trip on the American people and pleading for independence. For example, the Rev. Dr. Kaleo Patterson published an article entitled "Hawaiians Yearn Still for Freedom" in February 2001 in the Christian Social Action Magazine of the United Methodist Church (President Bush's own church).[138] The Honolulu Star-Bulletin on March 3, 2001 described his article this way: "Patterson contends Hawaii's status as one of the 50 states has been "emptied of any legal or political legitimacy," and accuses the United States of separating "a friendly nation from its history, cultural roots, land, language and destiny. Hawaii today is literally a kidnapped nation." The magazine's issue, on the theme of colonialism, includes other articles criticizing the "lack of political autonomy and freedom" for Puerto Rico, a U.S. commonwealth, and advocating self-determination for Guam, a U.S. territory."[

Many churches in Hawaii have politically liberal ministers and congregations who strongly endorse Hawaiian sovereignty as part of "liberation theology" morality. The United Church of Christ issued an apology to

Native Hawaiians for its role in condoning the overthrow of the monarchy, and gave money and land as "reparations." The American Friends Service Committee (Quakers) has been very active in supporting Hawaiian sovereignty, demilitarization, and gay rights (the three topics are indeed related in Hawaiian culture and history). Most of the liberal churches are also "peace" churches; i.e., they are anti-military. They think U.S. foreign policy in Iraq, Israel, and around the world is immoral. But in addition to opposing the use of military force for current U.S. (immoral) foreign policy, they also oppose the whole idea of military force.

Anti-military activism – push the U.S. military out of Hawaii as a first step toward ripping the 50th star off the flag

Environmentalists are political liberals who are also anti-military. And of course the Hawaiian sovereignty activists oppose the U.S. military's presence in Hawaii. Thus, all these groups cooperate in opposing the existence of military bases in Hawaii and especially the use of Hawaii lands for live-fire training. A coalition of environmentalists, "peace" activists, and Hawaiian independence activists filed lawsuits which crippled the Army's ability to use Makua Valley for training;[139] and which also crippled combat training with a Stryker brigade in other parts of Hawaii.[140]

Anti-military sentiment among sovereignty activists, and a desire to achieve international recognition of Hawaiian independence, combine to raise the question whether independence activists might cooperate with foreign governments hostile to the U.S. to engage in espionage or sabotage against military bases in Hawaii, in return for recognition. This topic will be dealt with later in this chapter, because it is the most extreme sort of anti-American activity along the continuum we are exploring.

During the mid-1990s there was a popular T-shirt worn by Hawaiian sovereignty activists, imprinted with the slogan "Last star on, first star off" (referring to the fact that Hawaii is the 50th state, and thus the 50th star on the U.S. flag). That slogan got attention in relation to a proclamation read from the steps of 'Iolani Palace on January 16, 1994, purporting to be a declaration of independence.[141] The slogan also got national attention in an article in the Baltimore Sun of August 8, 1998, regarding a Hawaiian sovereignty march in Washington D.C. on the 100th anniversary of Hawaii's annexation to the United States. Interestingly, both of those articles are made available on the very large website of an organization claiming to be the "Nation of Hawaii."[142]

The Hawaiian independence movement at the national and international levels

One section of Chapter 4 dealt with the decolonization of Hawaii and discussed the question whether Hawaii is legitimately the 50th state. As noted in Chapter 4, that question has been taken by Hawaiian sovereignty activists to United Nations offices and meetings at various venues in New York, Geneva, and in the Pacific.

One Hawaiian independence activist who has worked both domestically in the U.S. and also internationally is David Keanu Sai. His focus has been entirely on "legal" theory. He has extensively studied the domestic laws of the Kingdom of Hawaii, although sometimes he has suppressed information about Kingdom law which turned out to be devastating to his theories when the truth was exposed. For example, he claimed for many years that voting rights in the Kingdom were only for ethnic Hawaiians, plus those few newcomers who were naturalized or (later) denizized. He claimed the rule of "jus soli" (birth in Hawaii confers status of fully equal citizenship) was not part of Hawaiian Kingdom law; until he was forced to acknowledge the findings of attorney Patrick Hanifin.[143]

Sai followed a convoluted procedure to declare himself at various times the Regent Pro-Tem of the Hawaiian Kingdom, and the Minister of Interior, and the Ambassador. He helped create the "Perfect Title" land title company which did title searches. The theory was that because the overthrow and annexation were illegal, all title transfers since 1893 were improperly recorded under improper government seals at the Bureau of Conveyances, but Keanu Sai as Regent Pro-Tem had the authority to condone and to "perfect" the chain of title transfers (for a fee, of course). He also claimed that ethnic Hawaiians have a continuing right to assert ownership of any one parcel of land up to a certain size for their own residence and subsistence farming, so long as the parcel deed is not properly registered and the parcel is not occupied by a Hawaiian Kingdom subject. Eventually, after collecting hundreds of thousands of dollars in title search fees, and messing up thousands of titles and title transfers, he was found guilty of a felony in a jury trial and his company was disbanded. The land title scheme was a very useful ploy to get many people to believe in his theories of a continuing, living Hawaiian Kingdom and to try to assert the existence of the Kingdom through the land title recording process of the

State of Hawaii. The Perfect Title scam will be described more fully in Chapter 9 on Hawaiian sovereignty frauds.

With the help of far-left radical law professor Francis Boyle (University of Illinois) Keanu Sai filed two lawsuits against the United States directly in the U.S. Supreme Court, arguing that the Supreme Court had original jurisdiction in cases where a foreign government (Hawaii) sues the United States. His theory was that the Supreme Court should order (writ of mandamus) the President to enforce a treaty between the U.S. and the Kingdom of Hawaii that had promised perpetual friendship and commercial relations.[144] When those lawsuits were dismissed, he then moved to the international level, filing a claim at an arbitral tribunal associated with the world court at the Hague (See Chapter 9). After the Hague case failed, he then filed a "complaint" against the U.S. at the United Nations Security Council.

Other Hawaiian independence activists have been working at the international level for many years, including medical doctor and professor Kekuni Blaisdell, attorney Hayden Burgess (alias Poka Laenui), and attorney Mililani Trask.

Poka Laenui tends to work quietly, behind the scenes. He is a disciple of Johan Galtung, founder of the European University Center for Peace Studies (EPU) in Stadtschlaining, Austria. Poka has sponsored several visits to Hawaii by Mr. Galtung in conjunction with the local Spark Matsunaga Institute for Peace. He has made trips to the United Nations in New York, and various international organizations elsewhere. On his regular two-hour radio broadcast (sponsored by the "Hawaiian National Broadcast Corporation"!!), Poka did an hour long interview with one of the judges from the Nuremberg trials of 1945, discussing the war crimes of President Bush. Poka was principal author of a resolution that passed the Senate of the State of Hawaii in 2001, calling into question whether the Statehood plebiscite of 1959 was properly conducted under "international law," and calling upon the United Nations to come to Hawaii to revisit the issue. These topics were discussed at greater length in Chapter 4.

Dr. Kekuni Blaisdell has a long history of Hawaiian independence activism. He helped organize the revival of the Kingdom holiday Ka La Hoihoi Ea in an annual commemoration at Thomas Square on or near the date when Hawaiian sovereignty was restored by Admiral Thomas of the British navy (July 31, 1843, "Ua mau ke ea o ka aina i ka pono"). Unlike some independence activists who concede that people of no native ancestry were subjects of the Kingdom with fully equal rights, Dr. Blaisdell insists that only ethnic Hawaiians can have full rights in a restored independent Hawaii. Thus, he and his followers engage in ethnic cleansing of Kingdom holidays, refusing to acknowledge the non-native heroes of the Kingdom.[145]

In 1993, the 100th anniversary of the overthrow, Dr. Blaisdell organized an international "tribunal" of leftists and "international law" scholars (Ka Ho'okolokolonui Kanaka Maoli, The Peoples' International Tribunal) to visit Hawaii and hold a "trial" (empty chair for defendant United States) finding the U.S. guilty of violating international law. The infamous professor Ward Churchill was one of the judges.

Kekuni Blaisdell has attended many meetings of Pacific island nations, including delegations from colonial territories seeking independence (such as "Kanaky" – French Territory of New Caledonia). Some of the groups hosting such meetings are NGOs (non-governmental organizations), some of which are sponsored or supported by the United Nations. Occasionally United Nations "rapporteurs" in attendance write reports to be sent to official United Nations agencies. For example, in 1997 Dr. Blaisdell was unable to gain official observer status at such a meeting, so he attended a "parallel" (unofficial, informal) meeting at the same place and time, in Rarotonga, which was also attended by Deputy Secretary General of the South Pacific Forum Secretariat. He was successful in getting the forum to pass a resolution calling upon the United Nations to reinscribe Hawaii on the list of non-self-governing territories eligible for decolonization.[146]

Attorney Mililani Trask has been active for many years both locally in Hawaii (as one of the founders and long term governor of Ka Lahui sovereignty group) and also internationally. She served as a trustee of the Office of Hawaiian Affairs (but failed to win re-election). She hosted a visit to Hawaii by Rigoberta Menchu of Guatemala, the Nobel Peace Prize winner for her work on indigenous rights – the concept was that ethnic Hawaiians in Hawaii suffer the same sort of violations of their "indigenous rights" as the indigenous tribes of Guatemala (who were burned out of their lands and murdered by government troops). During the early 2000s Mililani Trask served a 3-year term as one of only 16 directors worldwide of the U.N. Permanent Forum on Indigenous Issues. At the behest of Hawaiian activists, the Hawaii Legislature during the 2003-2004 biennium passed a resolution inviting that Forum to hold its next annual meeting in Honolulu. In May 2004 Mililani Trask led a delegation of 18 Hawaiian independence activists to New York for two weeks of meetings.[147]

Niklaus Schweizer, the honorary Swiss consul in Honolulu, has also been active in local organizations favoring Hawaiian independence. He is

Professor of German at the University of Hawaii, and has no ethnic Hawaiian ancestry. But he is an honorary member of The Royal Order of Kamehameha I (only ethnic Hawaiians can be full members), and a member of the board of directors of the Friends of Iolani Palace. He frequently shows up at Hawaiian sovereignty events, and participates in forums at the UH Center for Hawaiian Studies. It should be noted that the Swiss Confederation had a full-blown treaty with the Kingdom of Hawaii ratified in 1864. Today's independence activists consider all such treaties to be still fully in force because the overthrow and annexation were illegal under "international law." The activists hope someday to persuade one of the Kingdom's treaty partners to make a public declaration that it still recognizes Hawaii as an independent nation.

Hawaiian independence activists like to compare the political status of Hawaii to the political status of Puerto Rico and Guam. Those two entities were acquired by the United States at roughly the same time as Hawaii, during the Spanish-American war. Since Puerto Rico and Guam are not (yet) states, it is possible they could eventually become independent instead of becoming states. The current in-between status of Puerto Rico and Guam seems to make people nervous, including the United Nations. Hawaiian activists cheer whenever the subject of United Nations action or a political status plebiscite is raised regarding Guam or Puerto Rico, because they hope similar action might be possible in the case of Hawaii. Some activists for Hawaiian sovereignty are also active in the movement for independence in Puerto Rico and Guam, and there is considerable exchanging of information and inspiration among the three independence movements. While February 24, 2004 was remembered by historians as the golden anniversary of the Great Hawaii Statehood Petition of 1954,[148] the Hawaiian sovereignty activists and Puerto Rican nationalists celebrated a date less than a week later as the golden anniversary of a terrorist attack on Congress. On March 1, 1954 four Puerto Rican independence terrorists seated in the visitors' gallery shot and almost killed 5 members of Congress on the floor of the U.S. House of Representatives. An essay praising and justifying this "brave and noble revolutionary effort" was circulated among Hawaiian independence activists.[149] One of the terrorists, pardoned by President Clinton after 18 years in prison, received great applause and warm embraces as a speaker at a Hawaiian Sovereignty Restoration Day rally in July 2000.[150]

A surprising number of nations have laws establishing racial supremacy.[151] The government of Zimbabwe (formerly Rhodesia) under the only President it has had since independence, Robert Mugabe, has been pushing multigenerational white settlers out of their land holdings in order to give the land to the indigenous inhabitants. Hawaiian activists take note of what's happening in Zimbabwe, but apparently have no relationships with the native Zimbabweans. Closer to Hawaii is Aotearoa (New Zealand), where the Maori, sharing their Polynesian race with native Hawaiians, have special political rights and control over racially designated lands. There are frequent cultural exchanges between the Maori and Hawaii's "kanaka maoli." Televised discussions wistfully compare Maori success in achieving special rights, with the slower pace of "Maoli" efforts in Hawaii. Blame it on the missionaries for not giving Hawaiians the letter "r."

On May 18-19, 2005 the East-West Center of the University of Hawaii hosted the annual meeting of the Pacific Islands Conference of Leaders. What made the 2005 meeting special is that Oscar Temaru attended. He was the then-new President of Tahiti, and is an activist seeking the independence of Tahiti from France. Hawaiian independence activists were not invited to attend the meeting, because they do not represent any official government. However, Hawaiian activists met informally with President Temaru, who made public statements of solidarity with them.

The Haleakala Times, a leftist newspaper on Maui, published a lengthy article about the Temaru visit to Hawaii in its edition of June 8-21. The Times article said, *"After a brief, less than two-hundred-year interruption by the West of the region's dynamic, advanced and ancient civilization, Pasifika seem ready to take up the steering paddle once again. Temaru doesn't consider the struggle by Hawaiians for full independence from the U.S, to be an unrealistic dream, given his own historical efforts. Temaru's ultimate victory came as a culmination of decades of activism that defined him as one of the most ardent spokespeople for full independence for his country. But he is equally passionate about the need for independence activists to bury their differences and work together in order to achieve that goal. About his meetings with Hawaiian leaders, which included Kekuni Blaisdell and Henry Noa among others, Temaru said, ". . . my message to them is first of all, to get united. They have to get united – there is no other strategy. Don't stay divided – this is what the colonial powers would wish! . . . they divide to rule. No matter what difference [Hawaiian independence activists] have between themselves, get together.""*

The Honolulu Weekly, Vol. 15, No.3 of June 8-14, 2005, page 5 also published an article reporting on the conference at the East-West Center. Gretchen Currie Kelly, "Where Are The Hawaiians?" This article has a different spin, claiming that the East-West Center deliberately downplayed media coverage of this conference and did not invite the participation of Hawaiian activists, because the East-West Center, funded by the U.S. government, does not want to encourage the Hawaiian independence movement. *"One observer noted that several of the visiting leaders expressed surprise at the fact that no indigenous Hawaiians – with the exception of Kumu Keola Lake who welcomed the leaders with a chant – had been invited to be part of the proceedings. Rapa Nui representative Mahina Rapu declined to enter the conference chamber when she learned that no Hawaiians had been invited to participate. She spent the two days of the meeting outside the building. "Linda Lingle is not an indigenous leader," Rapu said. "Where are the Hawaiians?" Lingle is the designated representative from Hawaii to the Conference of Leaders. When questioned about how the East-West Center, which gets half its funding from the U.S. State Department, sees Hawaii's role, director Charles Morrison made it clear that Hawaii was not considered an indigenous entity in and of itself but rather as a conduit for information about the Pacific to the U.S. government."*

On June 13, 2005 the Honolulu Advertiser reported that a United Nations official had just concluded two weeks in Hawaii visiting with Hawaiian independence activists, listening to their views and offering advice on how independence might be achieved. *"A U.N. expert on indigenous peoples is encouraging those seeking an independent Hawaiian nation to press their case for self-determination at the United Nations, saying the body could provide an international forum to air their grievances. Julian Burger, coordinator of the Indigenous Peoples Unit of the U.N.'s Office of the High Commissioner for Human Rights, is speaking to college classes and Native Hawaiian groups as well as visiting key sites during a two-week trip sponsored by the Hawaii Institute for Human Rights and other organizations.*

"Please come and make as much noise as possible," Burger told a gathering of Hawaiian independence movement leaders at the home of activist Kekuni Blaisdell last week. "Use the space that exists to talk about the problems, speak from your hearts, give the evidence ... make sure the story is known as widely as possible." ... Blaisdell, convener of the Kanaka Maoli Tribunal Komike and a separate group known as Ka Pakaukau, said he was inspired by Burger's visit. The United States won't relinquish its grip on Hawaii unless compelled to do so, not something that will happen anytime soon, Blaisdell said. "That's why we have to appeal to the rest of the world, as well as to those with a conscience in the

United States, to recognize who we are and to support re-establishment of our government under our control," he said. "We're calling on the United Nations to use its own law, international law, to support our cause."[152]

The possibility of Hawaiian espionage or sabotage in collaboration with foreign governments hostile to the U.S. in order to get diplomatic recognition of an independent Hawaii, or to weaken the U.S. thereby causing U.S. abandonment of Hawaii

The title of this section sounds like it belongs on a novel by Robert Ludlum or Tom Clancy. Are such treasonous activities actually plausible in Hawaii?

As of early 2007 there have been no reports of Hawaiian sovereignty-related espionage or sabotage. The sovereignty movement has a reputation of non-violence which is actually undeserved, as noted in a previous section of this chapter. The activists like to point to Queen Liliuokalani's decision in the revolution of 1893 to surrender peacefully, under protest, rather than to shed blood. However, it should be noted that the Queen's peaceful surrender is not the whole story about Liliuokalani. She conspired with Robert Wilcox in two very violent events in which men were killed and considerable property damage occurred.[153]

Supporters of the Akaka bill are seeking tribal recognition to make ethnic Hawaiians wards of the federal government within the framework of U.S. law. However, evidence was presented in an earlier section of this chapter regarding the simmering feelings of anger toward the U.S. for historical grievances. Those historical grievances are incorporated into the preambles of every piece of federal legislation providing ethnic Hawaiians with healthcare, housing, education, etc. The festering wounds of history are constantly poked and prodded by sovereignty activists who love to portray Hawaiians as poor downtrodden victims entitled to huge government handouts as reparations for U.S. crimes against the Hawaiian people. Several film production groups busily churn out movies like "Betrayal" and "A Nation Within" showing guns, bayonets, and an American warship assisting the overthrow of a beloved Queen.

But even if the movement remains non-violent, sabotage is a possibility. The U.S. military is seen as an enemy of the Hawaiian people, both historically and at present. The sovereignty activists say, and the U.S. 1993 apology resolution (falsely) says, in 1893 the U.S. military helped overthrow the Queen. Throughout the 20th Century the U.S. military burned, bombed, and polluted the sacred lands of Hawaii – Kahoolawe Island (a living embodiment of the god Kanaloa) was used as a target island for Naval and Air Force bombardment for many years, and still has not been adequately cleaned up. Makua Valley (sacred – the word "Makua" means "parent") was used for live-fire military training until a lawsuit by Hawaiian and environmental activists forced an environmental impact statement resulting in a settlement severely restricting such training there. Similar arguments were made about environmental and cultural impacts of a Stryker brigade, forcing delays and occasional shutdowns of construction and training.

Independence activists portray Hawaii as being under a century-long belligerent military occupation, and they demand its removal. It would seem quite plausible to imagine non-violent sabotage of military bases and military vehicles by Hawaiian independence activists, along with pacifists and environmentalists. The obvious immediate benefit of sabotage would be to prevent military activity from taking place. The strategic political long-term objective of sabotage would be to make military planners in Washington feel that Hawaii is an unreliable host for military bases, and the military should withdraw from Hawaii. Then, once the military is gone, it would be easier to get a complete political divorce.

Espionage is usually non-violent. Hawaii has a high concentration of military bases and training areas for all five services. There are thousands of civilians working on those bases, many of whom may be morally opposed to U.S. policy in Iraq and Israel, and opposed to the American military presence in Hawaii. Hawaiian independence activists Keanu Sai and Hayden Burgess both repeatedly state in public that they served in the U.S. military, until they realized they were "fighting for the wrong country." A family of activists living Kaneohe are known for various resistance actions against local police and government, including refusal to have government license plates or drivers' licenses. The mother styles herself as "head of the Spiritual Nation of Ku" and has a cable TV program. But according to one of the family's TV broadcasts, a daughter in this family did have a drivers license, license plates, and insurance; because she worked as a vehicle driver on the Marine Corps base. Quite strange. Also, Poka Laenui, on his weekly radio program, occasionally suggests that his (rabidly anti-American) listeners, especially in ethnic

Hawaiian Apartheid

Hawaiian neighborhoods like Waianae where jobs are hard to find, should get jobs on the military bases. Very suspicious indeed.

In an earlier section it was pointed out that there is considerable Hawaiian independence activism at the international level, including meetings of worldwide non-governmental organizations and various agencies of the United Nations. Clearly there is "diplomatic" contact between Hawaiian activists and representatives of foreign governments. Some of those governments are hostile toward the United States, just as the Hawaiian independence activists are.

Diplomatic activity between Hawaiian sovereignty activists and governments of nations hostile to the United States could very well result in secret agreements for sovereignty activists to engage in espionage or sabotage in return for formal diplomatic recognition of Hawaiian independence. While most opposition to the Patriot Act among Hawaiian activists is due to their generally leftist political orientation and support for civil rights, some of that opposition is undoubtedly due to a fear that the Patriot Act could thwart their future ability to organize and carry out espionage, sabotage, and other forms of treason.

The Kingdom of Hawaii had diplomatic relations with nations that are now opponents of the United States, including China; and a full-fledged treaty with Russia. There was also a treaty with Hong Kong, whose foreign affairs have now been reabsorbed into China. A chronological list of Hawaiian Kingdom treaties can be found on the "Hawaii Nation" website.[154] Today's independence activists believe that Kingdom treaties and diplomatic relations are still legally binding, due to the illegality of the overthrow and annexation.

Regardless whether a nation had relations with the Kingdom of Hawaii prior to 1893, any nation today could choose to help Hawaiian independence activists, including the possibility of formally recognizing an independent Hawaii, as a way of embarrassing the United States at the United Nations or other international forums. For example, mainland China regards Tibet and Taiwan as belonging to China. Next time the U.S. protests Chinese actions in Tibet, China could retaliate by filing a diplomatic protest over U.S. failure to allow self-determination for native Hawaiians. Next time the U.S. sends warships to patrol the Taiwan Straits, or sells military equipment to Taiwan, China could retaliate by sending a delegation to Hawaii to meet with Bumpy Kanahele, Kekuni Blaisdell, or Poka Laenui and publicize an offer to give them guns (for pig hunting, of course!). The aggressively anti-American governments of Cuba, North Korea, Iran, or Venezuela might gladly agree to help Hawaiian independence activists by publicly extending diplomatic recognition to a "Nation of Hawaii", sending an ambassador to Honolulu, and making speeches about Hawaii in the United Nations and other international venues.

The possibility of trading espionage and/or sabotage for diplomatic recognition is not at all far-fetched.

In 1776 a few American independence activists decided they would take action against the belligerent military occupation of their homeland by Britain. Those American independence activists sent Ben Franklin to Paris to engage in diplomatic relations, and he persuaded the French to send thousands of troops, dozens of warships, and tons of guns and ammunition to assist the American revolution. The French helped the American independence activists not only because the French loved the Americans, but more importantly because the French needed to use America to divert British military power from other places where France and Britain had ongoing struggles.

In the early 1940s, while Germany was occupying northern France and running a puppet Vichy government in southern France, French patriots engaged in sabotage and espionage to help American and British forces liberate their country.

Today there is speculation that the governments of Saudi Arabia and Pakistan might be providing safe haven, training facilities, and billions of dollars to help Al Qaida and other Islamist extremists attack America, Spain, Indonesia, and other countries. Some American citizens (of Arab ancestry and also not of Arab ancestry) have served as anti-American terrorist soldiers.

There are many Hawaiian websites, e-mail lists, and bulletin-board discussion forums that are anti-military and anti-American. Some of those are owned and operated by Hawaiian independence activists. One such forum that was especially troubling was called "Educate Hawaii," founded in 2002. It was created and moderated by Preston Kealoha Yoshioka, who is very skilled at computer programming and website design and management. In Spring 2004 he had a job in California and frequently traveled to Japan and occasionally to Hawaii. "Educate Hawaii" was also created in collaboration with Professor Kiope Raymond of Maui Community College, who teaches the introductory course Hawaiian Studies 107 whose content is provided by and monitored by the UH Manoa Center for Hawaiian Studies. Each semester Professor Raymond required his students to register as members of the bulletin board, where they could read and post messages about Hawaiian sovereignty, Hawaiian culture, etc. Each section of the course had its own private password-protected area where students presumably exchanged information about class assignments and perhaps participated in chat rooms. Students were required to read selected items posted on the main public forum, and could also receive extra credit for being brave enough to post their own comments there.

The "Educate Hawaii" forums were extraordinarily anti-military and anti-American. As of July 2004 there were 382 registered users, who had posted about 3500 messages; but only a few participants were posting frequently (perhaps because it was summer vacation at the colleges). The ONLY participant loyal and patriotic toward America was Ken Conklin.

Ken Conklin decided to do a survey of the members regarding "the treason question": "Would you spy for a foreign nation against the United States, in return for that foreign nation's help in "liberating" Hawaii through diplomatic means?" Before asking the question, there were four paragraphs of explanation describing the history of American patriots collaborating with the French to win independence, as above. Then the question itself was asked.

The moderator, together with the most active and aggressive anti-American member, decided almost immediately to remove the question because it was too dangerous! Anyone patriotic toward America would be very glad to say no. At the time this question was posted there were over 300 registered members of this forum. But nobody on this forum said no (although, to be fair, perhaps the question was pulled before most of them had a chance to see it).

Obviously, the moderator and his most frequent contributor realized that nobody would answer "no." And answering "yes" might cause problems in future years for students who might want to get a job with the government, especially one requiring a security clearance. Eventually the website was closed to the public due to abusive language, threats of violence, and threats of lawsuits, although it might very well continue to function under a new internet location accessible only to students and professors.

Tribal status as a pathway to independence and a threat to national security

Many Hawaiian sovereignty activists who seek total independence for Hawaii oppose the Akaka bill because it would seem to place ethnic Hawaiians more firmly than ever under the thumb of the plenary power of

Congress. However, some of the most militant independence activists with very long track records, including Hayden Burgess (Poka Laenui) and Charles Kauluwehi Maxwell, favor the Akaka bill as a pathway to independence. They see that the money and political power arising from the Akaka bill would make ethnic Hawaiians stronger as a group than they are today, and would empower their tribal government to speak on behalf of 400,000 people. Furthermore, tribal sovereignty would open a path to establishing political relations with foreign governments, thus smoothing the way for eventual secession of Hawaii from the United States. In international forums the new "Nation of Hawaii" as a tribe inside the United States would be comparable to the former status of Algeria or Tunisia, or the current status of Tahiti or Kanaky (New Caledonia), as "Departments" of France – Algeria and Tunisia are now independent nations; while Tahiti and Kanaky are currently agitating for independence.

As sovereign political entities, Indian tribes have the ability to circumvent federal and state law and to engage in economic and political relationships with foreign governments. Elaine Willman, Chair of Citizens Equal Rights Alliance, produced a book in 2006 "Going to Pieces: The Dismantling of the United States of America."[155] She is an enrolled member of an Indian tribe, and personally visited many tribal reservations. Among many topics in her book is a discussion of threats to U.S. national security posed by tribal sovereign immunity, including illegal border crossings facilitated by tribes living along the borders with Canada and Mexico, harboring fugitives, money laundering, and actual negotiations with foreign governments.

In February 2007 Professor John Warren Kindt presented a paper at a conference on international business at Harvard. The paper was entitled "Gambling With Terrorism: Gambling's Strategic Socio-Economic Threat To National Security."[156] His paper focused on the way gambling casinos foster crime including international money laundering. He gave special attention to Indian gambling because the tribes enjoy political sovereignty which allows unsavory international activity to go unchecked. He took special note of an article in "Indian Country Today" on August 31, 2006[157] describing Navajo President Joe Shirley's announcement of "a trade agreement between two sovereign nations" – the Navajos and Fidel Castro's Cuba (despite the long-standing U.S. trade boycott of Cuba). Kindt says "Tribes are using billions of gambling dollars for legal test cases and strategies expanding "tribal sovereign immunity" – superseding federal/state laws and opening U.S. borders."

Chapter 8

Indigenous Rights and Religious Fascism in Support of Hawaiian Racial Supremacy

Introduction

Are ethnic Hawaiians indigenous to Hawaii? Do they have a special relationship to the land of Hawaii that is different from any actual or possible relationship which non-ethnic-Hawaiians might have with the land? Are there legal or moral reasons why the status of being indigenous would entitle ethnic Hawaiians to special political rights?

Both methods for achieving Hawaiian apartheid rely upon claims that ethnic Hawaiians are entitled to special rights on account of being "indigenous." The Akaka bill justifies racial separatism by making frequent use of the words "aboriginal", "indigenous", and "native" in referring to ethnic Hawaiians.[158] If Hawaii were to become an independent nation with roughly the same population as today, ethnic Hawaiians would be only a 20% minority; thus they need a theory of "indigenous rights" to justify why they should have guaranteed political supremacy.

When enumerating the powers of Congress, the U.S. Constitution includes something known as the "Indian commerce clause." Article 1, Section 8, paragraph 3 says Congress shall have the power "to regulate commerce with foreign nations, and among the several states, and with the Indian tribes."

Legal theorists known as originalists, or strict constructionists, would argue that the Indian commerce clause specifically refers to TRIBES, and not the broader category of indigenous people. The majority of Indians today are not members of any tribe and would not be eligible to join one. The Indian commerce clause specifically equates tribes with foreign nations and with the several states of the United States, because they all are political entities having governments which exercise substantial authority over members. They have existed continuously from before the U.S. was created through the present, and they are separate and distinct from other nations, states, or tribes. The Constitution does not give Congress power to round up all Indians and treat them as a single group; nor does it give Congress the power to arbitrarily round up a group of unrelated individual Indians "on the loose" and call them a tribe.

But other legal theorists say the Constitution is a "living document." It is like a tree that must bend in the wind. The Constitution means whatever the nine Justices of the Supreme Court say it means. Particular tribes have been recognized, de-recognized, and re-recognized. The Pueblo Indians never were organized in a tribal structure, yet the U.S. government recognized them. These liberal legal theorists say the term "Indian tribe" really means "indigenous people." When Captain Cook first arrived in Hawaii in 1778, he and his crew used the word "Indians" when writing in their journals about the native Hawaiians. Since Cook's "discovery" of Hawaii happened within about a decade of the writing of the U.S. Constitution, that shows the word "Indian" was used at that time to refer to all aboriginal or indigenous people and was specifically applied to ethnic Hawaiians.

Do ethnic Hawaiians qualify as an indigenous people by historical standards?

Anthropological research suggests that the Polynesian islands were settled by people originating from Asia, spreading through the south Pacific, and arriving in Hawaii very late in the process. Tahiti and Samoa were settled long before Hawaii. But China, Africa, and even the Americas had indigenous peoples living in those places for tens of thousands of years before anyone ventured into any of the Polynesian islands. So, among the peoples of the world, Polynesians have one of the shortest tenures in their so-called indigenous area. And within the Polynesian triangle, Hawaii is probably the most recently settled island group.

The Hawaiian islands had no humans before the first Polynesian (or other?) explorers arrived. Some scientists say the first settlers came from Marquesas, sometime around the year 400. There are also stories of a group of people of particularly small stature, known as "Menehune." However, research reported in the Honolulu Advertiser of March 10, 2006 indicates that Polynesians did not arrive in Hawaii until as recently as years 800-1000 AD. "Kirch and University of Hawaii archaeology professor Barry Rolett agree that Hawaii was probably first settled between 800 and 1000 A.D. — perhaps before the Marquesas."[159] Whatever the year of first arrival, ethnic Hawaiians certainly did not spring forth from the lands of these islands.

Evidence also suggests that the final wave of Polynesian voyagers, from Tahiti, arrived around 1300-1400, conquering and largely destroying the original settlers. In that sense, modern ethnic Hawaiians are local to these islands only from about 1300. The tenure of ethnic Hawaiians in Hawaii after the Tahitian invaders established their genes and their culture is shorter than the tenure of Englishmen in England after the Norman invaders defeated the Saxons.

Some might say that the issue of Tahitians vs. Marquesans is irrelevant, because all were Polynesians. But neither the laws of Hawaii, nor the views of the sovereignty zealots, recognize ethnic Samoans or Tahitians or other Pacific islanders as having any rights to sovereignty in Hawaii.

Even if ethnic Hawaiian tenure in Hawaii is considered to be the tenure of Polynesians as a whole, that would still be only since about 400, or perhaps as late as 1000 – which is shorter than the tenure of the Anglo-Saxon-Celtic race as a whole in England-Ireland. Yet, most people recognized as indigenous would think it very odd if English or Irish showed up at indigenous people's conferences claiming to have indigenous rights. Some sovereignty activists like to say that ethnic Hawaiians have been in Hawaii since time immemorial. But that's false, as the memories contained in their own genealogies tracing through Tahiti can testify.

Do ethnic Hawaiians maintain an indigenous lifestyle?

One argument often heard is that indigenous people are entitled to special rights regarding the use of land, because they are in close contact with the land on a daily basis. For example, some indigenous tribes in Africa, Asia, and the Amazon river basin are very remote from modern civilization. They continue to maintain a subsistence lifestyle of hunting, fishing, gathering, and farming in the same tribal area where their ancestors survived for thousands of years. Continued survival depends on a delicate balance between the people and their ecosystem. Indigenous people who have continuously maintained their cultural traditions as their primary and regular way of life, and who are unable to defend themselves against encroachment from modern civilization, clearly deserve special protection against outside pollution or cultural disruption.

Some African tribes continue hunting with bow and arrow; fishing with net, spear, and individual hook; planting and harvesting by hand or animal-drawn plow; speaking their ancestral language from childhood as their main (and often only) way of communicating. That is quite different from what well-assimilated African-Americans sometimes do as a hobby when they learn traditional skills, or study Swahili, in their spare time.

In Fall 1998 television networks and newspapers around the world followed a controversy over the Makah Indian tribe in the Pacific northwest that was reviving whale hunting. The Makah claimed that "indigenous rights" entitled them to override both U.S. law and international law that prohibited the killing of whales. But the Makah in 1998 did not grow up watching fathers hunting whales, and they did not need whale meat to survive. They started hunting whales both for the enjoyment of the chase and kill, and for the pride they took in "preserving the culture." The Makah's use of the "indigenous rights" claim was clearly bogus, especially in comparison with a primitive African tribe's claim of a right to hunt endangered elephants for food and ceremonial ivory despite a modern law prohibiting it.

Very few ethnic Hawaiians live a traditional subsistence lifestyle, or have any desire to do so. They cannot claim they need land or water to grow taro as a matter of physical survival, since poi is not their primary food as it was 200 years ago. Ethnic Hawaiians might want to grow taro because it makes them feel closer to the land, helps them relearn an almost-forgotten lifestyle, and gives them a source of food free from dependence on the supermarket. But those reasons are more akin to voluntarily choosing to pursue a hobby. Almost all modern-day ethnic Hawaiians live in houses with electricity, plumbing, computers, and food from supermarkets; unlike true indigenous tribes whose dependence upon the land is direct, immediate, and inescapable.

On one hand there are people born and raised in an indigenous lifestyle who learn their culture through the normal activities of daily living, and who may not even be aware of how that culture would be described. They are like fish swimming in the ocean. Fish might never have heard about water, and would be surprised if someone told them about the water passing through their gills and sustaining them at every moment. On the other hand there are people born and raised in a modern lifestyle who voluntarily choose to adopt elements of an indigenous lifestyle. It really makes no difference whether the lifestyle hobbyist has genealogy from the tribe whose lifestyle he imitates. With or without Hawaiian native ancestry, and regardless whether someone is sincere or merely a dilettante, the lifestyle hobbyist is only an inauthentic indigenous wannabe.

Jocelyn Linnekin, a student of famed ethnohistorian Marshall Sahlins, spent a year (ending in 1975) living among ethnic Hawaiians on the isolated Keanae peninsula in windward Maui, along the picturesque road to Hana. She focused on the persistence of tradition. She studied whether traditional Hawaiian practices were still followed, including "exchange-in-kind" and mutual networks of informal obligation as the economic model. She concluded that even in 1975, in that isolated community where almost every resident was ethnic Hawaiian and living on land passed down for generations, ancient rituals and cultural practices do not survive in ancient forms.[160]

Cultural practices are often invented and then used for asserting political claims. For example, in the case of the awa ceremony, Kamakau (writing in the mid-1800s) stated that even in his time it was no longer practiced and only a dim memory.[161] In modern times that ceremony has been reinvented by Hawaiians following Samoan style, and the ceremony is used on public occasions to impress people with their alleged indigenousness. It seems inauthentic when a modern ethnic Hawaiian assembles his political supporters for an awa ceremony, describes the trade winds as the breath of the ancestor of all Hawaiians, passes around the awa bowl and some food and says that drinking and eating these things is a spiritual communion (hinting at the wine and wafers of the Catholic communion). What makes the ritual outrageously inauthentic is that the food is being passed to a mixed audience of men and women, and it includes pieces of banana and coconut. In ancient times there was a strict taboo against men and women eating together; and any woman eating either coconut or banana would be put to death. Today's Hawaiian sovereignty zealots pick and choose which portions of the ancient culture to honor, while dishonoring other elements that were inherently integrated with it. The new or reinvented cultural forms may be beautiful and inspiring, but are used for political purposes rather than spiritual ones. They are not the authentic or spontaneous expressions of people functioning with continuous indigeneity.

The ancient Polynesian tradition of voyaging canoes navigating by the stars had been completely lost and forgotten throughout all of Polynesia. It was revived at the initiative of a white man from California, Ben Finney, who organized the construction of the Hokulea canoe. Finney located a traditional Micronesian navigator, Mau Piailug, who taught the skill to a part-Hawaiian politically-connected man, Nainoa Thompson, in the 1970's. Part of the training for navigating by the stars took place not at night in the open ocean, but indoors in the planetarium of the Bishop Museum in Honolulu.

The author of this book has personally observed occasions when Hawaiian sovereignty zealots want to perform some sort of ceremony for political purposes but do not know any appropriate ceremony from actual personal experience; so they look up the words of an ancient chant as written in Fornander's book[162] and invent hula motions and music to accompany it. This was the procedure followed in 1999, when activists wanted to assemble a welcoming party on a beach in Hilo for the World Indigenous People's Conference on Education. Numerous training sessions were held on several islands with printed instructions, prayers, and chants to be memorized – in traditional indigenous culture these things would already be known to the participants from childhood and would be passed down through oral tradition and apprenticeship. The participants later got on airplanes and flew to Hilo, stayed in motels, drove by car to the beach, and performed their "indigenous" welcoming ceremony. Anyone would be able to do this sort of thing, regardless whether they have native blood, even without having cultural experiences of that sort in ordinary life. In that sense, most modern ethnic Hawaiians are only "wannabe" indigenous, just like white American hippies who sometimes come to Hawaii and try to adopt an "indigenous" lifestyle. This is not to disrespect ethnic Hawaiians or their ancient (or modern reinvented) culture – it is only to recognize a cultural discontinuity that would not be present if the people were truly indigenous.

Some individuals may be more attuned than others to the Cosmic Spirit that lives inside us all. Each culture has practices and rituals which evoke that spirit in ways unique to that culture. Individuals growing up in a culture experience those practices and rituals and become familiar with them. As adults, individuals may unthinkingly persist in following the cultural practices of their upbringing. Some individuals find that practices of other cultures more easily or profoundly evoke awareness of and communion with that inner spirit.

But indigenous people do not choose their culture – they are born into it, live it in everyday practice, and stay in it routinely. Indigenous people are either unaware of other possibilities, or reject and withdraw from whatever external forms might intrude. When indigenous people embrace new cultural forms, language, religion, and lifestyle, they are no longer indigenous.

Hawaiian Apartheid

An example of tribes invented out of thin air, for recreational purposes, was shown on a popular television "reality" series in the summer of 2000 (and continuing every year since then). The program was called "Survivor." In the 2000 series sixteen middle-class American men and women of various ages were placed on a remote island in the South China Sea, and divided into two "tribes" called the Pagong and the Tagi. Each tribe had its own zone of jungle and beach (a Hawaiian ahupuaa!), and was expected to survive through subsistence fishing and hunting. Competitions were held between the tribes, and the losing tribe had to vote one of its members off the island. The program's producers created a carved wooden totem that gave immunity from elimination to the tribe that possessed it. A torchlight ceremony was held each time a tribe had to vote one of its members off the island. After the vote, the person chosen to be sacrificed had his torch snuffed out and was told: "Fire is the symbol of life. Your torch is now extinguished. It is time for you to leave."

The "Survivor" TV series has "tribes" that are completely fictitious, engaging in ceremonies that are completely invented, featuring people who come from thousands of miles away and have no claim to being "indigenous" in the place where the show is filmed. But for a few weeks these contestants lived in a manner more indigenous than most modern ethnic Hawaiians. They were living off the land, exchanging goods and services cooperatively in a moneyless economy, building their own shelters from local materials, and engaging in torchlight ceremonies symbolic of life and death.

Other artificially staged events today are not so obviously phony, and are worthy of comparing with ethnic Hawaiians' reinvented cultural practices. These indigenous-style religious-appearing events are staged in the same places where similar events took place hundreds or even thousands of years ago. Some of today's participants belong to the same ethnic group or might actually be descended from the ancient worshipers. Today's participants often claim they truly believe in the old religion and are engaged in worship. For example, new-age "witches" have sorcery meetings in various New England towns including Salem Massachusetts. A group of "Druids" assemble for religious ceremonies at Stonehenge every year at dawn on the vernal equinox. Should they be taken seriously? How do their authenticity and level of sincerity compare with ethnic Hawaiians?

In January 2007 it was reported that a group of about 25 Greeks participated in a 90-minute program of prayers and ceremonies at the ruins of the ancient Temple of Olympian Zeus in Athens. Both Honolulu newspapers covered the event.[163] Mary Adamski very perceptively said the following in her weekly religion column in the Star-Bulletin:

"Makahiki season, 21st century style? Nope. But the self-proclaimed Greek pagans who honored Zeus at an Athens temple do have some things in common with Hawaiians who have revived the practice of giving reverence to the god Lono at Makua Valley and elsewhere. Some of it is just the liberating fun – oops, make that the serious religious ritual – of dressing up in retro robes. For those Greeks to bare their knees and shoulders was no doubt a bigger deal than Hawaiians donning kikepa and pa'u, which are standard gear for activist demonstrations and Hawaiian society processions. A step back to the past is also a way to define yourself as different and special in the midst of the globalized, homogenized population. The little band of Greeks cherish the glorious time when Greece was the center of philosophy and learning, its scholars and authors quoted to this day, its language still in use in science and medicine. Hawaiian culture did not have that timeless global impact, but there is the same longing to be "the way we were" before outside influences tainted the purity."

Let's briefly explore the continuum of religious authenticity, sincerity, and indigeneity in the above examples as compared with ethnic Hawaiian circumstances today.

Certainly ethnic Hawaiians have the same rights as anyone else to dress up in costumes, to say prayers to whatever gods they choose, to invent ceremonies, etc. The right to do such things does not depend on whether the costumes, prayers, or ceremonies are authentic, nor on whether the participants are sincere. Furthermore, ethnicity and indigeneity are irrelevant – anyone is entitled to participate.

The contestants on "Survivor" are hoping to win lots of money. But the same can be said of some of the ethnic Hawaiians who use the old religion and ancient ceremonies to try to impress politicians and the general public that they are entitled to be treated as "indigenous" people and should have a phony tribe created for them so they can get huge awards of land and money. Hawaiian language is one of the most important weapons in the arsenal of Hawaiian sovereignty activists. The language is used for ceremonial purposes in front of audiences who don't speak the language, to impress listeners with a sense of mystery, power, and authenticity – much like Latin was used in Roman Catholic churches throughout the world for many centuries after Latin became a "dead" language. For example on March 31, 2005 an informational briefing on the Akaka bill was given to the Hawaii legislature by Senators Akaka and Inouye, and Representatives Abercrombie and Case. The event was opened with a Hawaiian language prayer and the singing of the Christian "Doxology" in Hawaiian language. A transcript is available, with analysis.[164]

Some new-age hippies create prayers and ceremonies just because it makes them feel good. So do some Hawaiians. The modern witches at Salem enjoy the spine-tingling feeling that comes from chanting their magic incantations – the same is true for some ethnic Hawaiian "traditional practitioners." In both cases it's fair to ask whether the prayers, potions, spells or ceremonies are efficacious – do they have any actual effect in either the spirit world or the material world, beyond mere psychological titilation? And regardless of actual effect, do the performers sincerely believe the prayers and ceremonies are efficacious, or are the performers simply enjoying activities they know are merely recreational?

The modern "Druids" at Stonehenge, and the modern worshipers of Zeus, have a great deal in common with most ethnic Hawaiians. They are probably sincere; not trying to make money; believing they are indigenous; believing their ceremonies are at least somewhat authentic and somewhat efficacious. The Druids, Zeus-worshipers, and Hawaiians might also share uncertainty over whether "outsiders" should be allowed to participate. Some might worry that ancient secrets should not be shared; and some might feel sad or angry if outside wannabes imitate them.

But among all the examples cited, ethnic Hawaiians are the only ones who have zealous subgroups using religion as one of the justifications for demanding a race-based government or racial supremacy in an independent nation.

Where the bones are

In Hawaiian language the word for "ancestral homeland" is "kulaiwi." It is composed of two words: "kula" which in this context means "field", "plane", "source" or "container"; and "iwi" which means "bones." Thus, the very word for "homeland" literally means "the field where the bones are buried."

A well-known song in Hawaiian language uses that word "kulaiwi." The song is "Hawaii Aloha." Many residents who do not normally speak Hawaiian learned this song when they were children, or more recently after coming to live here. It is sung frequently at the end of social events as a form of bonding or fellowship, with everyone standing in a circle and holding hands. Even at a public ceremony marking the start of a renovation project at Windward Mall in Kaneohe in 2006, a large multiracial group of total strangers pushed aside their chairs, rearranged themselves in a circle, held hands and sang the song before going their separate ways. This is the kind of thing which makes Hawaii a special place, where the Spirit of Aloha is felt strongly.

The first two lines of the song have literal meanings which make it technically incorrect for many residents to sing it.

"E Hawaii e kuu one hanau e" "O Hawaii, sands of my birth" is clearly inaccurate for anyone who was not born in Hawaii.

"Kuu home kulaiwi nei" "My beloved ancestral homeland" is inaccurate, even for many "local" people born and raised in Hawaii, if their parents, grandparents, etc. are either still living or were buried outside Hawaii. "Kuu home kulaiwi" means "my ancestral homeland," so technically a lawyer could argue that it's OK for anyone to sing this song who has at least one parent or grandparent or great-grandparent who is buried in Hawaii. But emotionally "kulaiwi" runs deep, like "ancestral home."

Of course this song is sung in a spirit of feel-good togetherness. Newcomers to Hawaii can sing it in the same way Buddhists, Jews, or atheists can sing "Silent Night" at a Christmas party even though they do not believe in the song's lyrics about the birth of a holy Jesus to a virgin mother.

But at a deeper level the song "Hawaii Aloha" is a gentle reminder that anyone lacking a drop of Hawaiian native blood is merely a guest in the ancestral homeland of the ethnic Hawaiians. The song implies that the natives are very generous in welcoming outsiders; but those outsiders should never imagine they have standing as anything more than guests. It is a subtle assertion of a right to race-based political power.

Ethnic Hawaiians have ancestors whose bones have been in the land of Hawaii for hundreds of years. However, most ethnic Hawaiians have more ancestral bones outside Hawaii than they have native Hawaiian bones in the land of Hawaii. That's very obvious for either of two reasons. (1) Most ethnic Hawaiians have more English or Asian blood than they have Hawaiian native blood. If more than half of someone's genealogy is not Hawaiian, then more than half of the bones of his ancestors are not in Hawaii. (2) Even if someone were 100% "pure Hawaiian," his ancestors were in Hawaii for less than 2,000 years. But before that all his ancestors for tens of thousands of years were in other Pacific islands or in Asia from whence came the settlers of the Pacific islands.

Where the bones are is also used by Hawaiian sovereignty zealots to claim a "right of return." The nation of Israel has a policy that all Jews (born to a Jewish mother) worldwide have a right to "return" to Israel as their homeland, even if they and their mother have never been there. The theory is that Israel is the ancestral homeland of all Jews – all people descended from Abraham through Isaac. Israel is the "Promised Land" – literally, the land promised to the Jews by God who named them as his chosen people. In a similar way the Hawaiian sovereignty activists claim that every person worldwide who has even one drop of Hawaiian native blood is entitled to come to Hawaii in possession of full voting rights and property rights. The ethnic Hawaiian "returning" from "diaspora" would step off the airplane with rights far superior to the rights of anyone lacking native blood, even if their family has been born and raised in Hawaii for many generations. The next section in this chapter will describe the Hawaiian religious theory which explains why the Hawaiian islands are, in effect, the land promised to ethnic Hawaiians by the Hawaiian gods.

For the moment let's wrap up the bones this way. Where the bones are should not determine either indigenous status or political rights for ethnic Hawaiians. We have seen that most ethnic Hawaiians have most of their genealogy from outside Hawaii, and even a "pure Hawaiian" has 99% of all the bones of all his ancestors for tens of thousands of years buried outside Hawaii (from before the first voyaging canoes arrived in Hawaii less than 2,000 years ago). The right of return is also inappropriate. Perhaps a hundred million Americans have ancestors whose bones have been buried in England for many centuries, but that does not give those Americans political rights in England. Indeed, the ethnic Hawaiian who is 15/16 Chinese has China as his true ancestral homeland, but nobody (including the United Nations) would give him the right to go to China to live, own land, or vote.

A beautiful creation legend now used as a basis for religious fascism

All cultures have one or more creation legends to explain how the world and its people came into existence. There are several such legends for Hawaii. The most famous and beautiful one, "Kumulipo", is now used for political purposes as a religious basis to justify political fascism.

Kumulipo is a chant composed of 2102 lines, describing how the world began and how its various lifeforms evolved, all the way to modern man. In ancient times there was no written language, so the chant had to be memorized. Because it was so important, the chant had to be sung without error to an audience that maintained absolute silence. As Christianity took hold following the arrival of the American missionaries in 1820, Kumulipo receded into the cultural background and was nearly forgotten. But Kalakaua revived it and used it for political purposes during his campaign against Emma for the royal crown in 1874. Genealogy had always been important when asserting a claim to political power. And so Kalakaua hired a genealogist to use Kumulipo as the beginning of a pedigree emphasizing his alleged royal heritage tracing all the way back to the gods. Dowager queen Emma, wife of King Alexander Liholiho Kamehameha IV, was a grandchild of Englishman John Young. So she had only 3/4 native blood. Her genealogy worked against her. Kalakaua's use of Kumulipo was perhaps the first time Hawaiian religion was used to assert racial supremacy as a basis for political power in Hawaii. But it was not the last time religion was used that way.

The gods, the land, and the ethnic Hawaiians – How Hawaiian religion is (ab)used to assert an inherent right to racial supremacy

The old religion was abolished in 1819 by Liholiho Kamehameha II and his regent stepmother Kaahumanu. They ordered the destruction of the heiau (stone temples) and burning of the wooden idols. A few diehard deadenders refused to let go of the old religion and started a civil war, but were quickly defeated.

A few years before, several native adventurers had traveled to Yale University. They were taken in by professors at the divinity school and became Christians. One of them, Opukahaia (Obookiah), was a powerful speaker in both Hawaiian and English, as well as a fervent Christian.[165] One day he was found weeping on the steps of the Yale library. When asked why, he pleaded with his professors to send missionaries to Hawaii to lift up his fellow natives out of their heathen ways. And so as luck would have it (or was it Divine Providence?) the first boatload of Christian missionaries arrived in Hawaii at exactly the right historic moment, in 1820, a few months after the natives had unknowingly prepared the way for them by overthrowing their own native religion.

Although the Hawaiian religion was abolished nearly 200 years ago by the natives themselves, it has been making a comeback lately among Hawaiian "traditional practitioners." Most ethnic Hawaiians today are Christians, but many also embrace the mysticism of the old religion, particularly regarding the special relationship between the land and the natives. Even some Catholic priests and Protestant ordained ministers of Hawaiian ancestry practice elements of the old religion, telling their church members that there is no conflict between Christianity and many of the ancient beliefs. They say it's OK to pray to the Christian God while also recognizing the 400,000 Hawaiian gods. It's OK to believe in Hawaiian family or ancestral aumakua (guiding spirits) who may take the form of mano (shark), honu (turtle), or pueo (owl). After all, Christians believe in spirits (angels); and some alleged Christians believe in reincarnation as well as the concept that God is manifested in animals and plants. People of all faiths are confused about theology, including priests and theologians themselves!

Hawaiian "traditional practitioners" hold religious views that are clearly in conflict with Christianity. But what's more important for the future of Hawaii is that Hawaiian traditional practitioners hold religious views that are strongly in conflict with democratic political principles.

According to the creation story in Kumulipo, people of Hawaiian native ancestry have a family relationship with the gods and the land; and that relationship is not shared with anyone lacking Hawaiian ancestry. Thus, ethnic Hawaiians are inalienably entitled to racial supremacy in Hawaii. Furthermore, some ethnic Hawaiians have inherently higher spiritual standing than other ethnic Hawaiians, because of genealogy. That higher spiritual standing based on genealogy translates into an inherent right to superior political power. Thus, it is NOT true that all persons are equal in the eyes of the gods, and it is NOT true that all persons should be treated equally by the laws or the government. According to this religious belief all ethnic Hawaiians have inherent racial supremacy over anyone lacking native ancestry; but in addition, ethnic Hawaiians have different levels of genealogy and "mana" (spiritual power) which establish an inherent pecking order within that ethnic group.

The interpretation of Kumulipo favored by Hawaiian cultural practitioners and sovereignty activists goes like this (tremendously shortened): Sky father Wakea mated with earth mother Papa. As a result of those matings Papa gave birth to the Hawaiian islands as living beings. Later they mated again and produced the goddess Hoohokukalani (she who placed the stars in the heavens). Later, Wakea had a sacred niaupio mating with his own daughter Hoohokukalani (a normal cultural practice among high-ranking alii for the purpose of preserving genealogical power), but their baby Haloa was deformed and stillborn. They buried it, and from that source grew Kalo, the taro plant. Wakea and Hoohokukalani mated again, and produced a perfectly healthy baby, to which they gave the same name

Haloa; and he was the primordial ancestor from whom all other ethnic Hawaiians are descended.

The question of greatest concern for Hawaiian sovereignty is: was Haloa the first Hawaiian, or the first Polynesian, or the first human being? The sovereignty activists interpret the myth to mean that Haloa was the first Hawaiian, and the entire Kumulipo took place in Hawaii. Therefore the gods, the Hawaiian islands, and the ethnic Hawaiians are all related as members of a family. The highest seniority and rank in this family belongs to the gods; later come the Hawaiian islands (land and reefs) as living creatures; later the taro plant; and later the Hawaiian people. Hawaiians owe greatest loyalty and service first to the gods, then to the land, then to their elder brother the taro plant, and finally to each other. Creatures higher on the scale have a responsibility to feed and take care of lower creatures, while those lower on the scale owe loyalty and service to those higher up. Among ethnic Hawaiians, some are more closely related to the gods than others, having a genealogy which can be traced more clearly and directly. Thus there is a natural, inborn hierarchy among ethnic Hawaiians placing some as high-ranking alii, some as lower-ranking alii, some as makaainana (commoners, literally "on the land" or "looking to the land"), and some as kauwa (outcast slaves). The concept of pono is understood in this context – pono is not merely justice, or righteousness, but more fundamentally it is the balance of nature in which everything has its proper place and functioning. Kapu (taboo) is a set of rules for maintaining pono. Breaking kapu disrupts the stability of the whole family, threatening the security of each person and the productivity of the land. Pono can only be restored through some form of sacrifice.

Behavior considered normal today was regarded as a serious breach of kapu in precontact times. For example, women were forbidden from eating banana or coconut, because those were the kinolau (embodiments) of the god of masculinity – the shapes of bananas and coconuts are clearly suggestive of the male ule (penis) and the male hua (testicles). Stepping on the shadow of a high-ranking alii, or touching his clothing, was considered an infringement on the chief's sacredness which could result in a loss of the chief's mana (spiritual power) and therefore would have negative effects on the chief's ability to maintain pono between people and the gods. Men and women were forbidden from eating together. Women were required to live separately from the rest of the community for several days each month, at the time of their menstrual flow. A person who breaks the kapu (law) disrupts pono and thereby threatens the whole society. It is appropriate that the lawbreaker be killed and his body be placed on a lele (raised platform) in a heiau (stone temple). If things in general seem to be going badly, or there's a famine, then human sacrifice must be made to restore pono. The severity of the problem determines the number and rank of the humans to be sacrificed – it is possible that a high-ranking alii or even a king might need to be sacrificed. For further explanation of the relationships among kapu, pono, and mohai kanaka (human sacrifice), see a book by Valerio Valeri entitled "Kingship and Sacrifice."[166]

Was Haloa the first Hawaiian, or the first Polynesian, or the first human being? The biggest political bang for the theological buck would come from claiming that Haloa was the first Hawaiian, and the entire Kumulipo is confined to the Hawaiian archipelago (including the 1200 miles of the Northwest Hawaiian Islands). That way, only ethnic Hawaiians are descended from Haloa; and only ethnic Hawaiians have that special family relationship as children of the gods and brothers to the land.

But that interpretation logically contradicts the great pride today's Hawaiians take in the voyaging canoes. Human beings did not spring up directly from the lands of Hawaii. The first settlers in Hawaii came from other places, by voyaging canoes that used only the stars for navigation. It is believed those first settlers came from other Polynesian islands. All Polynesian islands share the most important legends, gods, and demigods in common – the gods Wakea, Papa, Hoohokukalani, Kane, Lono, Ku, Kanaloa; the demigods Maui, Pele, Kamapuaa, etc. Thus an interpretation of Kumulipo that would be consistent with anthropology and would incorporate the voyaging canoe history of Hawaii would be that Haloa was the primordial ancestor of all Polynesians (not merely of Hawaiians). However, acknowledging that Polynesians of other islands are also descendants of Haloa would imply that they too are children of the gods and brothers to the islands and therefore should share in racial supremacy and political power in Hawaii. Hawaiian sovereignty zealots refuse to allow such an outcome, and have reasons other than Kumulipo for keeping the scope of race-based political power limited to ethnic Hawaiians alone.

What about the idea that Haloa was Adam – the primordial ancestor of all human beings? It's just one story seen through different cultural lenses. Jews told the story of Adam set in their part of the world and using their metaphors; Polynesians told the story of Haloa set in the Polynesian triangle and using Polynesian metaphors. All human beings are indigenous people of the Earth; we are all children of the gods and brothers of the land. Can't we all just get along? But such an interpretation of Kumulipo would remove any religious basis for racial supremacy, and thus is summarily dismissed by Hawaiian sovereignty zealots.

Most scholars who carefully study Kumulipo conclude that it is at least as broad as Polynesians in general, and probably includes all mankind. For example, Chapter 21 of Martha Beckwith's book[167] describes the prevalence of this legend throughout Polynesia, and on page 119 Beckwith says David Malo (ethnic Hawaiian historian and political activist of the mid 1800s) calls Haloa "progenitor of all the peoples of the earth." Rubellite Kawena Johnson, a greatly respected ethnic Hawaiian kupuna and professor of Hawaiian language and literature at University of Hawaii, has made her own translation of Kumulipo. She stated publicly at Iolani Palace in 2003, during a performance of her own operatic play based on Kumulipo, that she recognizes Kumulipo is not racially exclusionary.

But regardless of arguments over how to interpret Kumulipo, it is simply unacceptable for a thoroughly integrated multiracial society to allow one race to claim permanent legal and political supremacy. Whether that race is in the majority, as whites were in the Southern United States during slavery, or whether the superior race is in the minority as the whites were in South Africa under apartheid, racial supremacy is no longer acceptable today. Claims for racial or ethnic political supremacy have caused tremendous suffering within the past few years. Rwanda: Tutsi vs. Hutu. Zimbabwe: indigenous Africans evicted and sometimes killed miltigeneration white farmers, with government approval. Fiji: native Fijians staged a military coup against a democratically elected government headed by Asian Indian descendants of sugar plantation workers who had been imported by the British several generations previously. The world will never forget the German Holocaust based on a theory of Aryan supremacy over the Jews.

Those who choose a racially exclusionary interpretation of Kumulipo are following a very dangerous path. For example, some Zionists defend Israeli brutality toward the Palestinians by claiming that the Jews are God's chosen people. Jews are the descendants of Abraham who had a covenant with God that forever gave the land of Israel to Abraham's descendants through Isaac. This religious justification for race-based control over land is similar to the Hawaiian claims under Kumulipo, except that Hawaiians claim to be in a family relationship with the land and gods whereas the Zionists claim to have a legal or contractual grant of sovereignty from a single all-powerful God. Other examples of religious claims to racial supremacy include the white supremacists who claim blacks are cursed by God with the mark of Cain; or followers of minister Farakhan (and the early Malcolm X) who claim white people are embodiments of the Devil. Can't we all just get along?

An interesting example of Hawaiian religious fascism concerns how the summit of Mauna Kea should be used.[168] Mauna Kea is the highest mountain in the pacific. It is widely regarded as the best place in the world for doing astronomy. There are many large telescopes on the summit. But Mauna Kea is regarded as a sacred place in Hawaiian legend. It's name is a shortened form of "Mauna a Wakea" which means the mountain belonging to Wakea (sky-father). It is the place where Wakea mated with Papa (earth mother), producing daughter Hoohokukalani (she who placed the stars in the heavens). Many years later, Wakea mated repeatedly with his daughter Hoohokukalani, producing first a stillborn baby whose body was buried and from which the first taro plant grew; and then producing the primordial ancestor of all ethnic Hawaiians, Haloa. Because of the fact that these enormously important events took place on Mauna Kea, the mountain is sacred. Therefore, say the Hawaiian zealots, it is a sacrilege and an abomination to corrupt and pollute that place with telescopes. Long ago when the telescopes were put there, the ethnic Hawaiian community was more mellow. But now they have had years of practice in political activism and are pressing for sovereignty.

When NASA made a proposal a few years ago to place additional telescopes on Mauna Kea, the zealots made very noisy protests starting in 1999 and continuing into 2006 when the plans were abandoned due to budget cuts at NASA. The zealots claimed that because the mountain is sacred to them, and they are the indigenous people of Hawaii; therefore what the rest of the world wants counts for nothing. It doesn't matter that spectacular discoveries are being made on Mauna Kea that shape our understanding of the how the universe got started – the zealots already know all about that through their Kumulipo legend. They claimed the right to assert political control over land use policy based on their religious belief and their indigenous status.

The author of this book presented testimony, partly in Hawaiian language, citing the creation legend as a reason why the use of Mauna Kea for astronomical observatories is a fulfillment of its spiritual essence.[169] That's because it is sky-father's mountain, and telescopes are the way we worship him today. Also, it is where Hoohokukalani was conceived, who is the mother of all Hawaiians and "she who placed the stars in the sky." Thus telescopes are how we give honor to her. Also, in ancient times, native Hawaiians had used the summit for an adz (axe-blade) quarry and workshop, thus showing that it was perfectly OK to dig into the ground there and use the place for technological purposes unrelated to religion.

But the zealots were not interested in the true meaning of their religious theory; or what the Ancients had done. They were merely interested in using the theory to bully the federal government and the State of Hawaii as a way to assert political power. As the controversy heated up, the Chairman of the Office of Hawaiian Affairs said everything would be OK if the astronomers would give $20 million to OHA.[170] So much for sacredness! Also, on July 31, "Sovereignty Restoration Day" (based on the restoration of sovereignty on July 31, 1843), a group of Hawaiian independence zealots walked to the top of Mauna Kea carrying huge Hawaiian flags in order to show the world that the Hawaiian flag flies higher than any American flag in all of Hawaii.[171] One wonders whether the gods were pleased.

Deep culture

The world has many unique and distinct cultures. Anyone who has traveled between Asia, North America, and Arabia has experienced radical differences in how people think, what values they hold dear, and what should be the relationship between a government and its people. Even within Europe there are important cultural differences among France, Germany, Italy, Spain, and England (although those differences are becoming less pronounced as the European Union melds them together). Each nation historically has produced unique styles of music, art, literature, and food. Governments come and go; wars are won and lost; fads erupt and fizzle; but the deep values that characterize a major culture survive for centuries with only glacially slow change. Is there such a deep culture in Hawaii? If so, how would it be described?

In ancient times each Hawaiian island had its own King and its own culture. Even different regions of the same island often had very different folkways. Perhaps the best attempt to describe the "deep culture" of Hawaii was a two volume book "Nana I Ke Kumu" whose principal author was the revered cultural expert Mary Kawena Pukui.[172] But in that book Pukui emphasized that cultural practices varied widely, and that she was describing the customs of one remote part of the Big Island (Kau) during bygone years. She noted that many of those customs were no longer practiced even forty years ago when she wrote the book. Another important book that tried to identify "Hawaiian values" was "Ku Kanaka" by

George S. Kanahele.[173] The book was written for the tourist industry, to help tourists and tour service providers understand how to explain "Hawaiian culture." But the book's subtitle, "a search for Hawaiian values", reflects Kanahele's admission that the values he identifies are more aspirational than descriptive.

Modern Hawaii has many different races, ethnicities, and cultures living side by side, participating in each other's events, intermarried, and assimilated. There is no majority – everyone in Hawaii is a member of a minority. It's a beautiful rainbow society. If there is a "deep culture" for ethnic Hawaiians, it seems that nobody is willing to describe it.

Hawaiian culture in ancient times (before Captain Cook) varied from place to place. But if there was a common core deep culture, it certainly would have included many elements practiced for a thousand years, which today's ethnic Hawaiians strongly reject – feudal land tenure; social caste system; total subjugation of individual rights under group communal rights; polygamy and polyandry; incest; infanticide; human sacrifice; death penalty for small infractions like a woman eating a banana or a man stepping on the shadow of a high chief. Those ancient practices survived for a thousand years, so they are certainly more appropriate descriptions of ethnic Hawaiian "deep culture" than current practices in place for only one or two centuries. Hawaiian sovereignty zealots love to complain about the destruction of "their" culture and way of life by Western values, which have allegedly caused today's allegedly bad health and welfare statistics. In making that complaint, they acknowledge that today's Hawaiian culture is not the "deep culture" which has now been lost.

"Hawaiian culture" seems to mean all the "good" stuff from all historical periods (as judged by present standards), and none of the bad. The vast variations in cultural practices in different parts of ancient Hawaii are set aside. Native historian David Malo, writing 175 years ago, complained that songs, chants, and genealogies were not being accurately handed down through the spoken language in the days before writing was created by the American missionaries and might (already at that time) be intentionally altered for political purposes.

Kenneth R. Conklin, Ph.D.

Hawaiian epistemology as justification for claiming indigenous status and for demanding racial separatism in education

"But will it also be thought strange that education and knowledge of the world have enabled us to perceive that as a race we have some special mental and physical requirements not shared by the other races which have come among us?" (ex-queen Liliuokalani, 1898)

Some Hawaiian sovereignty zealots are demanding that a group of a dozen Hawaiian "host-culture" charter schools (perhaps also to be joined by the Hawaiian language immersion schools) should be able to pull out of the Department of Education and form their own separate school district. This non-contiguous ethnic-based school district would have the authority to set its own standards for curriculum and teacher certification, radically different from the standards applicable to all other public schools. It would also have authority to create more such "Hawaiian" schools at taxpayer expense.[174]

Supporters of the "host culture" schools like to say that their children formerly had low attendance rates, poor self-esteem, and disciplinary problems when attending regular schools; but now have high attendance rates and very little misbehavior. Yes indeed. If parents are allowed to freely choose their children's schools; and if schools demand that parents making such choices must participate actively in school activities; and if the children get to spend long hours playing in the mud (taro patch), building rock walls (fishpond and heiau restoration), and generally doing hands-on projects outdoors rather than reading books and writing term papers – then the children will have high attendance and high morale. But they are not learning what they need for getting admitted to colleges and succeeding once they get there. They are learning ethnic pride and ethnic loyalty rather than pride and loyalty as Americans.

Children emerging from "host culture" charter schools will have low rates of success in the larger society of the state of Hawaii or the United States. But that's OK with the parents, and especially with the leadership of the "movement." They see the schools educating children for a future sovereign nation of Hawaii, either on the model of an Akaka tribe or on the model of an independent nation. "Success" for such children is defined very differently than for everyone else. Success means being able to speak Hawaiian, using Hawaiian to chant and pray to the old gods, to plant and pull taro, to catch fish and gather limu, to know the meanings of

Hawaiian Apartheid

place-names and the Hawaiian myths associated with them, to sail on a voyaging canoe, etc.

For decades America's schools struggled to achieve racial desegregation, even to the extent of court-ordered busing across district lines to produce racial mixing. Recent hard-fought Supreme Court cases gave state colleges the authority to engage in "affirmative action" so that ethnic minorities will achieve a "critical mass" of students to ensure diversity in college student populations. Why in the world would anyone want to re-segregate a public school system? Are we now wanting to endorse state-sponsored racial separatism?

Even if it is voluntary for parents to choose to send their children to schools that are overwhelmingly populated by one ethnic group, where the curriculum is tightly focused on a single subculture – is it a good thing for those children and for society as a whole? Would ethnic Japanese parents (plus a few non-Japanese who love sumo, ikebana, kendo and sushi) living in the state of California be legally permitted to create a group of Japanese-culture-focused public schools widely scattered throughout California and then create a separate non-contiguous "public" school district with its own standards?

Society has a responsibility to protect children against parents who make spectacularly bad choices for their children, even when such choices are "voluntary" (for the parents). Society also has a right to set uniform minimum standards for the schools it supports with tax dollars, whose children will end up on the tax supported welfare rolls if their schooling leaves them unprepared to earn a living. Parents who want radically different schools are expected to send children to private schools and pay tuition.

In the case of the Hawaiian "host culture" charter schools, society also has an obligation to defend itself against a radical group of zealots who are using government money to build a race-based nation hostile to that very government. The "host culture" charter schools are consciously and deliberately using children as pawns in a long-term political struggle for ethnic nation-building. Here are quotes from the 2002 version of the webpage of Kanu O Ka Aina, the school which is the spear-point of this consortium of charter schools. The webpage has been toned down since then, but the school's philosophy remains the same.

"The long-term goal of Kanu is to create a native designed and controlled system of Hawaiian education that will empower native communities throughout the archipelago to achieve political, cultural and economic self-determination. ... Kanu wants to empower Hawaii's native

people, who are direct descendants of earthmother Papa and skyfather Wakea, to once again assume our rightful stewardship over our archipelago. ... We believe that Hawaiian knowledge structure differs significantly from the Western system of education. We believe that as an indigenous people, Hawaiians have the right to design and control our own education. ... Probably the most unique and critical aspect of Kanu's educational foundations is the fact that Kanu wants to actively prepare native students to participate in - and perhaps even lead - Hawaii's indigenous sovereignty movement. ... Kanu wants to encourage Hawaiian students to become politically conscious, and individually and collectively tackle the problem of Hawaiian oppression by the United States and our subjugation to American law and a Western way of life. In that vein, Kanu has the potential of significantly contributing to the Hawaiian sovereignty effort. ... Kanu hopes to make our students realize that the occupation of Hawaii by the United States of America is not fatal and unalterable, but merely limiting – and therefore challenging. Additionally,

Kanu wants to empower our students to accept this challenge and find solutions to this and the many other dilemma, that face Hawaii's native people in their homeland today. By actively participating in finding solutions to native problems, it is envisioned that Kanu students will become an intricate part of the process of native liberation from American domination that nearly caused the demise of our native people and our way of life."[175]

Remember that Kanu O Ka Aina is a "public" school required by law to be open to children of all races. But imagine how children of no native ancestry would feel when exposed day after day, year after year, to a curriculum that constantly reminds them they are only guests in someone else's homeland; that they lack the magic blood which their classmates have.

It is not enough that such a model of education sounds really nifty, keeps the kids drug-free and off the streets, and parents like it. To make such a radically different kind of education palatable to a skeptical public who pay the bills, there must be a scholarly theory explaining why it is necessary.

The hope for scholarly respectability comes from a newly invented theory of Hawaiian epistemology, blended with John Dewey's discredited century-old "progressive" philosophy of education.

Professor Manulani Aluli Meyer of the University of Hawaii at Hilo has developed a description of the culture-based ways ethnic Hawaiians learn, based on her interviews with Hawaiian elders.[176] After describing her categories of ways of knowing, she then cites an eclectic hodgepodge of well-known mainstream philosophers, parts of whose theories support various categories of Hawaiian knowledge-sources. Underlying it all is Meyer's belief that anyone with a drop of Hawaiian native blood has genetically encoded unique ways of knowing and learning; and therefore ethnic Hawaiian children have special needs for uniquely tailored curriculum and instructional methods.

Meyer's theory has attracted the attention of radical educationists of other ethnic groups, who invited her to be the keynote speaker at a symposium at UCLA on Oct. 16, 2004. Perhaps these activists recognize that the public will easily buy the concept that "indigenous" people are so vastly different from the general population that it is easy to concede they have a need for a radically different, racially/culturally separatist education. Other ethnic minorities, less obviously different from the "dominant culture," perhaps can hope to develop their own culture-based epistemologies in order to demand ethnically separate culture-based activity-centered education, using Hawaiian epistemology as a sort of ideal model or guiding beacon for how to develop such a rationale.

Meyer's theory of Hawaiian epistemology was invented through a survey of Hawaiian culture-based ways of getting knowledge as told to her by ethnic Hawaiian elders. The theory includes a classification of different kinds of knowledge and the different methods whereby such knowledge is obtained and validated. Although Hawaiian epistemology is a theory derived from a study of Hawaiian culture, it is also claimed to be more generally descriptive of all indigenous cultures. That's because all indigenous cultures share a closeness of relationship to their ancestral land and a belief in ancestral spirits and gods who are constantly present throughout all aspects of nature.

The gods, the ancestral spirits, and the land itself speak to all living ethnic Hawaiians through racial memories encoded and passed down through genetic inheritance, and also through dreams and prayers. Thus, "ordinary" activities of daily life, as well as subject-matter knowledge and skill learned in school, are filtered through the lens of Hawaiian-ness and take on special meanings not available to those who lack a drop of native blood.

Ethnic Hawaiian elders, as the repositories of cultural wisdom and as people born in an earlier time when their upbringing was more culturally authentic, are regarded as authorities on Hawaiian ways of knowing. A survey of well-known and highly respected elders produced a list of ways of knowing, accompanied by illustrative examples given by the elders themselves.

Although the theory of Hawaiian epistemology is based on an empirical survey of cultural elders, it is put forward as being metaphysically true. Elements of this theory are explained by reference to the epistemological theories of well-known philosophers. Different philosophers' theories are more or less relevant to different aspects of the Hawaiian epistemology. But the empirically derived culture-based ways of knowing as revealed by the elders are the core of this theory. The epistemologies of well-known mainstream philosophers are used merely to illustrate or explain what is meant so that Western-trained philosophers will understand what is being said and will give recognition to the Hawaiian theory as being philosophically plausible.

Although the resulting theory of epistemology is obviously eclectic and lacks any coherence or credibility as would be judged by philosophers who specialize in epistemology, Meyer nevertheless defends it as a valid epistemology for an (allegedly) indigenous people. That's because, in Hawaiian culture, true knowledge comes from action in the material world and inspiration from the spirit world, but not from idle speculation or abstract logic. Accordingly, any valid theory of knowledge must arise out of cultural experience, must be described by the elders who are the repositories of wisdom, and must be vaidated by the authority of the elders and by the authority of being accepted within the culture itself. Hawaiian epistemology is a prime example of cultural relativism, and conventionalist descriptivism. It is cultural anthropology, not philosophical epistemology; despite a veneer of references to various philosophers.

The theory is valid for individual ethnic Hawaiians only to the extent that those individuals follow a particular kind of Hawaiian cultural upbringing in accord with the cultural patterns described by the elders who talked with Ms. Meyer. But very few ethnic Hawaiians today have that sort of upbringing either exclusively or predominantly. Indeed, there's a continuum of Hawaiian-style upbringing ranging from a small number of children brought up exclusively in traditional ways (hopefully without human sacrifice or brother-sister incest), to a vast majority of ethnic Hawaiians whose upbringing might include some elements of traditional lifestyle. There are an increasing number of ethnic Hawaiian children raised in families who simply don't care about tradition, and children who are raised in foster homes. There are also an increasing number of children with no native ancestry who are influenced by and engage in elements of traditional Hawaiian culture simply because those cultural elements are the core of Hawaii's multiracial rainbow society – things like hula, Hawaiian language, taro cultivation, and heiau restoration.

Professor Meyer's theory of Hawaiian epistemology might best be described as a dream or ideal for how children should be shaped in the future if only they could be completely decolonized. It can also be seen as a prediction for how ethnic Hawaiian children will actually become molded into an artificially created, radically different subculture if an apartheid school system already under development is allowed to become independent from the standards and supervision of the state of Hawaii.

One might wonder whether only ethnic Hawaiian children can be molded to fit into such a subculture. If Meyer is correct that racial memories and spirit communication are passed through genealogy, then presumably only ethnic Hawaiians could be fully molded into the newly emergent sovereign culture. However, if we exclude any belief in genetic inheritance of cultural knowledge, then even non-indigenous people could be molded by the educational system to become fully indigenous culturally, spiritually, and morally. Is it possible to "become" an indigenous person even without the native blood? If not, then "indigenous" is defined entirely by ancestry and by genetic transmission of cultural attitudes and behaviors. The claim that Congress has the power to create a government for a group of indigenous people then reduces to the claim that Congress has the power to create a government based on race and nothing else.

Polynesian voyaging: religion, epistemology, and racial politics

Are the Polynesian voyaging canoes, and their journeys, truly Polynesian? Is there such a thing as "deep culture" or "racial memory" which allows long forgotten skills and ceremonies to be revived with authenticity? Is the Polynesian Voyaging Society primarily a cultural organization focused on reviving an ancient skill, or is it primarily a political organization focused on ethnic pride, ethnic nation-building, and related public relations campaigns to solicit popular support for Hawaiian sovereignty? How important is it for PVS and the voyages it sponsors to be dominated by ethnic Hawaiians? What struggles were there over the role of people with no Hawaiian native ancestry in the founding of PVS and the voyaging trips of its canoes?

Surprising as it may seem, these questions were the primary focus of a "popular book" intended for a general audience by Ben Finney, the founding president of the PVS: "Sailing in the Wake of the Ancestors: Reviving Polynesian Voyaging."[177] Finney's book provides considerable depth about cultural authenticity and racial memory, including numerous footnotes to valuable resources on those topics.

Ben Finney, a Caucasian anthropologist from California, with no Hawaiian native ancestry, suffered what would today be called "racial hate crimes" in his work to revive Polynesian voyaging. Nevertheless, Finney maintains the "politically correct" view that ethnic Hawaiians are entitled by genealogy to exercise leadership in building canoes, navigating them, and running the Polynesian Voyaging Society; just as ethnic Hawaiians are entitled by genealogy to exercise leadership in building an independent nation of Hawaii, navigating the political waters toward sovereignty, and running the nation once it is operational. According to Finney people like himself, with no native ancestry, can contribute expertise, money, time, and political support. But they must always know their place in the canoe is to paddle, raise the sails, and swab the decks; not to be steersman or captain. Finney's view is that people with no native ancestry (about 80% of Hawaii's population) are rightfully relegated to second-class citizenship in the Polynesian Voyaging Society, on its canoe voyages, and also in a future sovereign nation of Hawaii.

Polynesian voyaging is intentionally used as a vehicle for promoting Hawaiian sovereignty. It does this by fostering a belief in cultural continuity from ancient times to now. Reviving Polynesian voyaging helps build ethnic pride in a collective consciousness of a deep culture that has been passed down from the ancestors. The spirits of the ancestors send their sacred breath to whisper cultural knowledge directly into the hearts and minds of today's ethnic Hawaiians, just as the genes of the ancestors have been passed to all who share a drop of native blood. Reviving the culture of the ancients is one way to revive the political self-determination and sovereignty they formerly enjoyed.

But in order for today's Polynesian voyaging canoes to succeed in building ethnic pride and reviving a long forgotten culture and sovereignty, it is essential to show that today's crews, canoes, and ceremonies are truly Polynesian. That's why Finney devotes most of his book to two topics: ethnic dominance inside the PVS organization and the voyaging crews; and cultural authenticity of the canoes and ceremonies.

That's why Finney feels it important to cite anthropological/ philosophical theories of deep culture and racial memory in order to provide scholarly support for the spiritual concept of the ancestors giving cultural knowledge to their descendants through genealogy. Otherwise,

Polynesian voyaging would be Polynesian only in the sense that there are a bunch of Polynesians having fun riding around the ocean on a canoe made of modern materials and navigating by a celestial system used by many cultures throughout the world.

Finney believes the PVS canoes have established beyond a doubt that it would have been possible for ancient Polynesians to build voyaging canoes and navigate by the stars, even against winds and currents, to find Hawaii intentionally. Finney thinks the PVS canoes prove the possibility of navigation by the ancestors using primitive materials – even though the modern canoes were not built with anciently available materials or tools. Finney thinks the voyages of PVS canoes prove that ancient Polynesians could have navigated by using the stars as guides, even though the modern Hawaiian navigators learned how to navigate by using the expertise of a Micronesian (not Polynesian) navigator, plus modern star charts and the Bishop Museum planetarium.

It's hard to imagine how the ancient navigators could have known the positions of the stars at a location where no human had ever been. Once the first guys made it to Hawaii and back to wherever they came from, they could have taught other people how to find Hawaii again; but how did the first guys know how to get here? Also, cross-Pacific voyages stopped visiting Hawaii centuries before Captain Cook arrived, and navigational knowledge was clearly forgotten for dozens of generations. So how could today's ethnic Hawaiians remember the wisdom of the ancient ones?

That's why a theory of "deep culture" or "racial memory" is necessary to maintain a belief in the authenticity of indigenous celestial navigation. Remember that all ethnic Hawaiians are descended from the goddess Hoohokukalani – "she who placed the stars in the heavens." Thus even the first guys who traveled to Hawaii could have used a star chart pulled up out of their racial memory encoded in their genes because Hoohokukalani was their ancestral mother.

Finney correctly describes today's Polynesian voyages as a way of reviving both ancient culture and modern ethnic pride. Voyaging can also be seen as an assertion of Hawaiian sovereignty – a way of controlling the future by controlling how the past is re-created and portrayed. That's why it is essential that leadership roles must be filled by people of Hawaiian native ancestry. That's why current construction practices and navigational techniques must be defended as "Hawaiian" even when they are mostly non-Hawaiian (just as 3/4 of all the people who call themselves "Hawaiian" have 3/4 of their ancestors being non-Hawaiian).

In summer 2004 Hokulea made a voyage throughout the Northwest Hawaiian Islands: a round trip of over 2500 miles from Hanalei Bay (Kaua'i) to Kure atoll and back, with numerous stops along the way at historically or culturally significant islands. This voyage was politically significant because it completes the joining together by canoe of all the Hawaiian islands that were once part of the Kingdom, and it comes at a time which coincides with the establishment of a Northwest Hawaiian Islands Reserve. The NWHI Reserve (President Bush declared it a national monument and sanctuary in 2006) is viewed as an effort to give government protection to a pristine environment and allow the fish and coral to regenerate. But NWHI Reserve is also politically controversial because it includes provisions giving special rights to ethnic Hawaiians for fishing and cultural purposes, even though fishermen with no native ancestry have used NWHI for subsistence fishing for many decades and even though Caucasian and Japanese sailors and pilots have their bones there (partly because of World War II).

The NWHI voyage was also interesting with regard to the issue of cultural authenticity. In all PVS voyages since the loss of Eddie Aikau, an escort boat accompanies the PVS canoe (either leading or following, but always within sight) to provide emergency assistance if needed. The canoes on their "voyages" are sometimes towed through part of their journey. During the NWHI voyage, Hokulea sailed with the prevailing trade winds to the west, but was towed most of the 1200 mile return trip against the wind. In addition there was an unprecedented amount of electronic gear including computers, internet connections, cellular phones, etc. The plethora of electronic devices prompted Star-Bulletin cartoonist Corky to show Hokulea under a starry sky (presumably using the stars to navigate) even while the crew members all held cell phones to their ears.[178]

Finney places the issue of ethnic dominance squarely at the beginning and end of his book, and discusses it at numerous places in between. He is a Caucasian scholar from outside Hawaii but with many years of residence and work in Hawaii. He has always believed in the "liberal" or "social justice" concept that ethnic Hawaiians are the indigenous people of Hawaii who are entitled to special rights in their ancestral homeland. Hawaiians are the hosts, and everyone else is merely a guest.

Finney and other Caucasians who founded the Polynesian Voyaging Society and led the first voyage to Tahiti were subjected to blatant, shocking anti-Caucasian racism by onshore Hawaiian nationalist radicals. Finney and other Caucasians on the canoe were badly abused by some ethnic

Hawaiian Apartheid

Hawaiian crew members, who went "on strike" during the voyage, did no work, and made life miserable for everyone else.

The Hokulea's first voyage, to Tahiti, was emotionally disastrous because of the racism, resulting in the resignation of Finney and of the thoroughly disgusted expert Micronesian master navigator Mau Piailug. The second voyage was physically disastrous. It was ill-conceived, racially exclusionary, and operated without any advice from the original crew. In less than 24 hours the Hokulea capsized. Eddie Aikau died while trying to paddle his surfboard to shore in a storm across many miles of open ocean to get help (yes, this is the Eddie about whom today's bumper stickers say "Eddie would go").

Nevertheless Finney rebounded from those troubling experiences and came to feel even more strongly as the years went by that the role of people lacking Hawaiian ancestry is to give help tirelessly but always to defer to the inherent "right" of ethnic Hawaiians to exercise cultural and political leadership. Finney is the sort of Caucasian the activists love. He knows his place.

A major portion of Finney's book is devoted to the great ceremony of March 18, 1995 at Taputapuatea Marae in Raiatea, when canoes from many Pacific islands assembled. Finney describes how one white British catamaran designer had come all the way from the Canary Islands, apparently at the invitation of the French Polynesian Ministry of Culture, but was not allowed to participate in the event on account of his being white. Finney expresses sympathy, not so much for the man from the Canary Islands, but for the feelings of the Polynesians seeking to rejuvenate their ethnic pride.

It is unclear what it means to call the Hokulea "Polynesian." The materials are not traditional, and the logs are not from Polynesia nor from any species of tree that existed in Polynesia. The style might somewhat resemble traditional Polynesian canoes, but would certainly cause "raised eyebrows" if the canoe sailed through a time warp into Waikiki of 1770. Some of the ceremonies used while cutting the trees in Alaska might have resembled ancient ceremonies; but there were probably enough inaccuracies that any ancient kahuna witnessing the ceremony would have called a halt and declared that the logs had been rendered unusable because of protocol errors – good intentions were not enough in old Hawaii, and death was the penalty for some protocol errors. Perhaps the canoe could be called "Polynesian" because some of the people who worked to assemble it were Polynesians.

Authenticity is a serious problem for today's Hawaiian "traditional practitioners." During a period of 120 years following the arrival of Captain Cook, the population of ethnic Hawaiians declined by at least 90%. The great decline of population, together with profound changes in religion and land ownership, produced a radical discontinuity in the transmission of culture. There was a shortage of kupuna to teach ancient knowledge, a shortage of students to learn, and a shortage of resources to allow free time for teaching and learning. There was also a shortage of desire to preserve the old culture, which many families regarded as either useless or as an actual hindrance to learning the skills needed for a new way of life.

If ancient knowledge and ceremonies are not passed from generation to generation continuously, then it is hard to claim their modern versions are authentic. Much of the ancient knowledge has been irretrievably lost. A few kumu hula claim to have an unbroken line of teachers going back to ancient times, just as Roman Catholics like to believe that the authority of today's Pope comes from an unbroken line of Papal succession since Jesus gave Peter the keys to heaven 2000 years ago. Some traditional knowledge was actually written down in the early to mid 1800s by native Hawaiians who knew it first-hand or directly from family members or kumu; but most such writings were produced by natives who were strongly influenced by Christianity and who often reported traditional concepts or ceremonies only for the purpose of denigrating their pagan-ness.

Today's "traditional practitioners" simply (re)invent much of their "ancient knowledge" by imagining what it must have been. Some claim to receive knowledge in dreams. All claim that cultural knowledge is somehow transmitted spiritually or genetically. "Mai ka po mai ka oia io." (Wisdom comes from the gods, or from the primordial darkness) The concept is that racial memory somehow allows small bits of accurately transmitted ancient knowledge to be authentically expanded, or it allows complete ignorance to be replaced by memories that flow like water once the tap has been opened.

There is nothing new about the concept of a "deep culture" being transmitted through some sort of collective "racial memory." Plato's theory of the Forms claimed that eternal Truth is found in an abstract world. Knowledge of that world is not accessible to the physical senses but is buried deep inside every soul; wise people can turn inward to find these Truths and then turn outward to apply them to this world of appearances. Immanuel Kant had a similar theory of the noumenal world of a priori knowledge, and the phenomenal world of fact. Buddhists talk about

Hawaiian Apartheid

Nirvana, and the role of a Bodhisattva in bringing perfect wisdom back to daily life. Catholic theologians Jacques Maritain and Pierre Teilhard de Chardin note that the gulf separating mortal man from a transcendent God can be bridged through faith bestowed as a gift from God. The concept of racial memories or "archetypes" is the central feature of the psychotherapy theory of Karl Jung. American poet William Wordsworth wrote an ode: "Intimations of Immortality from Recollections of Early Childhood" based on the Platonic concept that people are born with all the knowledge of the Forms deep inside. Wordsworth thought small children in their innocence are closer to wisdom than adults whose knowledge gets forgotten as life experiences focus attention on this world of appearances.

All the Platonic or mystical religious theories mentioned above have great respectability in Western intellectual tradition. All of them explain how knowledge from the world above can be brought down to the level of individuals in daily life.

But all these theories postulate universal values transcending race or culture, unlike the ethnocentric Hawaiian religious fascism. Sometimes these theories have been twisted to claim that different racial groups have inborn differences of perception or inclination – indeed, such ethnic-oriented interpretations of these great philosophers have been used to provide a rationale for blood nationalism and the evils of Hitler-style racial supremacy. That's a good reason to be cautious when we hear ethnic Hawaiians using theories of racial memory; because it would be very easy to slip from such a respectable theory into outright fascism.

The classical theories also allow for knowledge to flow only downward, and not up. They do not allow knowledge gained from daily life to flow upward to the racial oversoul, thereby changing the collective consciousness and then flowing down to individuals in later generations. Thus, these theories cannot be used to defend cultural authenticity. Knowledge or ceremonies created in ancient times could not become embedded in the racial memory and then retrieved by later generations.

Readers might recall a series of books by Jean M. Auel, starting with "The Clan of the Cave Bear." The novels are based on anthropological studies of the transitional period from Neanderthal to Homo Sapiens (modern man) about 30,000 years ago in the region now known as Europe. A modern girl is the sole survivor of a disaster, and wanders into a tribe of Neanderthals who adopt her. "Ayla" later mates with a Neanderthal and produces a half-breed son. A movie was made based on "Clan of the Cave Bear" starring Daryl Hannah in the role of Ayla. The series of novels are filled with stories about how the Neanderthals communicate big ideas with small gestures and limited speech, because they share "the memories." Although Ayla does not have "the memories," her half-breed son does have them, and later becomes the spiritual leader (Hawaiian kahuna nui) of the Neanderthal tribe. The concept as interpreted for the Hawaiian situation would be that if one parent is indigenous, then the child is indigenous and retains the indigenous racial memories, with full authority to use and interpret them. However many generations go by; however low the native blood quantum falls, it doesn't matter – the son or daughter of a tribesman is still a tribesman.

The recent movie "Whale Rider" was extremely popular in Hawaii and especially among ethnic Hawaiians. "Whale Rider" portrays a Maori girl on Aotearoa (New Zealand), living in a rural lower-class fishing village. She inherits the racial memories of a Maori cultural hero to the extent that she is able to recreate in real life a famous ancient legend about a spiritual leader riding a whale. The beautiful scenery, powerful spirituality, and humble lifestyle portrayed in the movie were deeply moving to the Hawaii audiences. And the movie seemed especially relevant to ethnic Hawaiians, because Aotearoa is an anchor of the Polynesian triangle; and the Maori are greatly respected by Hawaiians as having preserved more of the authentic ancient Polynesian lifestyle and having obtained greater race-based political power within their multiracial society.

Another less known novel has exactly the "feel" that Hawaiian sovereignty activists and Ben Finney would appreciate: Marlo Morgan, "Mutant Message Down Under"[179] Paraphrasing and expanding a blurb from the back cover: A white female American professor is summoned by a remote tribe of nomadic Australian aborigines who call themselves the "real people" to accompany them on a four month walkabout through the outback. While traveling barefoot with them through 1400 miles of rugged desert terrain, she learns a new way of life, including their methods of healing and hunting, based on the wisdom of their 50,000-year-old culture. Ultimately she experiences a dramatic personal transformation, and fulfills her aborigine-assigned mission of bringing back this story which has the potential of healing the troubles of civilization by putting us in touch with our deep culture and racial memories.

Finney's own book discusses the question whether the Hawaiian cultural renaissance is authentic. He points out that scholars have raised serious objections to modern-day reinvented ceremonies that probably bear little resemblance to ancient practices. My own analogy would be that today's activists complain when tourists create rock piles on heiau, or new-age hippies perform made-up ceremonies; and in the same way scholars complain that modern re-creations of awa ceremonies, hula, and chants are mostly fictitious. Activists who complain about wannabe Hawaiians may actually be little more than wannabes themselves – they have only the blood, but not the accurate knowledge – UNLESS Finney can rescue their authenticity by means of the theory of racial memory.

Finney defends the practice of cultural eclecticism in the Hawaiian renaissance. He points out that the European renaissance made use of architectural styles and philosophical concepts copied (often inaccurately) from ancient Greek and Roman ruins and books; and that European science and mathematics made use of Arabic concepts such as "zero" and "algebra."

So in the end, Finney seems to believe that "Hawaiian" culture is legitimately "Hawaiian" as long as it is created by ethnic Hawaiians using elements of ancient Hawaiian culture combined with other Polynesian, Micronesian, or Melanesian elements plus modern Western elements. He seems to consider modern ceremonies truly authentic even when they leave out important (indeed, essential) elements of ancient practice such as human sacrifice. Finney's concept of what makes a ceremony or newly built object genuinely Hawaiian is the same as the activists' theory of what makes a person genuinely Hawaiian – one drop of native blood is sufficient. Pay attention only to the native Hawaiian elements of genealogy and cultural products, and ignore all the other non-native elements that might actually comprise the vast bulk of it. Like the yeast in a loaf of bread. Like a fine perfume needs only a few drops of the essence of the fragrance mixed with a neutral carrier medium. Like a powerful medicine needs less than one percent of the active ingredient to be effective.

Finney's book spends considerable time discussing the absence of human sacrifice in the modern ceremonies in 1995 to lift the kapu at Taputapuatea. A lengthy book review includes Finney's gruesome account of the human sacrifice ceremonies at ancient Taputapuatea.[180] He concludes that the 1995 ceremonies are authentic mostly because they have the correct spiritual intention of honoring the ancestors and seeking to make things pono. And he provides numerous footnotes to the writings of anthropologists who discuss theories of racial memory as a basis for defending the authenticity of reinvented artifacts and ceremonies.

Indigenous intellectual property rights yes; but in Hawaii?

Copyright, patent, and trademark are the three best known ways of guaranteeing property rights for the intangible products of mental work, or for the value added by a producer's past performance and reputation.

In modern, Western societies such intellectual property rights are held by individuals or corporations. These rights are guaranteed by the legal system through formal registration of documents with government agencies. If one individual or corporation infringes on the property rights of another, the rights are enforced by courts.

But in primitive, indigenous societies knowledge and cultural products are created by informal interaction among all the members of the group in their daily relationships with each other and with their ancestral lands. Indigenous knowledge and property rights belong to the group rather than to any individual or corporation. Indigenous copyrights, patents, and trademarks are not written down, nor are they registered with any government agencies. It is not conceivable that individuals belonging to an indigenous group could infringe on the property rights of others – they spontaneously give their work product to the group, and freely take what they need from the group. Indigenous knowledge is owned by the group because it is a group product arising from spontaneous consensus and osmosis.

A major problem with indigenous intellectual property rights is that they are informal and unwritten, which makes it easy for outsiders to ignore, violate, and steal them. But indigenous intellectual property rights deserve respect. Simple respect for human rights imposes on civilized societies a moral obligation to treat indigenous intellectual property rights as though they were formally registered. Indigenous intellectual property rights should be thought of as comparable to aboriginal land title – not written down or formally registered, but deserving of moral respect and entitled to legal protection. Such protection would be delivered through the legal system of the modern nation which has engulfed the primitive tribe, or through "international law." Another problem with indigenous intellectual property rights is that they are the rights of a group, not an individual. But what happens if a tribal member steps out into modern society? Does he lose his indigenous property rights? Can or should he use his indigenous knowledge to get modern patents registered to himself as an individual?

Confusion arises when people living a modern lifestyle but claiming to be indigenous try to assert the special protections that might have been appropriate to the indigenous status of their ancestors. Knowledge created in ancient times, belonging to an indigenous group as a whole, is held today by individuals who are fully civilized and assimilated. Property rights belong to the people who own the property, not to the property itself. Therefore the decision whether to recognize indigenous property rights depends on whether today's property owners are indigenous today, not on whether the knowledge itself was created by long-ago indigenous ancestors.

Today's ethnic Hawaiians are fully civilized and assimilated individuals. They should not be treated as possessors of indigenous intellectual property rights. First, it's doubtful whether today's ethnic Hawaiians are descended from Hawaii's "first people." But regardless whether their ancestors were Hawaii's "first people," today's Hawaiians of native ancestry are now fully assimilated and widely dispersed throughout all neighborhoods and levels of society. They long ago gave up the religion, culture, lifestyle, group cohesiveness, and naiveté that might perhaps have qualified their ancestors as indigenous and might have entitled those ancestors to the special legal protections appropriate to indigenous societies according to modern legal and moral theories.

The assertion of indigenous intellectual property rights by modern ethnic Hawaiians is a political ploy in seeking racial separatism or ethnic nationalism. The Akaka bill seeks to authorize reimposing indigenous status on individuals of a racial minority who are descended from a people who long ago might have been indigenous. The Akaka bill might be useful in asserting claims to indigenous intellectual property rights, but only at the expense of taking today's fully equal citizens out of a unified multiethnic society and placing them under government wardship based on race and communal property.

For extended discussion of these issues see: "Indigenous Intellectual Property Rights – The General Theory, and Why It Does Not Apply in Hawaii"[181]

He alii ka aina, he kauwa ke kanaka
Land is the chief; people are its humble servants

The land and its spirits have been here for millions of years. Human beings have been living here for less than 2,000 years. The spirits speak constantly in the wind and rain, and in the rocks themselves. What they say can be heard by anyone whose ears are attuned. Race and genealogy are irrelevant. Some individuals can hear; others cannot. Some choose to listen; others choose to ignore.

The ancient Hawaiian proverb says: "He alii ka aina, he kauwa ke kanaka." Land is the chief; people are its humble servants. The Kumulipo legend makes that very clear. First the gods first mated and gave birth to the islands as living beings. Only later did the gods mate again and give birth to our primordial ancestor.

Those who say THEIR family, or THEIR race, should exercise supremacy in land use or land management are mahaoi – guilty of pride and arrogance – placing themselves above the land rather than as humble servants. We are ALL servants to the land. It is hewa (morally wrong) – a violation of the servants' trust relationship with their master – when some of the servants spend their time fighting the other servants to assert control over their master instead of humbly serving their master. The Hawaiian sovereignty activists demanding race-based land ownership are saying they outrank the spirits of the land, who speak freely to us all. The activists are shouting so loud they can no longer hear the spirits speaking to them.

The choice between religious fascism or religious freedom

One of the Constitutional principles that has made America strong is found in the First Amendment: "Congress shall make no law respecting an establishment of religion, or prohibiting the free exercise thereof." This principle is commonly called the "separation of church and state." The "free exercise" clause means that government cannot interfere with the right of Hawaiian religious zealots to practice their traditions, and the right of others to become their spiritual followers. However, the "establishment" clause means the government itself cannot adopt Hawaiian religion as an official state religion or as its basis for making laws governing how land shall be used, or who has the right to decide. The government cannot force anyone to adopt Hawaiian religion or to live under its authority.

Indian tribes can use religion to make tribal laws or to decide tribal policies. That's because the U.S. Constitution does not always apply to Indian tribes. Indians today join a tribe voluntarily and thereby agree to be subjected to tribal law even when it conflicts with the Constitution. An Indian tribe is free to establish a government religion which its members are required to obey. A tribe can prohibit any competing religions from being practiced on tribal lands. A tribe's religion can dictate what the tribe's civil and criminal laws will be, and religious leaders can outrank and over-rule elected officials; as is the case in some Islamic nations like Saudi Arabia and Iran.

When an Indian tribe has its reservation lands in a single place in a remote area, there is no conflict with "outsiders." But in Hawaii, people with a drop of native blood are scattered throughout all neighborhoods, and interracial marriage is commonplace. Ethnic Hawaiians live, work, play and pray side by side with non-ethnic-Hawaiians, at all levels of society and in all occupations. Lands that would belong to the Akaka tribe are scattered throughout the islands in large tracts and small parcels – they would certainly include several dozen Hawaiian homelands, huge portions of the ceded lands, large tracts of land purchased by private consortiums and recently deeded to OHA (Waokele O Puna on Hawaii Island, and Waimea Valley on Oahu), and probably all of the vast land holdings of Bishop Estate (Kamehameha Schools).[182] This scattering of ethnic Hawaiian tribal lands is a recipe for great jurisdictional conflict. Already Hawaii residents and tourists are being told not to enter into certain "sacred places," and not to dig below the ground in areas where native bones might be buried including sand dunes, public parks, and many other areas. Major highways and housing developments have been delayed or cancelled. Already legislation is proposed to ensure that ethnic Hawaiian children awaiting adoption should be adopted by ethnic Hawaiian families; and that there should be a presumption in favor of the ethnic Hawaiian parent when a judge must award child custody in a multiracial divorce.

The zealotry of ethnic Hawaiian sovereignty activism is quite frightening when viewed by Americans accustomed to religious tolerance. But the demand for American-style religious tolerance is (or logically should be) "foreign" and "rude" and "intolerable" from the perspective of Hawaiian activists who claim Hawaii is their homeland and everyone else is an uninvited guest. The conflict is not often visible, because most Hawaii residents (both with and without native ancestry) are not theologically sophisticated and do not practice their religions zealously. But to see the conflict expressed viciously, one need only read or listen to Haunani-Kay Trask[183]

Let's summarize why Hawaiian religious fascism is dangerous. The religious theory says ethnic Hawaiians have a family relationship with the gods and the land. The gods mated, giving birth to the Hawaiian islands as living beings. Then they mated again, giving birth to the primordial native Hawaiian from whom all other ethnic Hawaiians are descended. Thus anyone with even one drop of Hawaiian native blood is a child of the gods and a brother to the land in a way no outsider can ever hope to be. Hawaii is the ancestral homeland of ethnic Hawaiians; all others are merely guests and must know their place. Because of that genealogy ethnic Hawaiians are entitled to race-based political power. Hawaiian epistemology shows that ethnic Hawaiians have unique ways of knowing, thereby justifying racial separatism and control of the education system. The theory of racial memory shows that ancient knowledge and cultural expressions are genetically encoded and passed down from ancient ancestors to modern people, unbroken and authentic. The theory of indigenous intellectual property rights gives ethnic Hawaiians exclusive authority to control not only Hawaiian cultural knowledge like hula and Polynesian voyaging, but also all the uses of the products of their ancestral homeland including foods, medicines derived from native plants, etc. As we saw in Chapter 6, today's biological and cultural environment has been changed from ancient times in ways that are harmful to the health and prosperity of ethnic Hawaiians. Therefore ethnic Hawaiians have an inherent right to take control of the political, biological, and cultural environment and to change or restore it to the way it was when their ancestors were flourishing.

That summary makes clear why the Hawaiian religious theory as applied to politics is correctly called "fascism" and why it is so dangerous.

Hawaii as a whole must make a choice. Shall we be governed by non-sectarian U.S. law that allows free exercise of religion but prohibits any government-imposed religion? Or shall we acknowledge the racial supremacy of ethnic Hawaiians over other races and the genealogical supremacy of some ethnic Hawaiians over other ethnic Hawaiians? This is a fundamental conflict that cannot be set aside or compromised. It is a conflict between Hawaiian culture and Western culture. It is a conflict between religious fascism and religious freedom.

Chapter 9

Hawaiian Sovereignty Frauds

There have been many frauds perpetrated in the name of Hawaiian sovereignty. Some of them were mentioned in previous chapters of this book. For example, Chapter 3 briefly mentioned how Bishop Estate (Kamehameha Schools) was being used by its trustees for money laundering, personal enrichment, and political power instead of for educating children. A best-selling book about the scandal, "Broken Trust: Greed, Mismanagement & Political Manipulation at America's Largest Charitable Trust" was published in 2006.[184] Chapter 4 discussed tax evasion based on the claim that Hawaii is not lawfully part of the United States. Chapter 5 discussed several history frauds such as the claim that the U.S. overthrew the Hawaiian monarchy and imprisoned the Queen; the claim that Hawaiian language was made illegal; the claim that Mauna Ala (Royal Mausoleum) remains a piece of sovereign Kingdom territory where U.S. law does not apply; the claim that at the time of annexation (or was it the overthrow?) the Hawaiian flag taken down from Iolani Palace was ripped into pieces that were handed out as souvenirs.

Three scams are being singled out for special attention here in Chapter 9 because they provide extreme examples of pushing Hawaiian sovereignty claims to the limit. All are based on the theory that the Kingdom of Hawaii has unbroken continuity of existence from its founding 200 years ago right up until today. If Hawaii continues to be a living nation, then it would be wrong to use the words "fraud" or "scam." Anyone who enjoys science fiction, "Alice in Wonderland", "The Da Vinci Code", or conspiracy theories will love these. The three scams are interconnected, as will be seen.

Kenneth R. Conklin, Ph.D.

New Issue of $ 1 Billion of Hawaiian Kingdom Bonds in February 2002 (109 years too late)

In January 2002 Ken Conklin, author of this book, became aware of an internet website purporting to be the official government website of a reinstated Hawaiian Kingdom. There have been numerous groups over the years calling themselves reinstated Kingdom(s), but this one was unique. It was offering a billion dollars of newly issued Hawaiian Kingdom government bonds! The money was allegedly for the purpose of helping to finance the creation and operating expenses of the newly reinstated government.

Royal Kupuna Exchange had a website at www.royalkupuna.com (now no longer operating). According to the website a "Kupuna Action Council" had held a meeting on January 17, 2002 at which time the Kingdom was officially reinstated. The Royal Kupuna Exchange claimed to be offering digital financial services round the clock (presumably through the internet). The group apparently had no physical address but maintained a post office box at Century Center in Honolulu. The Kingdom's Prime Minister was Samuel Keolamauloa Kaluna II claiming to be a direct descendant of both Kamehameha The Great and Kamehameha Nui of Maui. The Kingdom's Finance Minister was John Paki Dudoit. Neither of these men was widely known in Hawaiian sovereignty circles. In fact hardly anyone had ever heard of them.

When attempts to reach the government "officials" named on the website failed, I contacted investigative reporter Rob Perez, who at that time was employed by the Honolulu Star-Bulletin. He conducted his own investigation, and also contacted State of Hawaii officials responsible for dealing with securities fraud, sales of unregistered securities, and sales of securities by unlicensed dealers.

Mr. Perez published an article in the Honolulu Star-Bulletin of Sunday February 17, 2002.[185] Here's some of what Mr. Perez reported.

"A note left by the Star-Bulletin at Royal Kupuna's mail drop at Century Center prompted a call from someone who originally said he was part of the organization, then phoned later to say he wasn't. He wouldn't identify himself (other than to give a first name) and said he would get a message to one of Royal Kupuna's principals, none of whom called the Star-Bulletin. Home phone numbers for Kaluna and John Paki Dudoit, listed as the kingdom's finance minister on the Web site, could not be located. A

search of registration records for the site indicated it was created in October 2001 and lists Steve Renner, a Minneapolis businessman, as a contact. He could not be reached for comment. Renner is founder of Cash Cards International, a company based in the Caribbean island of St. Kitts, part of a twin island federation known for its strict confidentiality laws pertaining to financial transactions and other matters. People who sign up as members of Royal Kupuna are linked to Cash Cards, which has an online system for conducting financial transactions worldwide."

A week or two after the Perez article was published the Royal Kupuna website removed explicit reference to sales of bonds. However, that was far from the end of the story. On July 16, 2003 the "Nation of Hawaii" published message number 526 by e-mail to its subscribers and also on its website (where hundreds more messages have been posted since then). This message was a forwarding of a "press release" from Samuel Kaluna Jr. on behalf of the Kingdom of Hawaii:

*http://groups.yahoo.com/group/hawaii-nation/message/526
From: "Hawaii Nation Info" <info@hawaii-nation.org>
Date: Wed, 16 Jul 2003
Subject: [hawaii-nation] Press Release: Declaration of Hawaiian Independence
----- Original Message -----
From: Kingdom of Hawai'i
<newsdesk@kingdomofhawaii.org>
Sent: Tuesday, July 15, 2003 9:16 AM
Subject: Press Release
Samuel Keolamauloa Kaluna, Jr.
Regent, Prime Minister
P.O. Box 359
96-3148 Pikake Street
Pahala-Ka'u, Kingdom of Hawai'i 96777
PRESS RELEASE JULY 15, 2003*

The Sovereign Kingdom of Hawai'i Announces Independence from all Foreign Powers

A Declaration of Independence, authored by His Majesty Edmund Kelii Silva, Jr. and signed by Prime Minister and Regent Samuel Keolamauloa Kaluna, Jr. and the Hawaiian House of Nobles, proclaims the Kingdom restored and states the intent of the Kingdom of Hawai'i to purchase back its lands and govern them under an independent constitutional monarchy. The Declaration calls upon the United Nations to supervise the transfer of power and monitor the attendant transactions under international law.

On January 17, 1893, armed forces of the United States overthrew the Hawaiian government. Since the taking of our beloved islands, the indigenous Hawaiian people have experienced the vicissitude of adverse foreign occupation and suffered a genocidal decline in population. Today we are but a mere fraction of our former numbers.

Now, however, the Kingdom of Hawai'i is, phoenix-like, resurgent. On November 22, 2002, the House of Nobles appointed His Royal Majesty Edmund Kelii Silva, Jr. – direct lineal descendent of King Kamehameha the Great – Ali'i Nui (High Chief and King) of the Kingdom of Hawai'i.

On June 24, 2003, the Hawaiian Declaration of Independence was hand delivered to the White House in Washington, D.C. On June 26, 2003 it was hand delivered to the United Nations.

The United States State Department responded quickly to the Declaration and contacted His Royal Majesty Silva and Prime Minister Kaluna to schedule talks. Response from the community of nations has been favorable.

Many Hawaiians have expressed support of the Declaration of Independence announcing the sovereignty of the Kingdom of Hawai'i. We fully expect that the United States shall endorse the principal of self-determination in this matter, ending more than a century of unlawful occupation. For further information contact: Samuel Kaluna, Jr. at (808) 928-6188.

For those who may want some fun, all the many hundreds of numbered messages of the "Nation of Hawaii" (a different and more widely respected Kingdom under convicted felon Bumpy Kanahele) including number 526 above can be found at
http://groups.yahoo.com/group/hawaii-nation/messages/
However, that July 15, 2003 press release was far from the end of the story. From 2003 into 2007 messages continued to be published on an

internet bulletin board at http://www.newmediaexplorer.org including a fascinating item about 50 pages long at http://tinyurl.com/irci

That one webpage includes many items of great interest showing a connection among important activists in the Hawaiian independence movement, the "Government of EnenKio", and Kaluna's reinstated Kingdom of Hawaii that was attempting to sell a billion dollars of Hawaiian Kingdom bonds. A letter to President Bush opposing the Akaka bill was signed by Kekuni Blaisdell [medical doctor], Kihei Soli Niheu, Terrilee Napua Keko'olani [Raymond], Puanani Rogers, Foster Kekahuna Ampong, Baron K.F. Ching [medical doctor], and allegedly also signed by "Robert Moore, Minister Plenipotentiary, Kingdom of EnenKio Foreign Trade Mission DO-MO-CO Manager, Remios Hermios Eleemosynary Trust, Majuro, Marshall Islands http://www.enenkio.org" Nearby is an open letter to all [ethnic] Hawaiians worldwide, from "Edmund Keli'i Silva Jr., Ali'i Nui Moi (The King), Ka Ho'iho'i hou Ke 'Aupuni Kumukanawai Mo'i o Hawaii (The Restored Constitutional Monarchial Kingdom of Hawai'i) Personal Email: HMKingdmofHawaii@aol.com, Kingdom website: www.KingdomofHawaii.org"

The webpage at http://tinyurl.com/irci includes the reinstated Hawaiian Kingdom's declaration of independence; His Royal Majesty Edmund Kelii Silva, Jr.'s genealogy and how he came to be King; his version of the history of Hawaii from the revolution of 1893 to the present; how Samuel Keolamauloa Kaluna, Jr. came to be named regent and prime minister; how letters containing all this information were delivered to President Bush and to U.N. Secretary General Kofi Annan; how the U.S. government mistreated the government of EnenKio by getting an injunction prohibiting the sale of EnenKio bonds, how Robert Moore became Minister Plenipotentiary, Kingdom of EnenKio Foreign Trade Mission. The webpage includes full text of a "TREATY OF PEACE, FRIENDSHIP AND MUTUAL UNDERSTANDING BETWEEN THE KINGDOM OF HAWAI'I AND THE KINGDOM OF ENENKIO"; although it is not clear who signed on behalf of Hawaii. Might it have been Silva and Kaluna?

What is EnenKio, and who is Robert Moore? EnenKio is another name for Wake Atoll, in the Marshall Islands. A small group of activists there claim EnenKio is an independent nation. During the 1990s they were trying to sell EnenKio government bonds in the United States, until the U.S. Securities & Exchange Commission filed an injunction to prohibit that. But they continue to do business from Wake Atoll, granting citizenship for a fee, selling bonds, and issuing passports. However, neither the Marshall Islands nor the United States recognizes EnenKio.

Irooj Murjel Hermios, Head of State of the Kingdom of EnenKio, revered Monarch over the islands of Eneen-Kio Atoll, esteemed Iroijlaplap and High Chief of the Northern atolls of the Ratak Archipelago, died. His brother Remios Hermios succeeded him as head of state. Robert Moore, already Minister Plenipotentiary, then became "Reagent, Kingdom of EnenKio."

In another item on that webpage at http://tinyurl.com/irci , Robert Moore claims he and Keanu Sai jointly sent a petition to the U.S. Supreme Court demanding U.S. withdrawal from Hawaii. The theory was that the Supreme Court should order the President to enforce a treaty between the U.S. and the Kingdom of Hawaii that had promised perpetual friendship and commercial relations.

Sorting through all this confusing nonsense, it appears that the bogus reinstated Hawaiian Kingdom under Silva and Kaluna is probably now collaborating with the bogus government of EnenKio to sell bogus government bonds, bogus citizenships, and bogus passports. It is unclear whether Hawaiian activists Kekuni Blaisdell, Baron Ching, Terri Kekoolani Raymond, and Keanu Sai are actual participants in that bogus activity with Robert Moore, Minister Plenipotentiary of EnenKio and/or with His Royal Majesty Edmund Kelii Silva, Jr of the reinstated Hawaiian Kingdom and Prime Minister Samuel Keolamauloa Kaluna II; or whether they are all merely linked by association on the same website and in the wild imaginings of Robert Moore.

"Perfect Title" land title search and registration scam

About 40% of the lands in Hawaii are "ceded lands" – government and former crown lands from the Hawaiian Kingdom. According to sovereignty activists the overthrow, annexation, and statehood were all illegal; therefore, the ceded lands belong collectively to the descendants of Hawaiian Kingdom subjects (nearly all of whom are ethnic Hawaiians). Regarding the privately owned lands in Hawaii, sovereignty activists make this claim: since the overthrow was illegal, therefore the Provisional government, Republic, Territory, and State governments have also been illegal. Therefore, officials of the Bureau of Conveyances were illegally appointed and had no valid authority to certify the transfer of land titles. Therefore, all deeds that changed hands after the overthrow were transferred illegally. In addition there are problems with land transfers between the time of the Mahele (1848-1850) and the overthrow (1893), so that many such transfers were also illegal. In other words, virtually all private land titles in Hawaii are invalid. For the most part, the only "safe" titles would be Royal Patent Deeds issued by King Kauikeaouli Kamehameha III during the Great Mahele for land which has subsequently remained within the family of the original owner and has been passed down through inheritance for 150 years.

People who buy real estate are accustomed to paying a title search and title insurance company to verify an unbroken chain of good title and to provide insurance that the title is valid. Mortgage companies require such title searches and insurance, and most fee-simple buyers paying cash also like to have them. But if there are problems in the chain of title, so the title is "clouded," then it may be impossible to sell a parcel of land or to get title insurance for fear the rightful owner will someday assert a claim and demand either the property itself or a large cash settlement.

In 1995 David Keanu Sai, a sovereignty independence activist who is part-Hawaiian, began a process to proclaim himself Regent pro-tem of the Kingdom of Hawaii. The Bureau of Conveyances of the State of Hawaii provides a repository where anyone can file documents that are officially recorded as having been filed. Most such documents are records of transfer of land title following legitimate sales. But some people file very strange personal declarations or ideological documents just for the pleasure of seeing them officially recorded. Mr. Sai laid a paper trail at the Bureau of Conveyances that he claimed would follow procedures under Kingdom law to make him the official Regent pro-tem of the Hawaiian Kingdom in the absence of the monarch, the cabinet, and the Kingdom legislature. In public speeches he gave the analogy of military chain of command: If the commanding general (Queen) and other officers (cabinet ministers and department heads) are all killed or captured, including the platoon sergeant, then even a corporal or private can take command until relieved by properly commissioned authorities.

Having declared himself Regent pro-tem, Keanu Sai launched a series of lectures throughout Hawaii, including on cable television, saying that all land title in Hawaii is clouded because of the history of illegal overthrow, annexation, and statehood. He further told people that "native tenants" during the Kingdom had special rights which were never extinguished, including the right to claim fee-simple ownership of a parcel of land for their own residence so long as that parcel did not already have a validly recorded deed. These lectures and TV shows were not merely academic in nature; they were actually sales presentations to persuade people to hire him.

Having declared himself Regent pro-tem of the still-living Kingdom of Hawaii, Keanu Sai then claimed the authority to officially condone and certify prior land title transfers that had been recorded at the Bureau of Conveyances during the periods of the Kingdom, (illegal) Republic, (illegal) Territory, and (illegal) State. People could pay a fee to Keanu Sai to have him research the chain of land title to their property and then to record a warranty deed signed by the "Regent pro-tem" at the Bureau of Conveyances, thereby assuring them that their property would be safe because the title had been "perfected." In addition, "native" tenants not already owning property could pay Keanu Sai a title search fee to discover the chain of title to any property they liked (including property where there was already a house with people living in it). If the title was not valid under Kingdom law (which probably always happened!) then they could have Sai file a warranty deed to the property in their name.

A real estate title search company was established under the name "Perfect Title" to manage the title searches, collect the fees, and process the paperwork. Each client ended up paying somewhere between $1500 to $2000 for the title search, warranty deed, and recording fees. News reports indicated there were at least 400 clients (perhaps considerably more).

Early in 1997 bad things started happening as people took action based on Keanu Sai's theories. Eventually several hundred people filed Perfect Title warranty deeds at the Bureau of Conveyances. Some of those deeds directly challenged previously-filed deeds to the same property, thereby casting a cloud on the title and causing realtors, title insurance companies, and mortgage companies to back away. Some real estate sales collapsed. Some people started refusing to pay mortgage interest on their homes, claiming they already owned them under Kingdom law; and banks began foreclosure proceedings.

A married couple who had lost their home through foreclosure relied on advice from Keanu Sai. Based on Sai's theories of land title, and based on title research and warranty deed done by "Perfect Title" company, the former owners claimed to be the rightful owners of that house and land, even after it had been subsequently purchased from the foreclosing bank and was occupied by a new owner. When the new owner left home one day, the previous owners broke in and attempted to replace the locks and to resume living there. After the police were summoned and the new owners retook possession, criminal charges were filed against the previous owners for the break-in. Felony charges of attempted grand theft (of a house) were also filed not only against the original owners but also against Keanu Sai and his "Perfect Title" business partner.

Mr. Sai demanded and received a jury trial. The multiracial jury on December 1, 1999 unanimously found Mr. Sai guilty beyond a reasonable doubt of attempted theft of title to a house (value approximately $300,000) for his role as an accessory to that man and woman. Not even one member of the jury had any reasonable belief that Mr. Sai's fanciful theories of history and Hawaiian sovereignty could possibly be correct. As Mr. Sai had argued during the trial, if his theories are correct then there would not have been any theft because the rightful owners of a house cannot steal it. The ordinary people of the multiracial jury gave their unanimous verdict beyond a reasonable doubt based on common sense. If the verdict had been appealed, then judges and legal scholars would also be able to sustain the verdict that Sai's theories are false. At first Mr. Sai said he would appeal the verdict as a way of proving his theories. If he truly believes his theories, that's what he should have done. But in view of his slap-on-the-wrist sentence, Mr. Sai apparently decided not to appeal for fear his theories would be discredited and perhaps for fear he would go to prison if the sentence was also appealed by the government. The married couple who were the former owners of the house did appeal, and their appeal was rejected by the Hawaii Supreme Court on July 20, 2004.[186] The author of this book has been unable to find any evidence that Keanu Sai ever appealed the decision of the trial court.

The maximum sentence for Keanu Sai's crime was 10 years in prison. But Judge Sandra Simms sentenced Keanu Sai to 5 years probation and a $200 fine. At sentencing on March 7, 2000 Ken Conklin, author of this book, was present in court. Perhaps a hundred Hawaiian sovereignty activists also packed the courtroom, including Bumpy Kanahele and Kekuni Blaisdell, while more stood in the hallway unable to fit inside. When Judge Simms entered the courtroom and the bailiff loudly proclaimed the customary "All rise!" the sovereignty activists defiantly remained seated to show their contempt for a court they consider invalid.

Judge Simms, playing to the crowd, said she admired Mr. Sai for his commitment to his cause, but that even the noblest protesters and seekers of social justice must be subject to the laws as they now exist. She then gave her absurdly light sentence, and apparently in response to a pre sentencing motion she also granted him permission to travel out of Hawaii and out of the United States for his anticipated hearing at the "World Court." So much for the rigors of probation! After the sentencing, the crowd spilled out into the hallway in a jovial and congratulatory mood. Judge Simms, a bleeding-heart liberal who gave light sentences even to hooligans who beat up tourists while robbing them, was later denied reappointment to the bench in May of 2004, probably because of her pattern of coddling criminals.[187]

To this day there appears to have been no accounting for the hundreds of thousands of dollars in fees charged to the several hundred clients of Perfect Title, and no apparent restitution or even apology to the hundreds of people who lost their homes to foreclosure or whose lives and finances were severely disrupted by having bogus clouds placed on their property titles because of Mr. Sai's activities. Many of Perfect Title's clients knew exactly what they were doing. They were sovereignty activists, convinced that Kingdom law still prevails and the State of Hawaii is illegal. They were happy to put their homes on the line for their hero, Keanu Sai. But other Perfect Title clients were victims of their own ignorance. Hundreds of innocent homeowners were victimized by having their property titles messed up by Perfect Title clients. A webpage provides a more lengthy analysis of Keanu Sai's theory of history and law that formed the basis for the Perfect Title scam, and also includes a compilation of news reports.[188]

There seem to be plenty of people in Hawaii, including Judge Simms, who give a wink and nod to the Hawaiian sovereignty zealots. It doesn't matter that the zealots threaten to rip apart the State of Hawaii by creating a racially exclusionary government, or that they seek to rip the 50th star off the flag. It doesn't matter that they cause tremendous political, financial, and emotional damage to thousands of innocent people. Perhaps part of this tolerance is a desire to "live and let live" and a reluctance to be "politically incorrect." But it runs deeper than mere tolerance. Public attitudes toward sovereignty zealots in Hawaii are perhaps comparable to public attitudes toward folk heroes of the old West like Jesse James, Doc Holliday, or Bonnie and Clyde – admiration for criminals defying the "system" and getting away with outrageous behavior. It's the seductive attraction some women feel for the "playboy" or "bad boy," like a moth drawn to the flame. It's also the "mascot syndrome" where one individual, or an entire racial group, is adopted as the favorite on account of a perceived combination of neediness, cuteness, and special knowledge or powers like those of a prodigy or savant.[189]

If the underlying theory of Perfect Title were correct, then it would apply to many other areas besides land title. The theory is that all land transfers since 1893 are nullified because the overthrow, annexation, and

Hawaiian Apartheid

statehood were all illegal. Land titles need to be "perfected" by Keanu Sai, who can give his official stamp of approval and make things right in his capacity as Regent pro-tem of the Kingdom of Hawaii.

What about marriages? The final sentence spoken by the minister, which makes everything official, is: "Now by the authority vested in me by the State of Hawaii, I pronounce you husband and wife." But marriages performed in Hawaii since 1893 are not legally valid, because the State of Hawaii is not legally valid. Thus all persons born in these islands are "illegitimate." As a matter of fact, the good news is that nobody ever dies (because death certificates are invalid); but of course the bad news is that nobody was ever born (because birth certificates are invalid).

Surely the Regent of the Kingdom would have the authority to confer legitimacy to marriages, births, and deaths, both present and past. Perfect Marriage Company could collect a fee for issuing a Regent's Proclamation that a current marriage is officially registered with the Kingdom of Hawaii. But of course that's not the end of the story. Every person born in Hawaii, and every marriage, must have proclamations issued for every generation of parents, grandparents, etc. all the way back to the overthrow, to certify that those ancestors were officially born and that their marriages are officially recognized. In some ways this would be analogous to the procedure used by the Mormons whereby modern-day believers can baptize their ancestors in absentia and seal the ancestors' marriages for all eternity.

There would also have to be a Perfect Birth Company to issue a Regent's Proclamation that each new birth from now on is recognized by the legal authority of the Kingdom. And there would have to be a Perfect Death Company to issue a Regent's Proclamation that someone really is officially dead. As a matter of fact, all those people who thought their land titles were repaired and guaranteed by the previous work of Perfect Title Company are in for a rude awakening. At any point in the last 150 years when a land title was passed through probate or inherited, there will now have to be repairs done by Perfect Death Company to certify that the deaths leading to probate really happened. And every owner along the way needs to be certified by Perfect Birth Company as having been really born.

So next time you attend a wedding in Hawaii, and the minister asks, "If anyone present knows of any good reason why these two should not be joined in holy matrimony, let him speak now, or forever hold his peace," stand up and say, "I object! This man and this woman do not legally exist because their birth certificates are invalid. And although you may join this couple in holy matrimony within your church, you lack any authority to join them according to law because the State of Hawaii does not exist."

Not only must Keanu Sai operate Perfect Title Company, Perfect Birth Company, Perfect Marriage Company, and Perfect Death Company, he must perform all the weddings himself, unless he also establishes Perfect Justice-of-the-Peace Company to issue Regent's Proclamations to certify the authority of agents to perform wedding ceremonies. Busy fellow! Oh, the fees that fellow is going to collect! Do you need money to pay for titles, birth certificates, marriage certificates, death certificates? Go visit Perfect Loan Company.

"World Court" allegedly confirms Hawaiian Kingdom still exists

Two friends agree that the Hawaiian Kingdom was illegally overthrown, and the annexation of Hawaii to the U.S. was done illegally. They agree that the laws of the Kingdom of Hawaii still are the rightful laws of Hawaii today. One of these friends, Lance Larsen, repeatedly gets arrested for driving a car in Hawaii while failing to have a license plate and drivers' license issued by the State of Hawaii. Larsen refuses to pay the fines, and continues to defy State law. He gets thrown in jail for 30 days. He claims the State of Hawaii is not the rightful government and has no jurisdiction over him. Meanwhile, his friend Keanu Sai claims to be the Regent pro-tem of the Kingdom of Hawaii, having followed the laws of the Kingdom to establish himself in that office. The two of them cook up a scheme whereby Lance will sue Keanu, as acting head of state, for failing to protect Lance, a subject of the Kingdom, against the illegal actions of an illegal State of Hawaii. And just to make it complete, Lance also sues the United States and all the other nations that had treaty relationships with the Kingdom, claiming that they also had a duty under their treaties of friendship and commerce to protect Lance against harassment from an illegal government. The lawsuit is filed in the U.S. District Court in Honolulu.

But the first action taken once the lawsuit has been filed is for Lance and Keanu to dismiss the lawsuit by agreeing to have the matter arbitrated. They don't want to undergo the rigors of proof and cross examination that would happen in a normal court. Instead they want to have their "dispute" arbitrated under an arrangement where every allegation of fact they agree upon (i.e., all the twisted history about the overthrow and annexation and belligerent occupation of Hawaii) will be accepted without further question by the arbitrators.

Lance and Keanu take their dismissal documents, and their agreement to submit to arbitration, to a senior (semi-retired) federal court judge (Samuel King) who still handles occasional matters, and who is himself ethnic Hawaiian and a supporter of Hawaiian sovereignty. Instead of laughing and dismissing the case outright as frivolous, the judge signs the order of dismissal including the agreement to arbitrate.

Lance and Keanu begin their propaganda campaign by publicly announcing that a federal judge has recognized the continued existence of the Kingdom of Hawaii. Of course the judge did no such thing, nor would he have the authority to do it. But if questioned on this issue, Keanu Sai would say the judge had recognized the Kingdom's continuing existence (and Sai's government title) by virtue of the fact that the judge signed a document in which the two individuals identify themselves as the Kingdom's Regent pro-tem and a Kingdom subject.

Since the case had the appearance of involving international law, Lance and Keanu were able to persuade the Permanent Court of Arbitration at the Hague (Netherlands) to provide a venue where hand-picked arbitrators can hear the case. Lance and Keanu each hired one certified arbitrator (fee $10,000 each), and those two arbitrators agreed upon a third arbitrator (another $10,000), thus comprising a three-man arbitral panel to hear the case at the Hague under the rules of international law governing commercial relationships (not the rules governing international political disputes). The arbitral panel heard the case, and issued a ruling that Lance and Keanu have no real dispute between them because they agree on everything (actual language of the ruling provided later). The panel said that if there is any real dispute capable of being arbitrated under international law it would be between Lance/Keanu vs. the United States over the issue of the alleged illegal occupation of Hawaii by the U.S. But the arbitral panel ruled that it was unable to consider such an issue because the U.S. was not a party to these proceedings (in other words, people are saying bad things about the U.S. and the U.S. was not present to defend itself since Lance and Keanu had dismissed the U.S. right from the start!). Case dismissed. In less polite terms: Where's the beef? Get out of here! In the language of international law, the notice of dismissal is called an "Award." Thus, Lance and Keanu now publicly proclaimed they had an "Award" from "the International Court at the Hague."

Gullible people see an opera and mistake it for real life. This staged performance had the backdrop of a building used for the genuine International Court at the Hague, where disputes between nations are resolved and where international war crimes trials are held. Naturally, Keanu and Lance refer to their arbitral panel as "The International Court at the Hague," which creates a false impression of grandeur.

At the beginning Lance Larsen flew to Europe to present his side of the "dispute" carrying two "passports" – one issued by the bogus Kingdom of Hawaii, and one issued by a bogus "international passport" company whose documents are not recognized by the Netherlands. He was denied entry to the Netherlands and had to return to the U.S., from where he participated in the hearings by telephone.

Keanu Sai flew to Europe carrying two passports: one issued by the United States to U.S. citizen David Keanu Sai, and one issued by the bogus Kingdom of Hawaii. He was admitted to the Netherlands and presented his case at the arbitral hearing in the Hague on December 7, 2000. His propaganda campaign announced that the Netherlands admitted him because it recognized his Kingdom of Hawaii passport. But of course, it was his U.S. passport which got him admitted to the Netherlands. The Dutch border guards didn't care what other identification cards he carried, including perhaps a membership card for the art museum or a booklet labeled "Hawaiian Kingdom Passport." Next time Mr. Sai wants to travel abroad, let him try traveling carrying no personal identification document other than his Kingdom of Hawaii passport!

An article in the Kauai Garden Island News (that island's only regular daily newspaper) by Lester Chang (who regularly writes about Hawaiian sovereignty topics with a very favorable slant) reported these events in excited tones on February 5, 2001 in an article entitled "Kingdom advocate predicts World Court victory" This article was published after the arbitral panel had finished its hearings but before the "Award" was announced.

"A case before an international court at The Hague, Netherlands will show the world the United States is responsible for the demise of the Hawaiian kingdom, said an acting agent for the kingdom. David Keanu Sai said the case before the World Court's Permanent Court of Arbitration will prove the U.S. illegally took over the Hawaiian Islands following the illegal ouster of Queen Lili'uokalani in 1893. ... Larsen said the kingdom failed to protect his right to drive on the Big Island without a driver's license. The kingdom said its hands are tied due to the control of Hawai'i

by the U.S. ... The revelations that come out of the international case could spur world powers to force the ouster of the U.S. from Hawai'i, Sai said. ... In pleadings and oral arguments before the international court, the United States, in its occupation of Hawai'i, has violated international law by administering its laws instead of kingdom laws, he said. ... The violations committed by the United States against the kingdom opens the door for claims for reparations by Hawaiians, Sai said."

This very lengthy article included major portions of Sai's claims about illegal overthrow, illegal annexation, illegal statehood vote, and continuing belligerent military occupation.

It's worth emphasizing the way arbitration works. Arbitrators must accept as valid everything that both parties agree with. Both sides in this trumped-up hoax agreed that the overthrow and annexation were illegal. Both sides agreed that the Kingdom of Hawaii continues to exist as the lawful government of Hawaii, and that the U.S. is engaged in a 108-year continuing illegal military occupation of the Kingdom. The whole point of this charade was to call attention to these claims, and to make it appear that an international court has validated them. But of course, all the arbitrators can truthfully say about these claims is that both sides agree to them, not that the claims are true. Contrary views were not presented. Exclusion of contrary views is precisely why an arbitration was set up by the two parties, and why all actual nations, including the United States, were "dismissed" from the "case" by agreement of the two remaining parties.

If a ruling were to be made in this case, it would clearly be that the Kingdom has no liability for failing to protect Mr. Larsen, for the obvious reason, agreed to by both Sai and Larsen, that the Kingdom is powerless to meet any obligations it may have. There are at least two conceivable explanations why the Kingdom is impotent. One is that the Kingdom is under military occupation by the United States and its puppet regime the State of Hawaii, and therefore the Kingdom cannot protect Mr. Larsen against the occupying power. The other explanation why the Kingdom is impotent is that the Kingdom died more than a century before Mr. Larsen was arrested and no longer exists. Which explanation of the Kingdom's impotence is correct could not be decided by the arbitration panel, because the two parties to the so-called "dispute" had no disagreement on that matter – both agree with the military occupation theory; and no contrary views were presented. Despite the name of the "court," this was not even an international arbitration, because the only two parties were an individual person and the ghost of what he claims to be his his own government.

What would be really funny is if the arbitral panel were to say that the Kingdom is liable for damages of ten million dollars. Lance Larsen could then try to collect. And Keanu Sai could then sue the United States (in the REAL International Court of Justice at the Hague) as being responsible to pay Larsen's damages because the U.S. is an illegal military occupier of Hawaii. Then there would be a genuine controversy for a court to settle, and Mr. Sai's absurd arguments would be contradicted by the true facts of history and law.

Here is the final "Award" of the arbitral panel, which became publicly available early in March, 2001. The panel refused to make any ruling regarding whether Sai owed damages to Larsen. The panel's wording is an extremely polite way of saying "This is baloney. Now get out of here."

AWARD

For the reasons stated above, the Tribunal determines as a matter of international law, which it is directed to apply by Article 3 (1) of the Arbitration Agreement:

(a) that there is no dispute between the parties capable of submission to arbitration, and

(b) that, in any event, the Tribunal is precluded from the consideration of the issues raised by the parties by reason of the fact that the United States of America is not a party to the proceedings and has not consented to them. Accordingly, the Tribunal finds that these arbitral proceedings are not maintainable.

SIGNED *as at the Permanent Court of Arbitration, the Peace Palace, Den Haag.*

JAMES CRAWFORD SC
GAVAN GRIFFITH QC
CHRISTOPHER GREENWOOD QC

As befits an opera or other public entertainment, a vast amount of publicity and "hoopla" surrounded this entire process for a period of about two years, right up until the result was announced. Large fundraisers were held, including a six hour extravaganza of speeches and music on the grounds of Iolani Palace, televised in Hawaii as a live paid infomercial, and simultaneously webcast over the internet. Numerous speeches and panel discussions were held throughout Hawaii, including the University, over a period of many months. Allegedly hundreds of supporters traveled to the Hague for the hearings dressed in Hawaiian-style clothing and bestowing beautiful, fragrant lei upon "court" personnel and spectators – the Hawaii Tourism Authority would have been proud! A good time was had by one and all.

The silence was deafening after the result was made known. Soon after, Keanu Sai and Lance Larsen announced they they would ask the arbitral panel to reconstitute itself as a fact-finding commission, so the propaganda circus could continue. But that never happened. Any genuine fact-finding commission would be obligated to find out the facts! Any respectable fact-finding commission would not limit itself to hearing only from Keanu Sai and Lance Larsen and other supporters of their revisionist view of history.

Even after the "Award" became known, the Hawaiian sovereignty zealots continued their propaganda campaign as though the event at the Hague was a great victory for their cause. To this day the zealots keep saying that the "International Court at the Hague" has "ruled" that the Kingdom still exists and is under illegal belligerent occupation by the U.S.

On April 18 2001, a month after the "Award" was published, the once-per-week "alternative" newspaper "Honolulu Weekly" explained the arbitration in a highly one-sided, glowing, full-page "news report" written by sovereignty zealot Anne Keala Kelly. Under the banner "International" the article had a double headline: "Citizens of an occupied nation seek international justice at the World Court" and "Kingdom Come."

"A series of traffic citations issued to Lance Paul Larsen in Hilo may one day be known as the tickets heard 'round the world. But for now, Larsen's refusal to display a license plate and safety tag and the subsequent 30 days of jail time he did should be looked upon as an act of civil disobedience powerful enough to bring the international court's attention to the subject of Hawaiian independence." The full-page article then describes the theory of illegal overthrow, illegal annexation, etc.; and the appropriateness of demanding massive reparations for damages. It concludes: *"The bottom line for the Hawaiian Kingdom is that even if U.S. leaders chose to ignore the convoluted way the United States has come to call these islands part of "America," international law still applies in*

matters of occupation - even a hundred years after the fact. The Hawaiian Kingdom's road is all about those laws, not America's perceptions."

Upon reading that article the author of this book composed a letter to editor. The letter was published April 25, 2001. The letter as submitted appears in its entirety below. However, the version that got published left out the final two major paragraphs about Santa Claus. Those two paragraphs are, of course, the most important from a public relations standpoint because they offer the public a simple and memorable analogy that deflates and ridicules Keanu Sai's fraud. The title submitted for the article was also changed to the much less attention-grabbing "Thy kingdom came." The spoof institutional affiliation was also published. The author continues to hope for offers of grant money from philanthropic organizations, Indian tribes, and U.S. government agencies, just as the sovereignty zealots continue to hope their Kingdom will come.

CONKLIN VS. SANTA CLAUS FOR NON-DELIVERY OF PRESENTS; U.S. TO PAY DAMAGES TO BOTH

Anne Keala Kelly's article about the Hague arbitration (Honolulu Weekly April 18-24) reminds me of those newspaper articles we see around Christmas time reporting that Santa's sleigh has been sighted somewhere over Alaska heading our way. Gullible children with big eyes get all excited, and even intelligent grown-ups give a wink and a nod.

The Larsen case was arbitrated. Arbitrators must accept as valid everything both parties agree with. Both sides in this trumped-up hoax agree that the overthrow and annexation were illegal (false). Both sides agree that the Kingdom of Hawaii continues to exist as the lawful government of Hawaii (false), and that the U.S. is engaged in a 108-year continuing illegal military occupation of the Kingdom (false). The whole point of this arbitration charade is to propagandize these claims, and to make it appear that an international court has validated them (false). But of course, all the arbitrators can truthfully say about these claims is that both Lance Larsen and Keanu Sai agree to them, not that the claims are true. Contrary views have not been presented. Exclusion of contrary views is precisely why an arbitration was set up and paid for by the two parties, and why all actual nations, including the United States, were "dismissed" from the "case" by Larsen and Sai.

The Kingdom has no liability for failing to protect Mr. Larsen, for the obvious reason, agreed to by both Sai and Larsen, that the Kingdom is powerless to meet any obligations it may have. One explanation why the

Hawaiian Apartheid

Kingdom is impotent: the Kingdom is under hostile military occupation (false) by the United States and its puppet regime the State of Hawaii, and therefore the Kingdom cannot protect Mr. Larsen (true). The other explanation: the Kingdom died 108 years ago and no longer exists (true). Which explanation of the Kingdom's impotence is correct cannot be decided by the arbitration panel, because the two parties to the so-called "dispute" have no disagreement – both agree with the military occupation theory; and no contrary views have been presented. Despite the name of the "court," this is not even an "international" arbitration (except that Larsen and Sai went to another country to present their "case") because the only two parties are an individual person (Larsen) and an alleged representative (Sai) of the ghost of what he claims to be his his own government.

Imagine this: I sue Santa Claus for failing to deliver my Christmas presents. A guy in a Santa suit agrees I have been nice and not naughty, and agrees Santa owes me Christmas presents. Santa and I agree the reason he couldn't deliver the presents is that a U.S. NORAD fighter jet shot down Santa's sleigh over Alaska. Santa and I agree the U.S. owes trillions of dollars in damages for destroying Santa's sleigh and for pain and suffering to us both. At first I file a suit against both Santa and the U.S., but then Santa and I agree to dismiss the U.S. and get our "dispute" arbitrated (What dispute?). We spend months explaining to the arbitrators why Santa owes me presents, and how the U.S. shot down Santa's sleigh, and why the U.S. owes us both big bucks. We agree on all those things, and therefore expect the arbitrators to publish them.

If the arbitrators were as gullible as Ms. Kelly, they might issue a ruling confirming everything we are saying (and incidentally deciding Santa doesn't owe me any money because failure to deliver wasn't his fault since the U.S. shot down his sleigh). After all, no contrary evidence was presented, and arbitrators are required to go along with whatever both parties agree upon. Fortunately, the Hague arbitrators weren't so stupid. Their conclusion clearly says CASE DISMISSED because (1) there was no real dispute between the two parties actually present; and (2) any real dispute would be with the United States government which is entitled to be present but was cleverly "dismissed" by the two parties. But a good time was had by all. Ho ho ho!

Kenneth R. Conklin, Ph.D.
President and Executive Director
Center for Hawaiian Sovereignty Studies

Disclaimer: The word "fraud" is being used in this book not in any formal legal sense, but in the customary informal moral or political meaning of "a deception deliberately practiced in order to secure unfair gain; a piece of trickery; a sham." Regarding the Hawaiian Kingdom bonds and EnenKio, actual securities fraud may have been attempted, but it is not known whether anyone was gullible enough to buy the bonds and also not known whether there was any prosecution for securities fraud by Hawaii or U.S. authorities. Regarding Perfect Title, piecing together published reports seems to indicate there was at least $600,000 (perhaps over $1,000,000) collected in fees by the company for title search and filing of documents. Keanu Sai was convicted only of attempted grand theft (of a house). He should have been prosecuted for filing official documents with the Bureau of Conveyances for fraudulent purposes, but no such charges were filed. Both his customers and the hundreds of victims who were inconvenienced by clouded land titles have apparently gone uncompensated. In the case of the Hague arbitration, no allegations of financial or legal fraud were made (although large sums of money were apparently raised for research, travel, and public relations through a tax-exempt corporation, whose financial records have not been made public). Rather, the accusation of fraud concerns political and moral fraud – one-sided historical claims, and claims that the "world court" has somehow agreed with those.

Chapter 10

Steps Toward a Positive Future

Quick review: What is Hawaiian apartheid? Why should it be of concern to people in Hawaii and throughout the United States?

The purpose of this book is to provide a wakeup call about Hawaiian apartheid. Racial separatism and ethnic nationalism have been gaining strength in Hawaii for several decades. The pace has been slow enough that most Hawaii people haven't noticed until recently. Hardly any anyone outside Hawaii knew there was a problem until the Senate spent four and a half hours debating the Akaka bill on a cloture motion in June 2006, carried live on C-SPAN television nationwide.

Hawaii's wall of apartheid is built of many bricks. The Lunalilo trust is more than 130 years old; Kamehameha Schools (Bishop Estate) is 120 years old; and the Queen Liliuokalani trust is 90 years old. For many decades they were truly benevolent institutions. They were always racially exclusionary, but on a small scale affecting relatively few people. Then Kamehameha turned evil as it converted some of its land holdings into enormous financial wealth which it used in a politically aggressive manner. Kamehameha, valued at $8-15 billion, is now an engine of racial separatism, educating (and propagandizing) thousands of students on its own campuses and in its ever-expanding outreach programs in the language immersion public schools, "host-culture" charter public schools, partnerships with numerous other public schools, and scholarships for college. Kamehameha's PASE division (Policy Analysis and System Evaluation) churns out a constant stream of "studies" claiming to show that ethnic Hawaiians have the worst statistics for income, disease, drug abuse, incarceration, etc. These victimhood claims are used to solicit public sympathy for the "plight" of the allegedly poor, downtrodden Hawaiians; and to support grant applications for millions of dollars in government and private money for large bureaucracies in wealthy institutions of the Hawaiian grievance industry; and to support demands for race-based political sovereignty.

A large brick in Hawaii's wall of apartheid is the Hawaiian Homes Commission Act of 1921. The increasingly powerful Department of Hawaiian Homelands operates dozens of racially exclusionary ghettos and is now becoming a major developer of industrial parks and shopping centers to generate revenue for further expansion of the homelands. DHHL easily manipulates the political activity of Homeland residents, sending busloads of them to rallies at the Legislature or Iolani Palace.

One of the largest bricks in the wall of apartheid is the Office of Hawaiian Affairs. It has spent many millions of dollars directly lobbying for the Akaka bill. It has spent more millions advertising for apartheid on TV, radio, and newspapers; and sponsoring "information booths" and rallies in Hawaii and on the mainland. It has spent millions getting people to sign up for a racial registry that will become the membership roll for either the Akaka tribe under federal recognition or a Plan B state-recognized tribe. OHA (sometimes in collaboration with Kamehameha) has paid for and produced feature films broadcast in Hawaii and throughout the U.S. portraying ethnic Hawaiians as an indigenous people victimized by the U.S. and entitled to political recognition. OHA recently acquired the entire 1875-acre Waimea Valley on Oahu, and the 25,856-acre (40 square mile) forest land in Waokele O Puna (Hawaii Island). OHA maintains a large staff working on governance plans for "nationhood" and aggressively lobbies the Legislature for its own package of bills.

The wall of apartheid has more than 160 additional bricks consisting of federally funded racially exclusionary programs, including powerful institutions based on them, such as Papa Ola Lokahi (ethnic Hawaiian healthcare); plus additional state-funded institutions such as the Native Hawaiian Legal Corporation. An additional dozen bricks are the "host culture" state-funded charter schools which openly teach children that ethnic Hawaiians are the rightful owners of Hawaii and they should liberate themselves from their oppression under American colonialism.

Although the wall of apartheid is currently limited to racial separatism within the United States, its institutions are also an increasingly powerful source of wealth and political power fueling a long-term movement toward total secession of all of Hawaii from the United States. By financing Hawaii's racial separatist institutions the U.S. government is an accomplice to Hawaiian apartheid and to the growing political power of groups who want to rip the 50th star off the flag.

As Hawaii goes, so goes the nation. Other ethnic nationalist groups are encouraged by the Akaka bill to hope that someday they too can have a piece of America for themselves. A prime example is MEChA, a group seeking recognition for a Nation of Aztlan that would encompass all the U.S. lands formerly owned by Mexico where indigenous people of Mexican ancestry live – they are indigenous because they possess at least one drop of Aztec or Mayan blood; and their lands were engulfed by the United States without their permission and without compensation (just like ethnic Hawaiians say happened to themselves). There are already 560 federally recognized Indian tribes; but the majority of Indians are not members of any tribe and would not be eligible to join one. However, if the Akaka bill passes it would set a precedent for further balkanization of America, as hundreds and perhaps thousands of new "tribes" would demand recognition. Perhaps other groups with no claim to being indigenous would also demand nationhood, such as the Amish, the Cajuns, and the largest of all – the Nation of New Africa.

Hawaii's racial separatism and ethnic nationalism are not merely political movements. They are also founded in religious fascism which makes them dangerous and potentially deadly. A beautiful Hawaiian creation legend has been perverted into a theory justifying racial supremacy.

Seeing the mass red-shirt marches in Honolulu of the 2000s brings memories of the brown-shirt and black-shirt marches and rallies in Berlin of the 1930s. Seeing the racial ghettos of the Hawaiian Homelands brings memories of the Bantustans of South Africa. Seeing the racial separatism in Hawaii, and the removal of Caucasians from the historic pantheon of heroes of the Hawaiian Kingdom, brings memories of ethnic cleansing in Bosnia and Rwanda. Seeing assertions of Hawaiian indigenous rights to control the land and exercise race-based political sovereignty brings images of Zimbabwe, Fiji, and Darfur. Of course what's happening in Hawaii has been non-violent so far. Nothing like those other places. Not yet.

If a frog is suddenly thrown into a pot of boiling water, it will jump right out. But if a frog somehow finds itself in a pot of lukewarm water which is then slowly brought to a boil, the frog will be cooked without a struggle.

Hawaii is not yet like Berlin, Bosnia, Rwanda, Zimbabwe, Fiji, or Darfur. That's because the frog in the pot of water is being brought to a boil very slowly. This book is a warning that our condition is dangerous. If we try to jump out of the water, the cook might try to grab us, tie us up, club us into submission, and throw us back into the pot kicking and screaming. Shall we go quietly into that long dark night, or shall we be brave and gather our remaining energy to jump out of the pot before it's too late? What kind of future is possible for Hawaii if we jump out of that pot? What can we do to succeed in jumping out?

What would a positive future look like for Hawaii?

This book is not intended to cover all aspects of a utopian society. The purpose of this book is limited to describing Hawaiian racial separatism and ethnic nationalism. If people understand what's happening to them, they can take action to work toward a better future.

A good future for Hawaii includes unity. The people of Hawaii should remain unified under the single sovereignty of the State of Hawaii, not divided into racially separate governments as the Akaka bill or Akaka Plan B would do. The State of Hawaii should remain unified with the United States of America, not seceding to become an independent nation.

A good future for Hawaii includes equality. Metaphysical equality means that all people are created equal in the eyes of God(s). Religious fascism would justify racial supremacy based a belief that ethnic Hawaiians are descended from the gods and are brothers to the land of these islands in a way nobody can be who lacks a drop of the magic blood. Religious fascism would also justify important inborn inequalities even among members of the master race based on differences in their genealogies. By rejecting religious fascism we affirm that every person is entitled to be treated equally by the government under the laws.

A good future for Hawaii includes aloha for all. Hawaii is a beautiful rainbow of races and cultures. Each is unique and distinct, while blending in beautiful ways. Each should be encouraged to preserve its traditions and thrive. All are held together by the Aloha Spirit, by a set of laws shared in common, and by a sovereign government which treats everyone equally. Hawaiian culture (in its modern form) is first among equals. It deserves special respect and encouragement because it derives from the oldest culture in these islands, and because everyone who lives permanently in Hawaii, regardless of race, participates in some of its elements to a greater or lesser extent. Most ethnic Hawaiians do not speak Hawaiian language; many do not participate in Hawaiian culture except superficially. Many people with no Hawaiian native blood participate, sometimes extensively, in elements of Hawaiian culture; some speak Hawaiian language. But in Hawaii other cultures also contribute to the stew, as people of all races share each others' foods, languages, and cultural traditions. We all leave our shoes outside the door. Some non-Japanese place kadomatsu by the door at New Years, and bring home omiyagi when returning from a trip. Some non-Filipinos send balikbayan boxes to relatives outside Hawaii. Anyone might greet anyone else saying "Mabuhay!" or "Kung Hee Fat Choy!" on appropriate occasions, even if neither person is Filipino or Chinese.

What steps can we take to rescue ourselves?

As we contemplate Hawaii's wall of apartheid and the Evil Empire it protects, we can take heart from what happened to the Soviet Union. On a visit to Berlin, President Ronald Reagan gave a speech to a huge crowd. He stood on a platform in front of the Berlin Wall, and said "Mr. Gorbachev – Tear down this wall!" Within a few years his words acted like "abracadabra," and the wall of separation was indeed torn down. Today pieces of the Berlin Wall are on display in museums and parks throughout the world (including Honolulu Community College), as reminders of the evils of government-created walls of separatism that divided a city and even tore families apart.

A Hawaiian proverb says "I ka olelo no ke ola; i ka olelo no ka make." In words there is life; in words there is death. Speaking is a form of action. Speaking words with conviction and faith can sometimes make a mountain move. So let's remember President Reagan and say his words, redirecting them toward Hawaii's wall of apartheid: "People of Hawaii – Tear down this wall!"

The first step toward tearing down Hawaii's wall of apartheid is to prevent it from growing even taller. There are three things to be done. (1) Stop the Akaka bill from passing. Stopping the Akaka bill by filibuster or procedural maneuvers (like defeating the cloture motion in June 2006) is good, but not decisive. We should work to get a large bipartisan majority in the Senate and House to decisively defeat the Akaka bill and drive a wooden stake through its vampire heart. Those pushing the bill should feel the sting of defeat and be so embarrassed by the public outcry against their racism that they will never bring it up again. (2) Stop Akaka Plan B in the Hawaii Legislature. The State of Hawaii must not create a state-recognized tribal government; and must not transfer money or land or legal jurisdiction to any such race-based entity. (3) Both Congress and the state Legislature should be lobbied to stop passing any new legislation to provide race-based benefits. They should defeat bills to reauthorize existing programs. They should pass bills to remove funding during the next budget cycle and to cancel existing programs.

The golden anniversary (50th) of Hawaii statehood will be celebrated in August 2009. Won't it? Statehood Day (formerly called Admission Day) has been an official holiday in Hawaii ever since 1959. State and local government workers get the day off with pay. But for many years there has been no actual celebration. Government officials fear to offend Hawaiian sovereignty activists who deplore the "illegal" overthrow of the monarchy, "illegal" annexation, and "illegal" statehood vote (when 94% of all voters said "yes"). In August 2006 a group of individuals led by one courageous state Senator, and with the participation of one state Representative, tried to hold a Statehood Day celebration; but were shouted down and physically threatened. Children in a high school marching band, seated and ready to play patriotic music, were removed by parents fearing for their safety after Hawaiian zealots shouted at them through a megaphone and intimidated them up close and personal.

There should be a joint resolution of Congress and a Presidential Proclamation commemorating the 50th anniversary of Hawaii's admission to the Union as a State. The joint resolution should rescind the apology resolution of 1993. Or, if that is too politically incorrect, then at least the resolution commemorating the golden anniversary of Hawaii statehood should include strong language affirming that Hawaii is the 50th state and that it proudly upholds the principles of unity, equality, and aloha for all. If our own Senators and Representatives are unwilling to sponsor such a resolution, or to include language affirming unity and equality, then those Senators and Representatives from other states who have rescued us by leading the fight against the Akaka bill should be asked to sponsor the resolution.

In Hawaii the Legislature should pass a similar resolution. There should be a first-rate celebration of the holiday, with marching bands and speeches, centered at the capitol building of the Republic, Territory and State, where both annexation and statehood took place.

The State of Hawaii has no provision for initiative, referendum, or recall. But the Constitution of the State of Hawaii has a provision requiring that a question must be placed on the ballot at least once every ten years – Should there be a Constitutional Convention? That opportunity comes again in 2008 when the question will be on the ballot whether or not the Legislature likes it. The most recent con-con was 30 years ago. In

1998 OHA spent big money advertising for a "No" vote, and the con-con was narrowly defeated. We must vote yes to hold a con-con.

Some of the amendments proposed by the con-con must include initiative, referendum, and recall. For example, it is unconscionable that the state Legislature has refused to place on the ballot a referendum for the people to decide whether to support the Akaka bill. The con-con should abolish OHA. It should include enabling language so that when Congress rescinds HHCA the State of Hawaii will then abolish DHHL and offer existing homestead lots in fee simple on very generous terms to the homeowners currently living on them. The con-con should carefully consider the "public trust" doctrine as applied to water and land, to remove all racial entitlements or preferences and to safeguard individual property rights. The con-con should carefully consider whether to maintain the ancient custom of limiting private property rights by guaranteeing shoreline access and gathering rights; and in any case the Constitution should make clear that shoreline access and gathering rights are not racially exclusive. The Constitution should prohibit the Legislature or the Governor from selling, leasing, or donating any land, or giving any money (whether tax dollars or land revenue), or transferring any legal jurisdiction, to any governmental or private entity that practices racial exclusion, discrimination, or preference.

It is possible that the strategies described above might be unsuccessful. Perhaps Congress and the Hawaii Legislature are unresponsive. Perhaps the water in the pot is getting close to the boiling point and Hawaii's people have lost the energy to jump out. If the wall of apartheid cannot be demolished all at once, then it must be dismantled brick by brick. There should be lawsuits against individual institutions that are especially evil such as OHA, DHHL, Kamehameha Schools. Removing the cornerstones might cause the entire wall to collapse.

For each institution to be attacked, including the smaller ones, a choice must be made between two strategies. Attack only the racially exclusionary or "preferential" policy of the institution, or attack the institution's very existence.

Some institutions have truly benevolent components which could continue to perform valuable public service. For example, Kamehameha Schools provides an excellent quality of education for the students on its campuses (except for the historical revisionism and religious fascism in its curriculum). Kamehameha helps needy children by offering tuition waivers and by providing room and board on campus for those who need it. If Kamehameha's racially exclusionary admissions policy could be abolished, much of the evil would wither away. If Kamehameha were open to children of all races on an equal basis, then the curriculum would probably change to include a more accurate version of history and a more egalitarian viewpoint on racial equality. Kamehameha might focus on financially and socially needy children, and those with learning disabilities, rather than the current focus on an elite group who must pass rigorous academic testing and personal screening. The PASE division (Policy Analysis and System Evaluation) would probably focus more on race-neutral studies of how to improve education and health rather than racial victimhood studies designed to bolster the Hawaiian grievance industry.

On the other hand, some institutions like OHA, DHHL, Alu Like, and Papa Ola Lokahi have racial separatism so firmly entrenched as their defining essence that they probably cannot be rehabilitated and must be completely abolished. If Papa Ola Lokahi and other racially exclusionary institutions are disbanded, that does not mean that needy ethnic Hawaiians currently receiving services through those organizations will lose their benefits. It simply means that ethnic Hawaiians must look to the same social service agencies as everyone else. Those wealthy or middle class ethnic Hawaiians who have been receiving free or reduced-price services merely because they are of the favored race will now have to pay for what they get, just like everyone else. Those ethnic Hawaiians who are truly needy will get help from government and philanthropic agencies, just like everyone else. Those professionals employed by the race-based institutions will find jobs at the race-neutral service agencies whose workload will of course now be at least 20% larger; while those bureaucrats whose jobs were focused on racial propaganda and grantwriting for racially exclusionary purposes will need to find some other line of work.

Civil War analogy

The U.S. went through a terrible time from 1860 to 1865. The Civil War was not only about abolishing slavery, but also about preserving the unity of the United States. The economic system of the South had to undergo profound change when slavery was abolished. The social system had problems that lasted for another century afterward, as former slaves found themselves deprived of fundamental rights through Jim Crow laws enforcing racial segregation and denial of voting rights. But the terrible times of the Civil War and its aftermath were not nearly so bad as the far more evil times of slavery. Should the South have been allowed to preserve its way of life? Didn't they have a right of self-determination? Should the South have been allowed to secede? Today most people throughout all of America believe the enormous costs of the Civil War, in blood and treasure, were necessary and worthwhile to secure the blessings of unity and equality.

It was not enough for the Union Army to win important battles in Virginia or Pennsylvania. It was also necessary for punitive expeditionary forces to rampage through the states of the very deep South so there could be no doubt about the decisiveness of the eventual victory. General Sherman's march through Georgia remains famous. He burned Atlanta to the ground. But today we are a unified nation, and even the people of Atlanta recall that history with gentle nostalgia. By the 1970s the old city of Atlanta lying under the modern city had been excavated and rebuilt as "Underground Atlanta" – a place for tourists and locals to gather in bars, restaurants, and souvenir shops. The "Burning of Atlanta Bar" featured drinks called "General Sherman" and "Scarlett O'Hara." The walls of the bar were covered with paper that moved in the breeze, lighted from behind with flickering orange and red lights simulating burning flames. In a town north of Atlanta there was a restaurant named "Aunt Fanny's Cabin" where 10-year-old "Negro" boys and girls wore blackboards around their necks with the menu selections written on them. These "slaves" stepped forward to each table of newly arriving customers and sweetly recited what was on their menu, as beautiful waitresses in antebellum dresses took the orders. The customers, both white and black, both tourist and local, enjoyed the ambiance.

In Hawaii today, civil rights lawyers are doing General Sherman's work. They are marching to cut through the wall of apartheid, and to utterly demolish those institutions whose racially exclusionary policies are so firmly entrenched that they cannot be rehabilitated.

As we move forward with resolution and perseverance, we must always remember to distinguish among ideology, institutions, and individual people. Our fight is primarily against an ideology of racial separatism, ethnic nationalism, and religious fascism. Some institutions serving those ideologies must be destroyed; but other institutions now following an evil agenda can be rehabilitated by weeding out racially exclusionary practices. Some people working in separatist institutions might be so zealous that it's unlikely they will change their hearts and minds. But many who work for the Evil Empire are "just trying to earn a living" – they are basically good people deserving respect and compassion as their institutions undergo great change or dissolution. The vast majority of ethnic Hawaiians are like everyone else, willing to play identity politics to get the most they can from their government, but happy to be Americans and deep-down opposed to racial separatism and ethnic nationalism. They are like the decent people of Germany trying to stay alive under Nazi rule. They are like the working white men and homemaker white women of Georgia during the Civil War, caught in circumstances they did not create, watching with dismay as General Sherman marches through, and able to adjust to changing conditions.

President Abraham Lincoln delivered a famous speech after the Battle of Gettysburg which schoolchildren today memorize and recite. Despite the bloodiness of that battle Lincoln's short speech was conciliatory, giving honor to all the men on both sides who had died. Lincoln understood that the purpose of the war was to preserve a unified nation, not to gloat over battlefield victories or to rub salt in the wounds.

Although the Gettysburg Address is remembered as Lincoln's greatest speech, his Second Inaugural Address has extraordinary ideas that speak to the people of Hawaii today. The closing paragraph is especially eloquent and relevant.

"Fellow Countrymen: At this second appearing to take the oath of presidential office, there is less occasion for an extended address than there was at the first. ... The progress of our arms, upon which all else chiefly depends, is as well known to the public as to myself; and it is, I trust, reasonably satisfactory and encouraging to all. With high hope for the future, no prediction in regard to it is ventured. ... [F]our years ago, all thoughts were anxiously directed to an impending civil war. All dreaded it – all sought to avert it. While the inaugural address was being delivered from this place, devoted altogether to saving the Union without war, insurgent agents were in the city seeking to destroy it without war – seeking to dissolve the Union, and divide efforts, by negotiation. Both parties deprecate war; but one of them would make war rather than let the nation survive; and the other would accept war rather than let it perish. And the war came. ..."

"Neither party expected for the war the magnitude or the duration which it has already attained. ... Each looked for an easier triumph, and a result less fundamental and astounding. ... Fondly do we hope – fervently do we pray – that this mighty scourge of war may speedily pass away. Yet, if God wills that it continue until all the wealth piled by the bondsman's two hundred and fifty years of unrequited toil shall be sunk, and until every drop of blood drawn with the lash shall be paid by another drawn with the sword, as was said three thousand years ago, so still it must be said, "The judgments of the Lord are true and righteous altogether."

"With malice toward none; with charity for all; with firmness in the right, as God gives us to see the right, let us strive on to finish the work we are in; to bind up the nation's wounds; to care for him who shall have borne the battle, and for his widow, and his orphan – to do all which may achieve and cherish a just and lasting peace among ourselves, and with all nations."

Conclusion

It seems fitting that the closing paragraph of this book should be the same as the closing paragraph of the U.S. Supreme Court's decision in Rice v. Cayetano.

"When the culture and way of life of a people are all but engulfed by a history beyond their control, their sense of loss may extend down through generations; and their dismay may be shared by many members of the larger community. As the State of Hawaii attempts to address these realities, it must, as always, seek the political consensus that begins with a sense of shared purpose. One of the necessary beginning points is this principle: The Constitution of the United States, too, has become the heritage of all the citizens of Hawaii."

Footnotes

[1] The most recent version of the Akaka bill will always be posted at http://tinyurl.com/4n64x

[2] U.S. Senate floor speeches and voting record for June 2006 are at http://tinyurl.com/k299m

[3] A spreadsheet showing each state's population of ethnic Hawaiians as determined in Census 2000 is at http://tinyurl.com/5vlp6

[4] 67% of respondents opposed the Akaka bill in a scientific survey of all 290,000 households having telephones, commissioned by the Grassroot Institute of Hawaii and conducted in Summer 2005. Furthermore, 45% feel strongly enough about this issue that they are less likely to vote for any politician who supports the bill. For details, including the actual questions that were asked, see: http://tinyurl.com/cwxgg On May 23, 2006 the results of another comprehensive GRIH survey were released. Once again, 67% of all responding households opposed the Akaka bill, and 70% wanted the issue to be placed on the ballot before Congress could consider the bill. For details of the 2006 survey see http://tinyurl.com/k5hxc

[5] A map of the Hawaiian islands showing some of the lands likely to be demanded by an Akaka tribe is available in pdf format at http://tinyurl.com/bgx25 There are large and small land parcels, SCATTERED throughout the islands, making jurisdictional issues a nightmare. Almost every current business would eventually come under competition from untaxed and unregulated businesses located within easy driving distance.

[6] "Hawaiian Nationalism, Chicano Nationalism, Black Nationalism, Indian Tribes, and Reparations -- Akaka Bill Sets a Precedent for the Balkanization of America" http://tinyurl.com/72214

[7] "Happy Holidays -- Not So Happy Anymore! Ethnic Cleansing of Hawaiian History" http://tinyurl.com/3gqgm

[8] "Three Choices For Hawai'i's Future: Akaka Bill vs. Independence vs. Unity and Equality" http://tinyurl.com/3sa2o

[9] "Native Hawaiian Racial Entitlement Programs Valued in the Billions of Dollars -- Description and List of Many" http://tinyurl.com/3walu

[10] For a description of these fundamental values in the context of Hawaii, see: http://tinyurl.com/2c49g

[11] One such lawsuit was Arakaki#1: "Arakaki vs. State of Hawai'i -- The Right to Run for Statewide Public Office Without Racial Restriction, Including the Right of Voters to Have a Full Range of Candidates Unrestricted by Race" http://tinyurl.com/4t339 Another was Arakaki#2: "A Multiethnic Group of 16 Hawaii Citizens File Suit Challenging the Constitutionality of Both the Office of Hawaiian Affairs and the Department of Hawaiian Homelands" http://tinyurl.com/3pkgg Another was Doe v. Kamehameha, seeking to desegregate Kamehameha Schools "Kamehameha 9th Circuit Decision: the Big Picture and Some Brush-Strokes (demolishing Hawaii's wall of apartheid one brick at a time)" http://tinyurl.com/bmtpr

[12] "Akaka Bill Controversy Draws Congressional Attention to Illegal Native Hawaiian Entitlements -- House Republican Study Committee Proposes Killing $40 Million Per Year" http://tinyurl.com/c3umj

[13] On December 5, 2006 an en banc panel of 15 judges of the 9th Circuit Court of Appeals issued an 8-7 decision overturning the previous 3-judge panel's decision. The majority opinion and the dissents make very interesting reading. See: http://tinyurl.com/y9xz4o

[14] One example is Professor Emeritus of Hawaiian Language and Literature at the University of Hawaii, Rubellite Kawena Johnson, who was also designated a Living Treasure of Hawaii by Honpa Hongwanji Buddhist Temple. Her testimony against the Akaka bill, and a partial summary of her achievements, is at: http://tinyurl.com/3mdmv

[15] Emmett Cahill, "The Life and Times of John Young (Confidant and Advisor to Kamehameha the Great)" (Honolulu: Island Heritage, 1999).

[16] George Avlonitis, "Legacy of One of Hawaii's Richest Men: Charles Reed Bishop" (Hawaii Reporter online, August 30, 2005) http://tinyurl.com/yutno5

[17] See sections 1 and 2 of "Happy Holidays -- Not So Happy Anymore! Ethnic Cleansing of Hawaiian History" http://tinyurl.com/3gqgm

[18] Henry Opukaha'ia (Obookiah) -- Native Hawaiian Travels to New England in 1809, Converts to Christianity, and Persuades Yale Divinity Students to Come to Hawai'i as Missionaries in 1820 to Rescue His People From Their Heathen Beliefs and Lifestyle. http://tinyurl.com/ygfnxh

[19] "How Thanksgiving Came to Hawaii" http://tinyurl.com/yeyf36

[20] "Was Hawaiian Language Illegal? Did the Evil Haoles Suppress Hawaiian Language As A Way of Oppressing Kanaka Maoli and Destroying Their Culture?" http://tinyurl.com/6zrka

[21] Gavan Daws, "Shoal of Time" (Honolulu: University of Hawaii Press, 1968), pp. 197-199.

[22] Daws, Ibid., pp. 245, 247, 253.

[23] For example, portions of the alleged new Constitution proposed by Liliuokalani were published in a royalist newspaper Ka Makaainana: Vol. 1, No. 21 (21 May 1894): page 4. Article 62 seems to set forth a racial restriction of voting for ethnic Hawaiians exclusively: "Pauku 62. O na kupa wale no ke hiki ke koho balota, a hoemiia mai hoi ke ana waiwai e kupono ai o na poe koho."

[24] http://morganreport.org

[25] An excellent book about Robert Wilcox and racial politics is Ernest Andrade, Jr., "Unconquerable Rebel: Robert W. Wilcox and Hawaiian Politics, 1880-1903" (University Press of Colorado, 1996). Chapter 14 describes the downfall of Wilcox and the reasons why Kuhio left the Home Rule Party to join the Republicans.

[26] Liliuokalani's legal document of complaint was filed in 1909, and the Court of Claims decision was handed down in 1910. Both documents are available in full, along with analysis, at http://tinyurl.com/56czl

[27] For more detailed information about Kuhio's villainy against Liliuokalani and her Trust to benefit Hawaiian orphans, see: Evelyn Cook, "100 Years of Healing," (Kauai: Halewai Publishing, 2003 (P.O. Box 460, Koloa, Kauai, HI, 96756)). ISBN 0-9723831-0-7; Library of Congress Catalog Card # 2003109480. The online syllabus for a course on elder law at University of Hawaii provides a short history and text of the court decision in Kuhio's complaint against Liliuokalani to have her declared mentally incompetent. http://www.hawaii.edu/uhelp/courses_EL.html

[28] A complete transcript of Trask's inflammatory racist speech, together with some analysis and commentary on the issue of mandatory lease-to-fee conversion, is at http://tinyurl.com/3vndu

[29] Gordon Y.K. Pang, "More are realizing homestead dreams" (Honolulu Advertiser, February 11, 2007) http://tinyurl.com/2fb59u

[30] Samuel P. King and Randall W. Roth, "Broken trust: greed, mismanagement & political manipulation at America's largest charitable trust" (Honolulu: University of Hawaii Press, 2006). A large website providing background information and documentation is at http://brokentrustbook.com/

[31] A webpage tracing the history of Kamehameha Schools race-based admissions policy is at http://tinyurl.com/e3mlm

[32] News coverage and photos of the huge march and rally are on a webpage at http://tinyurl.com/8aloj

[33] http://tinyurl.com/ytphkk

[34] The opinion of the 3-judge panel is available in pdf format at http://tinyurl.com/akqag

[35] Kahalekai v. Doi, 60 Haw. 324, 343, 590 P.2d 543 (1979). Search Google

[36] The Rice v. Cayetano decision was handed down in February, 2000. A webpage was published in March 2000 including excerpts, links to the complete decision, news reports, and commentary describing how State of Hawaii executives and legislators were scrambling to find ways to circumvent the decision. In July 2000 the Akaka bill was introduced in Congress as the best hope for undoing it. http://tinyurl.com/3wu78

[37] All plaintiff legal briefs at both the District Court and 9th Circuit Court of Appeals, and an amicus brief from the Pacific Legal Foundation; together with news reports and commentaries; are available on a webpage at http://tinyurl.com/4t339

[38] A webpage contains all legal briefs filed by plaintiffs and by 5 defendants including OHA, State of Hawaii, Department of Hawaiian Homelands, and the United States; plus many news reports and commentaries. http://tinyurl.com/3pkgg

[39] The decision is commonly known as PASH (Public Access Shoreline Hawaii). The ethnic Hawaiian Supreme Court Justice who wrote the decision, and has since stepped down to become attorney for OHA, is Robert Klein. A major legal commentary on the PASH decision by Honolulu attorney Paul M. Sullivan is available at http://tinyurl.com/23668n

[40] "Ceded Lands Belong to All the People of Hawaii; There Should Be No Racial Allocation of Ceded Lands or Their Revenues" http://tinyurl.com/356xy

[41] http://tinyurl.com/2hfjvs

[42] "Native Hawaiian Racial Entitlement Programs Valued in the Billions of Dollars -- Description and List of Many" http://tinyurl.com/3walu

[43] "The establishment of ethnic hawaiian charter schools -- the example of Kanu O Ka Aina" http://tinyurl.com/rthe2

[44] Public education for ethnic nation-building in hawaii -- a legislative bill to create a separate statewide school system for Native Hawaiians" http://tinyurl.com/2h6uo

[45] "The Progeny of Rice v. Cayetano: A Panel Discussion at University of Hawai'i Law School, And The Journal Articles It Spawned (Discussing The Lawsuits Following After and Based Upon Rice v. Cayetano)" http://tinyurl.com/2deusp

[46] "University of Hawai'i and Hawaiian Sovereignty -- A Case Study in Political Correctness Run Amok" http://tinyurl.com/3rlyk

[47] Historical information in this paragraph and the next one taken from Gordon Y.K. Pang, "The fight for Kaho'olawe" (Honolulu Advertiser, January 30, 2006) http://tinyurl.com/2a3cf6

[48] Akaka Bill -- U.S. Senate June 2006 (materials collected from the Congressional Record including transcripts of floor debates, plus roll call votes names and totals) http://tinyurl.com/k299m

[49] OHA Plan B -- full text of OHA memo plus news reports and commentary http://tinyurl.com/ez2ey

[50] Anthony Castanha, "The Hawaiian Sovereignty Movement: Roles of and Impacts on Non-Hawaiians" (Masters thesis, University of Hawaii, 1996; thesis title revised 1997) http://hookele.com/non-hawaiians/

[51] http://www.opihi.com

[52] http://HawaiianKingdom.org/info-registry.shtml

[53] The Hawaiian Kingdom Supreme Court Decision "Rex v. Booth" (1863) includes discussion of several such laws discriminating against natives in the interest of protecting them, citing such laws as evidence that the King was the sole possessor of sovereignty (and not the legislature or the people).

[54] Kanahele's Constitution for his Nation of Hawaii, written in 1995, is at http://www.hawaii-nation.org/constitution.html

[55] The United Nations Draft Declaration on the Rights of Indigenous Peoples is at http://tinyurl.com/2ha8w

[56] "Happy Holidays -- Not So Happy Anymore! Ethnic Cleansing of Hawaiian History" http://tinyurl.com/3gqgm

[57] "Fiji and Hawaii Compared -- Racial Supremacy By Law in Fiji Resembles What Hawaiian Sovereignty Activists Are Seeking (both Akaka bill and independence proposals)" http://tinyurl.com/34nvz The contents of this section of the book are based on news reports and commentaries found on that webpage.

[58] "Hawaiian Independence, Puerto Rican Independence, Guam Independence -- Conceptual Similarities, Political Cooperation, and Puerto Rican Terrorism Against U.S. Congress" http://tinyurl.com/2mjwlg

[59] The Hawaii legislature's own website archives for 2001 provide full text of Senate Resolution 98 at http://tinyurl.com/ypbpku

[60] Full text of the committee report for SR 98 can be found at http://tinyurl.com/2ef7km

[61] The 2002 resolution in support of holding a Statehood Day celebration, which did not even receive a committee hearing in either chamber, is at http://tinyurl.com/11w9

[62] "Hawaii Statehood Day 2006 -- Celebration at Old Territorial Capitol Building (Iolani Palace) Disrupted by Hawaiian Ethnic Nationalist Wannabe-Terrorists" http://tinyurl.com/pdt88

[63] Extensive information and internet links about people and events mentioned in this section is provided at "Income Tax Evasion Based on Claims of Hawaiian Sovereignty" http://tinyurl.com/3ojkw

[64] "John Philip 'Pilipo' Souza -- state income tax evasion by a man with no Hawaiian native ancestry claiming to be a native-born subject of the still-living Kingdom of Hawaii" http://tinyurl.com/5day5

[65] "The Akaka Bill And Secession: The Hawaiian Government Reorganization bill (Akaka bill) is seen by its supporters as a step toward total independence for all of Hawaii" http://tinyurl.com/4cho6

[66] Full text of the Hawaii Advisory Committee report to the U.S. Commission on Civil Rights is available on the USCCR website at http://www.usccr.gov/pubs/sac/hi0601/report.htm

[67] David Stannard, "Before the Horror" (Honolulu: University of Hawaii Press, 1989).

[68] Martha H. Noyes, "Then There Were None" (based on the televised docudrama by Elizabeth Kapu'uwailani Lindsey Buyers, Ph.D.). (Honolulu: Bess Press, 2003) ISBN: 1-57306-155-7 Hawaii Public Library call # H 996.9 No

[69] An essay-length book review, including the book's cover and full text of Shepherd's commentary, is at http://tinyurl.com/2z9dy

[70] Nolan J. Malone, Ph.D., "Native Hawaiian Population Forecasts for 2000 to 2050" (Kamehameha Schools, Policy Analysis and System Evaluation Division, September 2005). http://tinyurl.com/cwehb

[71] "Native Hawaiian Population To Double by 2050 -- Lilikala Says Use Population Bomb to Blow Up Current Non-Native Majority" http://tinyurl.com/clk7z

[72] 54.9% of Native Hawaiian mothers are unmarried compared to 17.1% for Whites -- taken from Hawaii Data Book 2002 as reported by the U.S. Department of Health and Human Services at http://tinyurl.com/34jdx9

[73] "Continuity of the Hawaiian Kingdom" by Dr. Matthew Craven http://tinyurl.com/2uxjys

[74] Kyle Kajihiro, "Hawai'i Report for the Asia-Pacific Consultation of Movements Against U.S. Military Bases" (American Friends Service Committee - Hawai'i and DMZ-Hawaii / Aloha 'Aina, November 6, 2006) http://tinyurl.com/y2ra7p

[75] Keanu Sai, Ph.D. candidate in Political Science: "A Slippery Path Toward Hawaiian Indigeneity" (University of Hawaii Indigenous Politics Colloquium, January 30, 2007) http://tinyurl.com/2a4ag6

[76] "Akaka Bill -- U.S. Senate June 2006 (materials collected from the Congressional Record including transcripts of floor debates, plus roll call votes names and totals) http://tinyurl.com/k299m

[77] For example, portions of the alleged new Constitution proposed by Liliuokalani were published in a royalist newspaper Ka Makaainana: Vol. 1, No. 21 (21 May 1894): page 4. Article 62 seems to set forth a racial restriction of voting for ethnic Hawaiians exclusively: "Pauku 62. O na kupa wale no ke hiki ke koho balota, a hoemiia mai hoi ke ana waiwai e kupono ai o na poe koho."

[78] http://morganreport.org

[79] Thurston Twigg-Smith, "Hawaiian Sovereignty: Do the Facts Matter?" (Honolulu, HI: Goodale Publishing, 1998). Chapter 10 deals with the apology resolution. The entire book can be downloaded free of charge in pdf format here: http://www.hawaiimatters.com/book/HawnSov.pdf

[80] "Hawaii Divided Against Itself Cannot Stand" (Essay by Constitutional lawyer Bruce Fein, as printed In the Congressional Record of June 14, 15, and 16 of 2005 by unanimous consent, by request of Senator Kyl) http://tinyurl.com/ajz9s

[81] Slade Gorton and Hank Brown, "E Pluribus Unum? Not in Hawaii" (Wall Street Journal online, August 16, 2005) http://tinyurl.com/exdg3

[82] The entire Morgan report, together with summaries and commentaries about it, is at http://morganreport.org A special essay was written compiling some of the Morgan Report testimony that repudiates the Blount Re-

port. See http://tinyurl.com/cfxbl One section of that essay includes a compilation of some Morgan Report testimonies in which witnesses swear under oath that Blount falsely reported what they had told him.

[83] Helena G. Allen, "The Betrayal of Liliuokalani" (Glendale California: The Arthur H. Clark Co.,1982).

[84] http://tinyurl.com/ldx4c

[85] Krischel's webpage thoroughly documenting the Cleveland proclamation as fake is at http://tinyurl.com/mgfo5

[86] http://tinyurl.com/k38tm

[87] The entire Morgan report, together with summaries and commentaries about it, is at http://morganreport.org A special essay was written compiling some of the Morgan Report testimony that repudiates the Blount Report. See http://tinyurl.com/cfxbl One section of that essay includes a compilation of some Morgan Report testimonies in which witnesses swear under oath that Blount falsely reported what they had told him.

[88] A special essay on the Morgan Report website describes the history of President Cleveland's relationship with Hawaii's Provisional Government and its successor the Republic of Hawaii. Following the U.S. Senate investigation of the Hawaiian revolution and the issuance of the Morgan Report, the Senate passed resolutions that there should be no further interference in Hawaii's internal affairs. President Cleveland then stopped his efforts to restore the Queen, and finally gave formal diplomatic recognition to the Republic of Hawaii. See "The Rest of the Rest of the Story" at http://tinyurl.com/9hg45

[89] "Letter of December 19, 1893 from United States to President Dole, Demanding That Liliuokalani Be Restored to the Throne" http://tinyurl.com/6zlct

[90] "Hawaii President Sanford B. Dole, Letter of December 23, 1893 Refusing United States Demand to Restore Ex-Queen Lili'uokalani to the Throne" http://tinyurl.com/8y6jo

[91] http://tinyurl.com/2g2bju

[92] Lorrin A. Thurston's 32-page report debunking the anti-annexation petitions is difficult to read because the typewriting has faded, and the documents were scanned as photographs. One way to see Thurston's report is on the University of Hawaii library's digital collection of anti-annexation documents. The trouble is that each of the 32 pages must be individually downloaded. Start at page 820, here: http://tinyurl.com/p293b Another way to see Thurston's report is to download a single 32-page pdf document; but it has the disadvantage of having a file size of 16 megabytes! http://tinyurl.com/26bcuj

[93] All points discussed in this section regarding Hawaiian language being illegal or suppressed are explained in more detail, and thoroughly documented, on a webpage at http://tinyurl.com/6zrka

[94] The contents of this section are described in detail and thoroughly documented on a webpage: "The myth of the shredded Hawaiian flag -- a false claim that the Hawaiian flag removed from Iolani Palace on annexation day August 12, 1898 was cut up into pieces distributed to the annexationists as souvenirs of their victory over the Hawaiian people" http://tinyurl.com/6hmb4

[95] The contents of this section are explained in further detail, and thoroughly documented, on a webpage: "Mauna Ala (Royal Mausoleum) -- History, Mystery, Ghost Stories, and A Claim of Continuing Hawaiian Sovereign Territory" http://tinyurl.com/5rtmy

[96] Gordon Pang, "Forced assimilation may hurt Hawaiians" (Honolulu Advertiser, June 20, 2005). An essay-length review of Pang's article by Ken Conklin is the basis for this section of this book, and can be found at http://tinyurl.com/8fz9q

[97] "Henry Opukaha'ia (Obookiah) -- Native Hawaiian Travels to New England in 1809, Converts to Christianity, and Persuades Yale Divinity Students to Come to Hawai'i as Missionaries in 1820 to Rescue His

People From Their Heathen Beliefs and Lifestyle"
http://tinyurl.com/ygfnxh

[98] http://www.healthtrends.org/health_status/lifeexpec.html

[99] National Cancer Institute, "Cancer in Native Hawaiian Women." http://dccps.nci.nih.gov/womenofcolor/pdfs/hawaiian-chapter.pdf

[100] Data for Tonga taken from the website of the U.S. State Department at http://www.state.gov/r/pa/ei/bgn/16092.htm
Additional information about incomes is available at http://www.finfacts.com/biz10/globalworldincomepercapita.htm

[101] The data for ethnic Hawaiians, taken from the U.S. Census Bureau and reported at the State of Hawai'i Department of Business, Economic Development and Tourism (DBEDT) can be found at http://www.hawaii.gov/dbedt/census2k/sf4profiles/xnhstate.pdf

[102] http://www.cdc.gov/tobacco/statehi/htmltext/hi_sh.htm

[103] http://www.drugabusestatistics.samhsa.gov/nhsda/2k1nhsda/vol3/Sect2v1_PDF_W_55-69.pdf

[104] http://dccps.nci.nih.gov/womenofcolor/pdfs/hawaiian_reference.pdf

[105] Kamehameha Schools PASE website: http://www.ksbe.edu/pase

[106] http://www.ksbe.edu/pase/pdf/Ka_Huakai/KaHuakai_ExecSummary.pdf

[107] Iwalani R.N. Else "The Breakdown of the Kapu System and Its Effect on Native Hawaiian Health and Diet." (Kamehameha Schools, PASE, 2004) http://www.ksbe.edu/pase/pdf/Hulili/Else.pdf

[108] "Legacy of a Broken Heart" http://www.hoolokahi.net/brokehrt.htm

[109] For "Native Hawaiians" separately (race alone[i.e., "pure"], or in combination with one or more other races -- i.e., the "one drop" definition as used in the Akaka bill) all the statistics are on:
http://www.hawaii.gov/dbedt/census2k/sf4profiles/xnhstate.pdf
Overall State of Hawaii, all from Census 2000 (including ethnic Hawaiians along with everyone else):
http://www.hawaii.gov/dbedt/census2k/h90_00_state.pdf
Median household income is $49,820 from middle of table at http://tinyurl.com/na53j

[110] The population of "Native Hawaiians" will more than double by year 2050. Gordon Pang's article is at http://tinyurl.com/8prrv The complete PASE report is at http://tinyurl.com/cwehb

[111] "Native Hawaiian Population To Double by 2050 -- Lilikala Says Use Population Bomb to Blow Up Current Non-Native Majority" http://tinyurl.com/clk7z

[112] 54.9% of Native Hawaiian mothers are unmarried compared to 17.1% for Whites (Hawaii Data Book 2002) http://tinyurl.com/34jdx9

[113] "Forbes Cave (Kawaihae Caves) Artifacts Controversy" http://tinyurl.com/82xqp

[114] "Akaka Bill and Ethnic Hawaiian Entitlements -- Dialog -- Jere Krischel vs. OHA Chair Haunani Apoliona and others, January 2007" http://tinyurl.com/2gn27m

[115] Patricia Reaney, "Left-handed women's risk of breast cancer higher -- study" (Reuters, Sunday September 25, 2005)
http://today.reuters.com/News

[116] Reuters Health, March 9, 2000. For more detail see "The journal Epidemiology" (March 2000; 11:181-184).

[117] "Akaka Bill Survey by Grassroot Institute of Hawaii released May 23, 2006" http://tinyurl.com/k5hxc

[118] "Attorney Hayden Burgess, Alias Poka Laenui -- Hawaiian Sovereignty Independence Activist Supports the Akaka Bill As a Way of Getting Federal Money While Continuing To Seek Independence" (a collection of essays he has written on this topic) http://tinyurl.com/4wkhu

[119] Herbert K. Pililaau of Waianae got the Medal of Honor for his heroic death in the Korean War. For the citation, see:
http://www.msc.navy.mil/inventory/citations/pililaau.htm

[120] In December 2003 USNS Pililaau arrived in Honolulu to pick up another load of supplies for delivery to Kuwait. While the ship was docked, more than 30 proud members of Private Pililaau's family from Waianae were given a tour of the ship with lunch onboard. To read a description of the ship and the family's day onboard, including photos, see http://www.msc.navy.mil/sealift/2004/January/pililaau.htm

[121] http://www.homeofheroes.com/moh/states/hi.html

[122] Ethnic Hawaiian Brigadier General Irwin K. Cockett, Jr., United States Army, Retired gave a speech summarizing the contributions of ethnic Hawaiians in the U.S. military. It is filled with interesting historical tidbits. http://www.thepaf.org/info/Cockett071502.htm

[123] http://akaka.senate.gov/~akaka/speeches/2002715A16.html

[124] "Professor Haunani-Kay Trask: Some Speeches and Writings Illustrating the Anti-American and Anti-White Attitudes of the Hawaiian Sovereignty Movement" http://tinyurl.com/2comb

[125] "A discussion of the UH propaganda factory known as the Center for Hawaiian Studies, and why its monolithic party line in support of racial supremacy has become the unchallenged orthodoxy in every academic department that shares students and curriculum with CHS" http://tinyurl.com/ypmnx

[126] "A review of Dobelle's tenure as President at UH, focusing on his aggressiveness in pushing the CHS agenda and his pledge to politicize UH

even further, harnessing UH as a partner in bringing about a racial supremacist government entity" http://tinyurl.com/3fhnd

[127] "University of Hawaii and Hawaiian Sovereignty -- A Case Study in Political Correctness Run Amok" http://tinyurl.com/3rlyk See especially the extended introduction, and sections 4 and 6.

[128] "Core Attitudes of Hawaiian Sovereignty Movement -- Racial Separatism, Ethnic Nationalism, Anti-Americanism, Racial Supremacy" http://tinyurl.com/3mjh3

[129] "Red-Shirt Pro-Apartheid March of September 2003 and Follow-Up Newspaper Articles" http://tinyurl.com/4jxan and "Red-Shirt Pro-Apartheid March of November 2003 -- A Clear Attempt to Intimidate Federal Judges and the General Public" http://tinyurl.com/ysapf

[130] "Red-Shirt Pro-Apartheid March of September 6, 2004 -- 'Die Jugend Marschiert'" http://tinyurl.com/3mfsw

[131] Gavan Daws, "Shoal of Time", pp. 255-256.

[132] "Anti-American Hawaiian activist protesters -- photos and links to explanatory webpages" http://tinyurl.com/8aloj

[133] "NATIVE HAWAIIANS AS THE STATE PET OR MASCOT: A Psychological Analysis of Why the People of Hawaii Tolerate and Irrationally Support Racial Separatism and Ethnic Nationalism" http://tinyurl.com/3he27

[134] "Racism in the Hawaiian Sovereignty Movement (with special focus on anti-white racism)" http://tinyurl.com/b5bef

[135] "Violence and threats of violence to push demands for Hawaiian sovereignty" http://tinyurl.com/2su9pa

[136] "Native Hawaiian Bank -- How Bumpy Kanahele and Activists Seeking Reparations for Slavery are Blackmailing Bank of America as it Seeks

to Merge With FleetBoston; followup coverage as Bumpy continues to publicize his concept of a Native Hawaiian Bank" http://www.angelfire.com/hi2/hawaiiansovereignty/bumpybank.html

[137] "Income Tax Evasion Based on Claims of Hawaiian Sovereignty" http://tinyurl.com/3ojkw

[138] http://www.umc-gbcs.org/getinvolved/viewarticle.php?csa_articleId=124

[139] http://www.angelfire.com/hi2/hawaiiansovereignty/makua.html

[140] http://www.angelfire.com/hi2/hawaiiansovereignty/strykerlawsuit.html

[141] http://www.hawaii-nation.org/proclamsum.html

[142] http://www.hawaii-nation.org/alohamarch-markcentury.html

[143] Patrick W. Hanifin "To Dwell on the Earth in Unity: Rice, Arakaki, and the Growth of Citizenship and Voting Rights in Hawai'i" (Hawaii Bar Journal, Vol. V, No. 13, pp. 15-44). http://www.angelfire.com/hi2/hawaiiansovereignty/HanifinCitizen.pdf

[144] Pat Omandam. "Isle 'illegal occupation' lawsuit hit dead end" Honolulu Star-Bulletin, Saturday, October 27, 2001 http://starbulletin.com/2001/10/27/news/whatever.html

[145] "Happy Holidays Not So Happy Anymore! Ethnic Cleansing of Hawaiian History" http://tinyurl.com/3gqgm

[146] http://www.inmotionmagazine.com/ngo1.html

[147] In May 2004 Mililani Trask led a delegation of 18 Hawaiian independence activists to New York for two weeks of meetings. http://the.honoluluadvertiser.com/article/2004/May/13/ln/ln29a.html

[148] "Hawaii Great Statehood Petition of 1954 -- 120,000 Signatures Gathered in 2 Weeks On a Petition for Statehood for Hawaii" http://tinyurl.com/68ygp

[149] http://www.angelfire.com/hi2/hawaiiansovereignty/puertoricoguam.html

[150] http://starbulletin.com/2000/08/22/editorial/letters.html

[151] For a general discussion of "Racial Supremacy Government Policies Worldwide, Compared To Hawaiian Sovereignty Proposals" see http://tinyurl.com/4hhrj

[152] http://the.honoluluadvertiser.com/article/2005/Jun/13/ln/ln14p.html

[153] Was Liliuokalani Really Like Martin Luther King and Mahatma Gandhi? What really happened in the 1893 overthrow of the Hawaiian monarchy?" http://www.angelfire.com/planet/bigfiles40/MLK-Liliu.html

[154] "Treaties, conventions and other international agreements of the Kingdom of Hawaii" http://www.hawaii-nation.org/treatylist.html

[155] Elaine Willman, "Going to Pieces: The Dismantling of the United States of America." (privately published, 2006, Equilocus, P.O. 1280, Toppenish, WA 98948). The Citizens Equal Rights Alliance has its website at http://www.citizensalliance.org/
To obtain a copy of Willman's book go to http://tinyurl.com/38och8

[156] John Warren Kindt, "Gambling With Terrorism – Gambling's Strategic Socio-Economic Threat To National Security" (Hawaii Reporter, February 13, 2007) http://tinyurl.com/2e6w4e

[157] Brenda Norrell, "Navajo Nation, Cuba negotiate trade agreement" (Indian Country Today, Aug. 31, 2006) http://www.indiancountry.com/content.cfm?id=1096413568

[158] Full text of the latest version of the Akaka bill is at http://tinyurl.com/4n64x

[159] http://tinyurl.com/yqgj4e

[160] Jocelyn Linnekin, "Children of the Land." New Brunswick, N.J.: Rutgers University Press, 1985.

[161] Samuel Kamakau was a native Hawaiian scholar, born in 1815, who thoroughly studied the Hawaiian culture as contained in ancient stories passed down from generation to generation through the oral tradition. Between 1865 and 1871 he published articles in the Hawaiian language newspapers describing some of these ancient stories. See Samuel Kamakau, "Na Moolelo a ka Poe Kahiko (Tales and Traditions of the People of Old) (translated from the newspapers Ka Nupepa Kuokoa and Ke Au Okoa by Mary Kawena Pukui), Honolulu: Bishop Museum Press, 1991

[162] Abraham Fornander, "Ancient History of the Hawaiian People to the Times of Kamehameha I" (Honolulu, Mutual Publishing, 1996).

[163] Derek Gatopoulos, Associated Press, "Zeus revivalists defying ban" (Honolulu Advertiser, January 20, 2007) http://tinyurl.com/yunx9h and Mary Adamski, "View From the Pew" (Honolulu Star-Bulletin, January 27, 2007) http://tinyurl.com/2h26c9

[164] "Hawaii Legislature Informational Briefing Regarding the Akaka Bill by U.S. Senators Inouye and Akaka, and U.S. Representatives Abercrombie and Case, on March 31, 2005 (Hawaiian language, Christian prayer, failure of Legislature to perform due diligence)." Transcript and commentary at http://tinyurl.com/9s8et

[165] For the story of Opukahaia, see http://tinyurl.com/ygfnxh

[166] Valerio Valeri (trans. Paula Wissing), "Kingship and Sacrifice." Chicago: University of Chicago Press, 1985. This book is an anthropological study of the role of ritual in the society of precontact Hawaii, focusing especially on the ritual of human sacrifice. Rituals are seen as mediating between people of different social classes, or between humans and spirits or gods.

[167] Kumulipo was translated, with extensive commentary, in a book by Martha Beckwith, published in 1951, entitled "The Kumulipo: A Ha-

waiian Creation Chant." Because the copyright to Beckwith's book was not renewed, its massive full contents are available on the internet at http://www.sacred-texts.com/pac/ku/index.htm

[168] "MAUNA KEA -- How the telescope campus serves the spiritual essence of this sacred place; how OHA and the sovereignty activists try to extort money and destroy Mauna Kea astronomy" http://tinyurl.com/4k3ys

[169] Ken Conklin's testimony at NASA Environmental Impact scoping hearing, January 12, 2004 http://tinyurl.com/4fhkx

[170] "NASA should set aside $20 million for education in Hawai'i as compensation for use of Mauna Kea as an astronomy center, Office of Hawaiian Affairs Chairman Clayton Hee said yesterday." Honolulu Advertiser, January 17, 2002 http://tinyurl.com/2ml2be

[171] Huge Hawaiian flags carried to the summit of Mauna Kea; photo http://tinyurl.com/hfn27

[172] Mary Kawena Pukui, E.W. Haertig, and Catherine A. Lee, "Nana I Ke Kumu" (Honolulu: Hui Hanai [Queen Liliuokalani Childrens Center], 1972).

[173] George S. Kanahele, "Ku Kanaka (Stand tall: a search for Hawaiian values)" (Honolulu: University of Hawaii Press, 1986).

[174] "Public education for ethnic nation-building in Hawaii -- a legislative bill to create a separate statewide school system for ethnic Hawaiians" http://tinyurl.com/2h6uo

[175] For more about Kanu O Ka Aina charter school see http://tinyurl.com/rthe2

[176] Manulani Aluli Meyer, "Ho'oulu -- Our Time of Becoming (Hawaiian Epistemology and Early Writings). 'Ai Pohaku Press, Native Books Inc. P.O. Box 3080, Honolulu HI, 96802, www.nativebookshawaii.com, (c) 2003. LCCN 2003110403. ISBN 1-883528-24-0. A web page includes extensive excerpts from Dr. Meyer's work, and excerpts from the UCLA

symposium program giving hints at how other ethnic groups might hope to piggyback on the Hawaiian style of theorizing. See: http://tinyurl.com/5lu9r

[177] Ben Finney, "Sailing in the Wake of the Ancestors: Reviving Polynesian Voyaging" (Honolulu: Bishop Museum Press, 2003). 168 pages. ISBN 1-58178-025-7 (hard) or 1-58178-024-9 (soft). Hawaii Public Library Call # H 910.9154 FI. An extended book review exploring the philosophical issues is at http://tinyurl.com/5hjah

[178] http://starbulletin.com/2004/05/24/news/corky.jpg

[179] Marlo Morgan, "Mutant Message Down Under" (Harper Collins 1991 and 1994; Harper Perennial 1995; ISBN 0-06-092631-7).

[180] http://tinyurl.com/5hjah

[181] For extended discussion of these issues see: "Indigenous Intellectual Property Rights -- The General Theory, and Why It Does Not Apply in Hawaii" at: http://tinyurl.com/2b77k

[182] A map highlighting the federal and state lands is at http://tinyurl.com/bgx25 However, that map does not show any of the very extensive land holdings of Bishop Estate (Kamehameha schools) that would almost certainly be incorporated into the territory of the Akaka tribe. Also not included are the huge land areas recently deeded to the Office of Hawaiian Affairs -- the entire Waokele O Puna (Hawaii island) and Waimea Valley (Oahu).

[183] "Professor Haunani-Kay Trask: Some Speeches and Writings Illustrating the Anti-American and Anti-White Attitudes of the Hawaiian Sovereignty Movement" http://tinyurl.com/2comb

[184] Samuel P. King and Randall W. Roth, "Broken trust: greed, mismanagement & political manipulation at America's largest charitable trust" (Honolulu: University of Hawaii Press, 2006). A large website providing background information and documentation is at http://brokentrustbook.com/

[185] Rob Perez, "Hawaiian royal bonds questionable," Honolulu Star-Bulletin, Sunday February 17, 2002. Article available at http://starbulletin.com/2002/02/17/news/perez.html

[186] The Hawaii Supreme Court issued a ruling on July 20, 2004 denying the appeal of Michael and Carol Simafranca. http://www.hawaii.gov/jud/23332sdo.htm The author of this book has been unable to find any evidence that Keanu Sai ever appealed the trial court's decision.

[187] A webpage opposed Judge Simms' reappointment to the bench and compiled some news reports about her absurdly light sentencing decisions. See: "Should Judge Sandra Simms Be Retained in Office for Another 10 Years? Speak Out Now Or For 10 Years Hold Your Nose" at http://tinyurl.com/6rnnj

[188] "The Perfect Title Scam -- Self-Proclaimed Regent of Hawaiian Kingdom Collects Huge Fees, Causes Grief to Property Owners, Messes Up Land Titles, Escapes With Probation and $200 Fine" http://tinyurl.com/4w2rt

[189] "NATIVE HAWAIIANS AS THE STATE PET OR MASCOT: A Psychological Analysis of Why the People of Hawaii Tolerate and Irrationally Support Racial Separatism and Ethnic Nationalism" http://tinyurl.com/3he27

CPSIA information can be obtained
at www.ICGtesting.com
Printed in the USA
BVOW03s0618181116
468277BV00001B/59/P